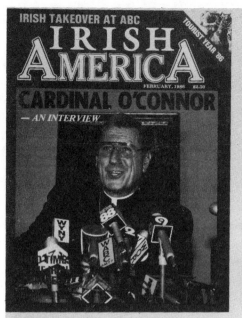

IRISH TAKEOVER AT ABC

IRISH AMERICA

CARDINAL O'CONNOR

— *AN INTERVIEW*

**THE PARADE —
THE POWER, THE POLITICS
AND THE PRIDE**

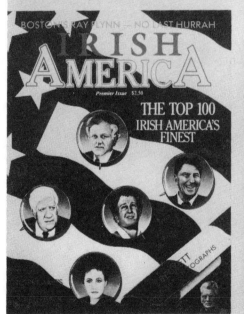

BOSTON'S RAY FLYNN — NO LAST HURRAH

IRISH AMERICA

Premier Issue $2.50

THE TOP 100
IRISH AMERICA'S
FINEST

IRISH AMERICA
M A G A Z I N E

**JOE
KENNEDY**

*Born
To Run*

THE
IRISH-AMERICAN
ALMANAC
&
GREEN PAGES

First Edition
1986

Managing Editor:
Brian E. Cooper

Contributing Editors:
Martha Moore Battles
Ann Kathleen Bradley
John Vincent Cody, Ph.D.
Karen S. Daugherty
Joan Moody
Timothy Rogus

PUBLISHERS

New York

First edition 1986
Second printing: February 1987

Printed in the United States of America

2 3 4 5 6 7 8 9 10 11 12 13 14 15 16 17 18 19 20

In preparing this publication, Pembroke Press, its staff and consultants have taken reasonable care to assure the accuracy of all information included. Much of the research is based on secondary sources, which are themselves sometimes in disagreement. Other information has been provided by a wide variety of respondents and sources and accepted in good faith, subject to reasonable discretion. Pembroke Press therefore cannot assume responsibility for errors or inaccuracies, whether of commission or omission. Nor does it make any warranties or representations regarding the nature, quality, performance, authenticity or availability of any product or service mentioned herein. Descriptions are provided for information purposes only, based on information available to the editorial staff. Where errors are found or presumed, the Publisher asks that they be brought to its attention so that future editions of this publication may be amended as appropriate.

ISBN   0-911159-01-0

Cover design: Edgar Blakeney
Typography: MacTypeNet™, Livonia, MI

CONTENTS

The Green Pages:

————————

ACKNOWLEDGMENTS

Rare is the publication that results from solitary effort. Far from being one of these few, *The Irish-American Almanac & Green Pages* is a collective work in the broadest sense. Nearly two dozen bills from New York Telephone Company eloquently attest this. What merits this book has are in direct proportion to the contributions made over the past two years by hundreds of individuals throughout the United States and in Ireland.

The editors gratefully acknowledge, in particular, the information, ideas and suggestions we have received from those listed below. So many have given so much, however, that we fear more than one name has been inadvertently forgotten. Even one such omission we profoundly regret.

Tom Bayne, American Irish Historical Society, New York, NY
Bob Burns, Editor, *The Irish American News*, Chicago, IL
Angela Carter, Keshcarrigan Book Shop, New York, NY
Drew Crosby, Alicorn/Irish Books & Things, San Francisco, CA
Fr. John Daly, St. Patrick's Church, San Francisco, CA
Patrick C. Dowling, San Francisco, CA
Evean Fitzgerald, Consulate of Ireland, New York, NY
Jim Ford, Boston Public Library, Boston, MA
Maxine Graham-Olson, Houston, TX
A. G. Haworth, Dept. of Geography, Trinity College, Dublin
Donna Reid Hotaling, Genealogist, Vienna, VA
Aidan Kirwan, Former Vice Consul of Ireland, New York, NY
David Monagan, Cold Spring, NY
Fr. Kevin O'Brien, St. James Church, New York, NY
Denise O'Meara, Irish Arts Center, New York, NY
Michael O'Shea, Cockeysville, MD
Coilin Owens, The Gaelic League, Washington, DC
Prof. Joseph Peden, City University of New York, NY
George Ryan, Editor, *The Pilot*, Boston, MA
John Clement Ryan, Irish Distillers Corporation, Dublin
David Wadsworth, Historical Society, Cohasset, MA

In addition to the information provided by those above, we benefitted from research, editorial suggestions, proofreading, graphic design and other assistance by several individuals including, most notably:

Edgar Blakeney, New York, NY
Josephine Danna, Palomino Press, Briarwood, NY

Arnold Davis, New York, NY
Betty Dornheim, Bronxville, NY
Patricia R. Heidenry, Queens, NY
Carolyn S. Knight, Esq., New York, NY
Loren Moss, RSW Concept & Design, New York, NY
Edward O. Raynolds, Short Hills, NJ
Steven M. Roffwarg, New York, NY
Leslie Safford, New York, NY
J. Carlisle Spivey, New York, NY
Jane Van Norman Turano, New York, NY

I am deeply grateful to my typographers, MacTypeNet™ of Livonia, Michigan: Suzi Lee, Renée Stevenson, and particularly Frank Lee. They showed that the centuries-old professional standards of traditional typography are still very much alive. These standards, combined with their thorough grasp of the art and science of computerized typesetting, made possible the special formats required for this book.

Finally, I would like to acknowledge the support and patience of our advertisers and that of my parents, James and Virginia Daugherty Cooper. Without their material assistance the fruit of so many other efforts might not have come to publication.

Brian E. Cooper
Managing Editor & Publisher

INTRODUCTION

"Greater Ireland," the writer and sociologist Rev. Andrew Greeley has called the United States. It is, in many ways, an apt description.

The 1980 U.S. Census found that over 43 million Americans claim Irish ancestry, either wholly or in part. By comparison, the 32 counties of Ireland support a population estimated in 1981 at slightly over five million. A relative few in the Irish-American community have come to the United States in recent years. Some are descended from forebears who left Ireland two to three centuries ago. Most probably trace their Irish roots to immigrants who sailed sometime between the 1820s and the 1920s.

But the significance of Irish America goes far beyond its size. Never has there ever been any question of duplicating Ireland physically on this side of the Atlantic; the Emerald Isle shall always remain unique in some fundamental respects. Yet much that is best about Irish culture has been perpetuated or recreated in America.

Indeed, at a time when the use of Gaelic is declining in Ireland itself, growing thousands of Irish-Americans enthusiastically embrace a chance to learn the tongue of their forefathers. Irish-American folk festivals, some decades old, grow larger each year, and rare is the year that doesn't see the inauguration of at least one new event. On the material side, new businesses emerge to feed Irish America's hunger for tangible expressions of its heritage, offering a surprising variety of traditional Irish crafts and other products, some made here, others in Ireland. Students of all ages flock to courses in Irish and Irish-American history, literature, genealogy and the like, spawning an Irish studies association that numbers well over 1,000 scholars and teachers. And traditional Irish music becomes more popular in America every year, reckoning among its devotees many who have no Irish heritage whatsoever.

In short, traditional Irish culture is alive and well in America. Hence the occasion for this two-in-one book.

The idea for the **Green Pages** came to us about two years ago. Reviewing copies of several Irish-American newspapers, we noticed repeated cases where Irish-related products or services were advertised in only one or two local or regional publications. This made sense, of course, for businesses or organizations designed to serve only members of local Irish-American communities. Often, however, we encountered products and services that were likely to appeal to a national Irish-American audience; many of these were available through the mail, by telephone and other means. Soon we concluded that there was a need to be filled by bringing together information in a systematic, easily accessible way about the surprising range of "things Irish" available throughout the United States.

The idea for the *Irish-American Almanac* followed. As we began systematically researching the *Green Pages*, we came upon countless bits of cultural and historical lore that were as novel as they were fascinating. Even though we considered ourselves reasonably informed about the heritage of Irish America, we tested our hunch on a number of Irish-American friends.

By and large, the information we were uncovering proved as new and as interesting to other Irish-Americans as it had been to us. Indeed, as we began digging for more information on traditional Irish proverbs, drinking toasts, Irish-American historical landmarks and the like, we discovered just how difficult it was to find such information. It was soon clear that the cultural and historical lore we sought could be uncovered only through diligent research; but a wide audience, we were sure, would welcome the effort. For *The Irish-American Almanac*, like the *Green Pages*, would present in easily accessible form a wealth of information far greater than had ever been published before in one place.

While both parts of this work break new ground, we do not pretend they are the final word. Despite our earnest efforts, some readers may find errors or omissions.

We welcome your comments, suggestions, corrections and additions. As they come in, we will publish new and improved editions of *The Irish-American Almanac & Green Pages*, keeping the perishable information in it up-to-date, and adding new information and topics of broad interest and appeal. We invite you to use the form at the back of the book to let us have your thoughts on this first edition.

Brian E. Cooper
New York, New York

The
Irish-American
Almanac

DID YOU KNOW...

...That County Mayo boasts a village with the longest placename in Ireland: *Cooneenashkirroogohifrinn*. For the record, it means "the little harbor sliding to hell." But please don't ask us to explain how it's pronounced!

...That the United States once had a ship named the *U.S.S. Shamrock*. Launched at the Brooklyn Navy Yard on St. Patrick's Day, 1863, she was christened with a bottle of Irish whiskey and presented with a souvenir wreath of shamrocks. The 240-foot steam gunboat carried eight guns, which she used during blockade duty with other Union ships along the Carolina coast.

...That San Juan, Puerto Rico, is one of at least 125 U.S. communities that honor St. Patrick with a parade every March 17th.

...That James Shields (1806?-1879), a County Tyrone man, is the only person ever to have represented three different states in the United States Senate. A hero of the Mexican-American War, in which he served as a brevet major-general, Shields was subsequently appointed governor of the Oregon Territory. Illinois elected him a senator first, and following Civil War service with the Army of the Potomac, he went on to win election as a senator for Minnesota and Missouri, respectively.

...That Irish women won the right to vote in 1919 — a year before their American sisters.

...That Ireland has more golf courses per square mile than any other country. Among these are several world-class links: for example, Ballybunion, County Kerry; Royal Dublin and Portmarnock, both in County Dublin; and Lahinch Golf Club, County Clare — Ireland's oldest course.

...That Halloween as it is observed in the U.S. is based on the ancient Celtic celebration, "Samhain."

...What the three Gaelic sports first played in Ireland are? We don't need to tell you the first two — Gaelic football and hurling (camogie is the women's version). But did you know that the third is international handball? This is the only one of the three that has become popular outside the world's Irish communities.

...That the 1840s blight that ravaged the potato crops of Europe — and especially Ireland — was an American import. So, for that matter, was the potato itself. Sir Walter Raleigh (1552?-1618) brought the plant back to Ireland from one of his voyages to the New World.

...That Briarwood Beach, Ohio, is currently the only community in the U.S. that observes a legal holiday on St. Patrick's Day, March 17th. And Mayor Leonard English (of Irish descent despite his name) has also proclaimed John Jameson Irish Whiskey as Briarwood Beach's official drink! (*National Hibernian Digest*, March/April 1984)

...That, according to some estimates, as many as two thirds of the forces fighting for the North during the Civil War were of Irish birth or descent. In the South, the comparable figure was one third. The North claimed several generals of Irish birth or heritage, including Philip Sheridan, Philip Kearny, Thomas F. Meagher, Michael Corcoran, C.C. Sullivan, George Croghan, John Logan and Robert Patterson. Generals Patrick Cleburne and Patrick Finnegan led Confederate troops.

...That Beethoven was fond of Irish music. He prepared arrangements of several traditional Irish tunes, including "Kitty of Coleraine." And those who know the tune of "The Sash My Father Wore" will recognize snatches of it in the composer's First Piano Concerto.

...That you don't have to pay taxes in Ireland — *if* you're a writer, painter, composer or other artist *and* your creative work is "generally recognized as having cultural or artistic merit," in the opinion of the Revenue Commissioners. This policy has helped stop the export of creative talent — long one of Ireland's most important national resources — and has even attracted well-known actors and authors from Britain and other countries.

...That an Irishman seems to have sailed with Columbus on his first voyage to the New World. When he returned to Spain, Columbus left 40 men to defend a fort on the island of Santo Domingo. Before the admiral could return, however, the entire group was massacred by local natives. But a list that survives reportedly includes the name of "William Ayres, native of Galway, in Ireland." Ayres' presence on the expedition would not have been that surprising. Galway had traded actively with Spain for centuries, and still retains traces of its Spanish connection. Galway tradition, in fact, says that Columbus stopped at the port on his first voyage and prayed at a local church before setting sail to the West. Another account has it that the name of Columbus' presumed Irish crew member was "Rice de Culvey."

...That Limerick-born John Sullivan, a New England schoolmaster during the mid-18th century, was the father of two state governors; two state attorneys-general; a major-general in the Continental Army; the first judge appointed by George Washington in New Hampshire; and four other sons who served as officers in the Continental Army.

...That the Irish wolfhound is the tallest breed of dog recognized by the American Kennel Club. Despite its size and strength, however, the wolfhound is well-known for its gentle and even-tempered disposition. Other breeds with Emerald-Isle roots include the Kerry Blue terrier, the Irish water spaniel and the Irish setter.

...That Irish-Americans still make up 25 percent of the seminarians studying for the Roman Catholic priesthood in the U.S. — more than any other ethnic group. But that's down from 34 percent in 1966, according to a survey presented to the National Catholic Education Association in 1986. (*USA Today*, April 3, 1986)

...That as many as one-third to one-half of American troops during the Revolutionary War were of Irish birth or descent. Among them were nearly 1,500 officers, including 26 generals (15 of them Irish-born).

...That the individuals below are the "10 Greatest Irish Men and Women in History." That, at least, is the opinion of Stephen Birmingham, author of the best-selling Irish-American history, *Real Lace*, who made the following selection for *The Book of Lists* (Morrow, 1977):

1. William Butler Yeats	6. Sean O'Casey
2. George Bernard Shaw	7. Al Smith
3. James Joyce	8. Thomas E. Murray, Sr.*
4. Eugene O'Neill	9. John O'Hara
5. John M. Synge	10. Rose Fitzgerald Kennedy

* Murray (1860-1929) was a U.S. engineer and inventor who held over 1,000 patents at the time of his death — more than anyone else but Thomas Alva Edison. He was particularly active in developing safety devices.

...That blue has an older claim to be called Ireland's traditional national color than green! The official color for several centuries was St. Patrick's blue, and one of Ireland's historic flags shows the harp on a blue ground, later changed to green. Green was commonly considered the national color by the 1800s, when it became associated with the nationalist movement in general, and the Catholic majority in particular.

...That the Declaration of Independence was written in the hand of an Irish-born patriot, Charles Thomson...first read to the people outside the hall where it was drafted by John Nixon, another native of Ireland...first printed by an Irish-born Philadelphian, John Dunlap...and signed by at least three Americans of Irish birth: James Smith of Pennsylvania, a native of Dublin; George Taylor, another representative of Pennsylvania; and Derry- born Matthew Thornton, who represented New Hampshire. At least five other signers had Irish-born parents or grandparents: Thomas McKean, George Read, Robert Treat Paine, Thomas Lynch, Jr. and Charles Carroll of Carrollton.

...That, despite the Catholic-versus-Protestant aspect of the current "Troubles" in Northern Ireland, Protestant Irishmen (and women) have played a disproportionately large role in leading the Irish nationalist movement, particularly before Catholics were given the right to vote in 1829. The honor roll of Protestant patriot leaders and martyrs might surprise you. Among its more prominent names are those of Isaac Butt, (Theobald) Wolfe Tone, Henry Grattan, Charles Stewart Parnell, Sir Roger Casement, Robert Emmet, Thomas Osborne Davis, Henry Flood, Henry Joy McCracken, John Martin, John Mitchel, Robert Erskine Childers, Beauchamp Bagenal Harvey, Countess Constance Markievicz (born Constance Gore-Booth), Douglas Hyde, William Smith O'Brien, Thomas Clarke Luby, James Brown Armour, Samuel Neilson, Thomas Russell, John Redmond and Maude Gonne MacBride (a Protestant-born convert to Catholicism).

...That, since the Congressional Medal of Honor was first awarded in 1863, 257 Irish-born Americans have earned this recognition for distinguished, courageous military feats. This is more than twice the number of winners born in Germany, the next highest contributor, with 126, and compares with 95 English-born recipients, 52 from Canada, 38 born in Scotland, and so forth. While these figures testify to the bravery and fighting abilities of Irish-born Americans, they also reflect the unusually large number of Irish immigrants who fought in the Civil War and later conflicts.

IRISH GRACE: A TOAST
FOR NEARLY EVERY OCCASION

Back in the 1500s, historians tell us, drinkers began to garnish their beer or wine with bits of toasted bread to add more flavor. Over the next couple of centuries, people found that some well-chosen words often added more to a drink than crumbs of overcooked bread. Even though they stopped putting toast into their drinks, this word stuck and has been used ever since to mean a special sentiment expressed before a drink.

Toasting special occasions is a routine custom today. And, with their love of words, the Irish have developed the art of toasting to a higher level than perhaps anyone else. In fact, we think you'll agree that toasts like the following might add a special touch to even the most commonplace drink.

We have reprinted these toasts with the kind permission of Irish Distillers International, Dublin. Our friend there, John Clement Ryan, had one observation, however. "If you really want the sentiments expressed in a toast to come true," he pointed out, "you can't be drinking anything but Irish whiskey!"

FOR GOOD WISHES (GENERAL)

Health and life to you.
The wife (or husband) of your choice to you.
Land without rent to you.
And may you be half-an-hour in heaven before the Devil
knows you're dead. Slainte!

May you live as long as you want, and never want as long as you live.

May the frost never afflict your spuds. May the outside leaves of your cabbage always be free from worms. May the crows never pick your haystack, and may your donkey always be in foal.

FOR AN ANNIVERSARY

I have known many,
liked not a few,
loved only one.
I drink to you.

FOR A WEDDING

A generation of children on the children of your children.

May you have as many children
and may they grow as mature in taste
and healthy in color
and as sought after
as the contents of this glass.

FOR GOOD HEALTH

The health of the salmon to you:
a long life,
a full heart
and a wet mouth!

FOR A BIRTHDAY

May you live as long as you want, and never want as long as you live!

May you die in bed at 95 years, shot by a jealous husband (or wife).

May you live to be a hundred years — with one extra year to repent.

FOR A RETIREMENT, A PROMOTION OR A FAREWELL

May the road rise to meet you.
May the wind be always at your back,
the sun shine warm upon your face,
the rain fall soft upon your fields,
and until we meet again
may God hold you in the hollow of His hand.

May your doctor never earn a dollar out of you
and may your heart never give out.
May the ten toes of your feet steer you clear of
all misfortune, and, before you're much older,
may you hear much better toasts than this.

HOLIDAY TOASTS

May you have warm words on a cold evening,
a full moon on a dark night,
and a smooth road all the way to your door.

In the New Year, may your right hand always be stretched out in
friendship and never in want.

May peace and plenty be the first to lift the latch on your door, and
happiness be guided to your home by the candle of Christmas. (NOTE:
This toast refers to the traditional custom of leaving the door unlatched,
and a lighted candle in the window, on Christmas Eve.)

FOR THE BACHELOR

May you have nicer legs than your own under the table before the new
spuds are up.

May you be poor in misfortune,
rich in blessings,
slow to make enemies,
quick to make friends.
But rich or poor, quick or slow,
may you know nothing but happiness
from this day forward.

FOR A WAKE

May every hair on your head turn into a candle to light your way to
heaven, and may God and His Holy Mother take the harm of the years
away from you.

FOR NO PARTICULAR OCCASION

May the grass grow long on the road to Hell for want of use.

May you have the hindsight to know where you've been,
the foresight to know where you're going
and the insight to know when you're going too far.

Here's to you, as good as you are.
Here's to me, as bad as I am.
As good as you are and as bad as I am,
I'm as good as you are, as bad as I am.

May the roof above us never fall in, and may we friends gathered below never fall out.

IRISH PROVERBS:
AN EVERGREEN SELECTION

"Comfort is not known if poverty does not come before it."

"Every invalid is a physician."

"Where the tongue slips, it speaks the truth."

"It's almost as good as bringing good news not to bring bad."

"Keep a thing for seven years and you'll find a use for it."

"A new broom sweeps clean, but the old brush knows all the corners."

"There is pain in prohibition."

"He who is bad at giving lodgings is good at showing the way."

"One person with a plan helps as much as two people can."

"Nearest the heart comes first out."

"What's got badly, goes badly."

"However long the road there comes a turning."

"The devil is good to his own in this world and bad to them in the next."

"While the cat is out the mouse will dance."

"Better the fighting than the loneliness."

"If you want praise, die. If you want blame, marry."

"The thing that often occurs is never much appreciated."

"A blessing does not fill the belly."

"Always touch a new-born baby, or when it grows up it will lift its hand against you."

"The worst, most damaging witness is a former friend."

"A constant beggar gets a constant refusal."

"A dimple in the chin, a devil within."

"He who can follow his own will is a king."

"It's the first drop that destroyed me; there's no harm at all in the last."

"Neither make nor break a custom."

"Beauty won't make the pot boil."

"A little help is better than a deal of pity."

"God never closes one door but He opens another."

"Sickness is the physician's feast."

"Pity him who makes his opinion a certainty."

"Don't say everything you want to lest you hear something you would not like to hear."

"Where there's love, there's enough."

Quoted in: Patricia Houghton, *A World of Proverbs* (Poole, Dorset: Blandford Press, 1981); Mary M. Delaney, *Of Irish Ways* (New York: Barnes & Noble, 1973); *The Irishman*, San Francisco, October 1985; Sean Gaffney & Seamus Cashman, Eds., *Proverbs & Sayings of Ireland* (Dublin: Wolfhound Press, 1974); and Selwyn G. Champion, M.D., Ed., *Racial Proverbs* (New York: Barnes & Noble, 1950).

SYMBOLS OF IRELAND

The Shamrock

This is, without a doubt, the most familiar emblem of Ireland. For centuries, every March 17th, Irishmen have worn shamrock sprigs in their hats to honor their patron saint, Patrick. The three-leaf, clover-like plant has traditionally been associated with the Welsh-born missionary saint.

While trying to convert a group of Irish people, we are told, St. Patrick had trouble explaining the concept of the Trinity. Seeing some shamrocks close by, he plucked one of the familiar plants. Holding it up for all to see, he explained that the three persons of the Trinity were like the three leaves of the shamrock — held together in one unit by the stem, which he used as a symbol of the godhead.

Tradition says that the shamrock never flowers, nor will it grow anywhere outside of Ireland. But just what species of plant is it? According to one Irish scholar, there is, in fact, no distinct plant called a shamrock. She cites, for example, a botanist, Nathaniel Colgan, who during the last century collected samples from various counties of what "competent local authorities" had certified as authentic "shamrocks" gathered for St. Patrick's Day. Of 35 specimens he examined on one occasion, all but two proved to be clover of various species, and the remaining two were black medick, a plant almost indistinguishable from clover during March.

But does it really matter whether shamrocks are really clover, black medick, wood sorrell or some other plant? Not really. Symbols have never been any less powerful for not being real. Welshmen, for example, fought under the badge of the red dragon for centuries, and this creature endures today as a symbol of their nation.

The Harp

Though not so popular as the shamrock, the harp is the oldest official symbol of Ireland. The instrument in question is, of course, not the concert harp used in today's orchestra, but the smaller, portable harp traditionally played by Celtic bards, or minstrels.

Before it was adopted as a symbol of Ireland as a whole, the harp had been used for centuries in the arms of Leinster (see below), the ancient Irish kingdom that endures as one of the island's four provinces. It seems first to have appeared in the Irish arms during the reign of the Tudor king, Henry VIII. Here it was depicted in gold on a field of "St. Patrick's blue," the color traditionally associated with Ireland until the early 1800s.

When it is used today, as it is quite widely despite not being constitution-
ally recognized, the harp emblem is modelled on the so-called Harp of
Brian Boru housed in Trinity College, Dublin. It appears on Irish coins,
the unofficial Irish state arms, the presidential flag, state seals, uniforms
and official printed documents and stationery. But the harp is perhaps
most often seen in connection with Guinness, the quasi-national brewery
that adopted it as a trademark back in 1862.

The Irish Tricolor

If the flag of present-day Ireland reminds you of the French tricolor, it's
no coincidence.

Throughout most of the last century, the official flag of British-ruled
Ireland retained the gold emblem of Brian Boru's harp. By then, the
traditional background of St. Patrick's blue had been replaced by a darkish
olive green. This was not yet the vivid green of the modern Irish banner,
however, but a shade said to have been produced by combining the
original blue with the orange that symbolized the Protestants of the north.

According to most accounts, the Irish tricolor made its debut in 1848, a
year of revolution throughout most of Europe. The Young Ireland
movement, which was particularly sympathetic to the revolution that
established the Second Republic in France, sent a delegation to Paris.
There the Irish nationalists were urged to adopt a tricolor of their own.

The model flag brought home by the delegation was based on the
French flag, comprising three vertical bands of solid color and equal
width. The colors, of course, were appropriately Irish. Farthest from the
flagstaff came a band of green, the color that had by now become a popular
national symbol among the Catholic majority. On the innermost side a
band of orange symbolized the Protestant minority. And between the two,
as Thomas F. Meagher explained in unveiling the flag, a band of white
was inserted to symbolize a peaceful union between the two chief elements
of the Irish population.

Since this flag was revolutionary and thus illegal, displaying it carried
risks. It soon fell into obscurity. During the first two decades of the
century the design was revived by Sinn Fein, the movement that was in the
process of adopting armed force as a means of winning independence.
The flag was first flown on the General Post Office during the Easter
Rising of 1916.

No one yet looked to this as a national flag — it was flown as the ensign
of "E" Company, 4th Dublin Battalion, Irish Volunteers, Patrick Pearse
commanding. Still, the flag had now (or certainly by 1920) assumed its
current form, with the colors reversed from their positions on the 1848

design: green was now nearest the flagpole and orange on the outer edge. As sympathy for Sinn Fein grew, more and more Irishmen came to regard this banner as a symbol of their solidarity with the militant nationalist group. The Irish constitution of 1937 recognized the the tricolor as the official flag of the Republic.

The flag of the President of Ireland resembles not the tricolor, but the quartering for Ireland in the Royal Arms of the United Kingdom, and the former Royal Arms of Ireland. It consists of a golden harp on a field of blue. The harp, however, is not the one used in the British arms or in Northern Ireland, but the model traditionally associated with King Brian Boru.

Symbols of the Four Provinces

For centuries before 1002 A.D., when Ireland was first united under King Brian Boru, the island had been divided into four rival kingdoms: Connacht, Leinster, Munster and Ulster. In general, a single, powerful family or clan dominated each kingdom. At times, however, this family fought for domination with rival families, occasionally having to share dominion or even losing out entirely.

When they weren't fighting local rivals for control of their own lands, the rulers of each province were often trying to expand at one another's expense.

In time, the arms or heraldic symbols of each kingdom's dominant family came to be linked with the kingdom it ruled. Thus, the "Red Hand of the O'Neills" came to symbolize Ulster, and was combined with the red cross of the De Burgos (Burke) family in the provincial arms. The family origins of the other three provinces' arms seem to have been lost. At various times, however, the arms of Leinster (a silver-stringed golden harp); Munster (three antique gold crowns); and Connacht (a black spread-eagle combined with an upright arm bearing a sword) have all served as the national arms of Ireland.

With Ireland's unification under King Brian and its gradual conquest by the Normans and English, the four kingdoms eventually disappeared as meaningful political or administrative units. But these centuries-old divisions had become ingrained. Even today, while they have little practical significance, Ireland's traditional kingdoms live on in the island's four provinces. Leinster, Munster and Connacht lie entirely within the Republic. Ulster's nine counties are divided between the Republic, which includes three, and Northern Ireland, which contains the remaining six.

The traditional arms of the four provinces live on in the official arms of the Republic, where they are quartered together on a shield.

The Wolfhound

The wolfhound figures in some of Ireland's oldest sagas. The hero Fionn, for example, had a favorite hound named Bran, and another called Sceolaing. During the first centuries A.D., the island exported choice specimens to Imperial Rome, which prized the dogs for "solemn shows and games." St. Patrick himself is said to have escaped from his boyhood enslavement in Ireland by hiding among a shipment of wolfhounds bound for the Continent.

Given their size, strength and noble bearing, we can easily imagine how these peculiarly Irish beasts came to be valued all across Europe. They were superbly suited for hunting wolves and deer, and probably ranked as status symbols as well. By the eighteenth century, however, wolves had become extinct in Ireland. No longer needed in their homeland, their numbers thinned by shipments abroad, wolfhounds themselves had nearly died out by the early decades of the last century.

Fortunately, an English dog-lover rescued the breed, crossing some of the few remaining specimens with Scottish deerhounds. By 1885, the newly formed Irish Wolfhound Club had compiled pedigrees for 300 of the dogs. Interest in the dog grew as the Irish rediscovered their past traditions in the so-called Celtic Revival. Artists began depicting the dog as an emblem of Ireland, usually grouped with a figure of Erin or Hibernia or in a trio with a round tower and shamrock. It also appeared on the sixpenny coin and was adopted by Belleek, the prestigious chinaware maker, as part of the company trademark.

Today, though the wolfhound remains a symbol among the Irish, it is mainly a token of a heroic past. Racing of greyhounds and hunting with foxhounds seem to monopolize Irish canine interests. It is in London, ironically, that the wolfhound endures as a living symbol of Ireland. There the Irish Guards, one of Britain's most distinguished regiments, keep one of the dogs as an official mascot and sometimes take it on ceremonial parade.

The Round Tower

The round towers of Ireland have been a familiar sight for centuries. Seventy of the structures dot the island, some in ruins, others well preserved. Nearly all stand next to churches, often amid the ruins of monasteries. Normally rising to between 90 and 110 feet, the towers are typically some 15 feet in diameter and are topped with conical caps. Particularly puzzling was the placement of their doors, which were generally set several feet above the ground, seemingly beyond reach of normal humans.

The questions of who had built the towers, when, and for what purpose remained subjects for unending speculation until the 19th century. Many bizarre theories were put forth, including the proposition that the towers were giant phallic symbols that had been worshipped by some ancient fertility cult.

Today scholars agree that their origins are much more straightforward. All the towers have been dated between the 9th and 12th centuries, and their proximity to early Christian monastic sites gave a further clue. They were, we now believe, nothing more than bell towers that were designed to double as places of refuge in time of danger. Given warning of a Viking raid, a common enough experience for monastic communities during this period, the monks and other inhabitants could flee to the local tower, climbing up a ladder that was pulled up behind them.

Like wolfhounds, round towers are a distinctively Irish phenomenon. Outside Ireland, only a handful exist, and these are in the west of Scotland, an area the Irish had much contact with during the period in question. So the structures were a natural choice to symbolize Ireland.

IRISH FAMILY NAMES:
THE 99 MOST COMMON SURNAMES *

1. Murphy
2. Kelly
3. Sullivan
4. Walsh
5. Smith
6. O'Brien
7. Byrne
8. Ryan
9. Connor
10. O'Neill
11. Reilly
12. Doyle
13. McCarthy
14. Gallagher
15. Doherty
16. Kennedy
17. Lynch
18. Murray
19. Quinn
20. Stewart
21. Casey
22. Foley
23. Fitzpatrick
24. Leary
25. McDonnell
26. McMahon
27. Donnelly
28. Regan
29. Burns
30. Flanagan
31. Mullan
32. Barry
33. Kane
34. Moore
35. McLoughlin
36. Carroll
37. Connolly
38. Daly
39. Connell
40. Wilson
41. Dunne
42. Brennan
43. Burke
44. Collins
45. Campbell
46. Clarke
47. Johnson
48. Hughes
49. Farrell
50. Fitzgerald
51. Brown
52. Martin
53. Robinson
54. Cunningham
55. Griffin
56. Kenny
57. Sheehan
58. Ward
59. Whelan
60. Lyons
61. Reid
62. Graham
63. Higgins
64. Cullan
65. Keane
66. King
67. Maguire
68. Nolan
69. Flynn
70. Thompson
71. Callaghan
72. O'Donnell
73. Duffy
74. Mahoney
75. Boyle
76. Healy
77. Shea
78. White
79. Sweeney
80. Hayes
81. Power
82. Kavanagh
83. McGrath
84. Moran
85. Brady
86. Maher
87. McKenna
88. Bell
89. Scott
90. Hogan
91. Keefe
92. Magee
93. McNamara
94. McDonald
95. McDermott
96. Maloney
97. Rourke
98. Buckley
99. Dwyer

* The list above was compiled in 1892 by the Registrar General of Marriages, Births and Deaths, which analyzed surnames listed during that year in departmental records. While it did not use scientific survey techniques, it is probably fairly accurate in suggesting the relative frequency of the most common Irish surnames at that time. You should not assume, however, that the rankings on this list are applicable to the Irish-American community, or even to Ireland at other times.

GAELIC GIVEN NAMES:
ORIGINS, MEANINGS AND EQUIVALENTS

MEN'S NAMES	ORIGIN AND/OR MEANING	EQUIVALENTS
Ailbhe	"Gentle one"	Alby, Albert
Ailin	"Of gentle birth"	Allen, Alan
Amhlaoibh	Norse, "Ancestral relic"	Olaf, Humphrey
Aodh	"Fire"	Hugh, Egan
Aonghus	—	Angus, Niece
Art	"Stone" or "bear"	Arthur
Brian	"Strong, sincere"	Bryan, Bernard
Buadhach	"Conqueror"	Victor
Caoimhin	"Sweet offspring"	Kevin
Cathal	"Strong in battle"	Cahal, Charles
Cian	"Ancient"	Kean, Cain
Colm	—	Colum
Conall	"Tall and strong"	Connell
Conchur	"High desire"	Connor, Cornelius
Conn	"Intelligence"	Constantine
Cormac	"Charioteer"	Charles
Criostoir	Greek, "Christ bearing"	Christopher

MEN'S NAMES	ORIGIN AND/OR MEANING	EQUIVALENTS
Deasun	"Of south Munster"	Desmond
Diarmaid	"A freeman"	Dermott, Jeremiah
Donal	"Power of the deep"	Donald, Daniel
Donnchadh	"Brown warrior"	Donogh, Denis, Duncan
Eamonn	Anglo-Saxon, "Blessed protection"	Edmund
Eoin	Hebrew, "Gift of God"	John
Eoghan	"Well-born"	Owen, Eugene
Fearghal	"Bravest of the brave"	Fergal, Virgil
Fearghus	"The choicest one"	Fergus, Ferdinand
Fionn	"Bright (like the sun god)"	Finn
Flann	"Blood red"	Florence
Liam	Germanic, "Strong protector"	William
Niall	"Champion"	Neil
Padraig	Latin, "Noble"	Patrick
Peadar	Greek, "Rock"	Peter
Piras	Norman form of Peter	Piers, Pierce, Pearse
Ruairi	Norse, "Famous ruler"	Rory, Roger, Roderick

MEN'S NAMES	ORIGIN AND/OR MEANING	EQUIVALENTS
Seamus	Spanish name, "Jaime," from Hebrew, "Supplanter"	James
Sean	Norman French, from Hebrew, "Gift of God"	John
Traolach, Tarlach	"Incarnation of the thunder"	Turlogh, Terence

WOMEN'S NAMES		
Aine	"Beauty" (A quality of the moon)	Anne
Aisling	"An epiphany; manifestation of the Divine"	Esther
Aoibheann	"Lovely shape"	Eavan
Blathnaid	"Little flower"	Florence
Brighid	"Strength"	Brigid, Bridie
Caitrin, Cait, Caitilin	Greek, "Pure"	Katherine, Kate, Catriona
Ciara	"The dark one"	Keary
Damhnait	"Little poet"	Devnet, Dymphna
Eibhlin	Greek, "Sunlight"	Eileen, Evelyn, Helen
Eilis	Hebrew, "Word of God"	Elizabeth

WOMEN'S NAMES	ORIGIN AND/OR MEANING	EQUIVALENTS
Eithne	"Kernel"	Ethna, Edna
Fionnuala	"Bright shoulder" (an attribute of the moon)	Finola, Nuala
Gobnait	"Small mouth"	Abigail, Deborah
Gormfhlaith	"The stranger lady"	Barbara
Grainne	"Perfect," "virginal" (attributes of the moon)	Grania, Grace, Gertrude
Ide	"Thirst"	Ida, Ita
Mairead	Greek, "A pearl"	Margaret, Marjorie
Muire, Maire	Hebrew, "Of the sea," "bitterness"	Mary, Maria, Maura, Miriam, Moya, May
Nora	Latin, "Honorable"	Norah, Honor
Orfhlaith	"The golden lady"	Orla
Proinnseas	Latin, "French, frank"	Frances, Fanny
Sile	Latin, "Blind"	Sheila, Cecily, Julia
Siobhan, Siun	Feminine of Sean	Joan, Joanna, Jeanne, Hannah
Sorcha	"Bright"	Sarah
Una	"The white one" (an attribute of the moon)	Agnes, Winifred, Freda

IRISH WORDS THAT HAVE ENRICHED
THE ENGLISH LANGUAGE

Banshee – In Irish tradition, a female spirit believed to foretell a death in the family by appearing to family members or wailing outside their house. (From Irish Gaelic, *bean sidhe*, woman of the fairies.)

Bard – A member of an ancient Celtic order of poets who wrote and performed verses in song recalling the legends and histories of their tribes. The word has come to refer, more generally, to any poet, but especially a revered national poet, such as Shakespeare. (From Gaelic and Irish, *bard*, and Welsh, *bardd*.)

Blarney – Words intended to flatter, beguile or cajole. (From the *Blarney* stone, located at Blarney Castle near Cork, which tradition says gives those who kiss it the skill of flattery.)

Bog – Waterlogged and spongy ground, whose soil consists mainly of decayed vegetable matter. The word also refers to an area of such ground, such as a marsh or swamp and, as a verb, "to be *bogged* down," means to be hindered, slowed or impeded, as if in a bog. (From Irish or Gaelic *bogach*, meaning soft ground.)

Boycott – To refrain from buying from, using or dealing with, usually as a group, in order to protest or bring pressure against. (After a 19th century English soldier, Captain Charles *Boycott*, who served as land agent for the Earl of Erne. To protest Boycott's refusal to lower their rents, the earl's tenants shunned him, helping give the world a new word for such nonviolent collective action.)

Brogue – A marked dialectal accent in pronouncing English, especially a heavy Irish accent. This use of the word comes from the older meaning of *brogue*, i.e., a heavy shoe made of untanned leather such as was formerly worn by Irish and Scottish peasants. (From Irish, *brog*, meaning shoe.)

Carrageen (Also, **carragheen, carageen**) – A purplish-brown North Atlantic seaweed, also called Irish Moss, which yields a gelatin-like extract used in medicine and cooking. (From *Carragheen*, near Waterford, where the plant is found in particular abundance.)

Colleen – An Irish girl, especially a young one. (From Irish, *cailin*, roughly little countrywoman.)

Donnybrook – A brawl or free-for-all; an unusually wild and uncontrollable fight. (From *Donnybrook*, County Dublin, where a fair held annually until 1855 was noted for riotous and large altercations.)

Galore – Occurring or available in abundant or plentiful amounts, or great numbers. (From Irish *go leor*, meaning roughly, to sufficiency.)

Hooligan – A young ruffian or hoodlum. (Generally thought to derive from an Irish family, the *Houlihans*, some of whom justly or unjustly became associated in the common mind with rowdy, violent behavior.)

Keen – A wailing lament for the deceased, or the act of so wailing. (From Irish, *caoine*, meaning lament.)

Limerick – A distinctive form of humorous or nonsensical verse consisting of five lines. The first, second and fifth lines rhyme with each other, while the shorter third and fourth lines form a separate rhyming pattern. (From *Limerick*, North Munster, where the verse-form was first practiced. At a social gathering, tradition says, each member of the party would invent a set of verses, after which the rest the group sang, "Won't you come up to Limerick?")

Lynch – To execute without benefit of due process, especially by hanging. (There are two theories about the origin of this term. According to one, it goes back several centuries to a lord mayor of Galway named *Lynch*, who was obliged by duty to hang his own son as a criminal. The second theory derives the term from Charles *Lynch*, an 18th-century Virginia planter and justice of the peace, who gained a wide reputation as a "hanging judge.")

Shanty – A crudely built, rickety cabin; a shack. (Probably from Irish, *sean tig*, old house.)

Shillelagh – A wooden cudgel or club, customarily made of blackthorn or oak. (From *Shillelagh*, County Wicklow, where these weapons were first made.)

Smithereens – Small pieces or bits of a larger object, usually one that has been violently broken. (From Irish, *smidireen*, diminutive of *smoidar*, small fragment.)

Whiskey – A liquor distilled from barley, rye, corn or other grain and typically containing from 40 to 50 percent alcohol by volume. (From *whiskybae*, derived in turn from Gaelic *uisgebeatha* or *usquebaugh*, water of life. NOTE: Whiskey is the usual spelling in the United States and Ireland, especially when referring to American or Irish liquor. The Scotch and Canadian liquors are generally spelled whisky, especially in their homelands.)

IRELAND IN THE WHITE HOUSE:
U.S. PRESIDENTS OF IRISH HERITAGE

For a people whose Old World forebears had typically lived in humble huts or cottages, Irish-Americans have made it in surprising numbers to the most prestigious address in America. Even for so-called Scots-Irish and other Protestant immigrants, who furnished most of the earlier Irish settlers and most of our presidents of Irish heritage, a move into the White House usually marked an almost incredible advance beyond the circumstances of their fathers, or their fathers before them. In all, from John Adams to Ronald Reagan, no fewer than 17 Presidents of the United States have traced all or part of their ancestry to Ireland. Three were sons of immigrants.

Indeed, the very architect of the White House was an Irish-Catholic immigrant. James Hoban (1758-1831), a native of Kilkenny who had settled in Charleston, South Carolina, was chosen for the assignment in competition with a large number of other architects. In planning the home of America's First Families, Hoban is said to have been strongly influenced by the design of Dublin's Leinster House, which serves today as the meeting place for Ireland's parliament.

The roster of U.S. presidents of Irish heritage reads as follows:

1. **John Adams** – His mother, Susanna Boylston Adams, was reportedly descended from a family that had been small farmers in Ulster for generations. The family name is thought originally to have been Boyle, embellished to Boylston, as was not uncommonly done.

2. **James Monroe** – Monroe's Irish antecedents are a little hard to pin down, but a direct ancestor named Monroe (or Munro) is said to have been a Scottish officer who married a local woman while serving in Ulster during the late 17th or early 18th century.

3. **John Quincy Adams** – As the son of John Adams, he naturally had his father's Boylston heritage.

4. **Andrew Jackson** – Both parents came from the village of Boneybefore in Carrickfergus, County Antrim.

5. **James K. Polk** – The family name had originally been Pollock, a common Ulster name since the Plantation of the early 1600s. His mother's family was also from Ulster.

6. **James Buchanan** – Both of his father's parents came from County Donegal, after having lived for a time in Larne, County Antrim. His mother's roots seem also to have been in Ulster.

7. **Andrew Johnson** – His Irish ancestors came from County Antrim.

8. **Ulysses S. Grant** – Grant's mother, Hannah Simpson, lived in a small farmhouse at Dergenagh, County Tyrone, before emigrating to America.

9. **Chester A. Arthur** – His father, William Arthur, was born in the Dreen, Cullybackey, County Antrim, in a house that still stands. His mother was reportedly also of Ulster ancestry.

10. **Grover Cleveland** – His mother's father was a Neal (or Neill) who had immigrated from Ulster.

11. **Benjamin Harrison** – Harrison had Ulster roots on his mother's side.

12. **William McKinley** – His father's family had come from Dervock, County Antrim, where the name had been spelled "McKinlay."

13. **Theodore Roosevelt** – TR's mother, Martha Bullock, came from a Scots-Irish and Huguenot family that had lived in County Antrim. His father's mother, Margaret Potts Burnhill, is said to have been born in County Meath.

14. **Woodrow Wilson** – Both his paternal grandparents -- James Wilson and Annie Mills (Wilson) – were from the Strabane area of County Antrim.

15. **John Fitzgerald Kennedy** – Kennedy's ancestors all came from Ireland. His paternal great-grandfather, Patrick Kennedy, had immigrated from Dunganstown, New Ross, County Wexford, to Boston, and there married Bridget Murphy, another immigrant. The paternal grandparents of Kennedy's mother – Thomas Fitzgerald and Rose Mary Murray – had also immigrated from County Wexford.

16. **Richard M. Nixon** – Nixon numbered Irish Quakers among his forebears. His great-great-grandfather, Richard Milhous, was born at Timahoe, County Laois. While in the White House, the Nixons owned an Irish setter they named King Timahoe.

17. **Ronald W. Reagan** – Reagan's paternal great-grandfather, Michael Regan, emigrated from Ballyporeen, County Tipperary, in 1829.

125 NOTABLE IRISH-AMERICANS, PAST AND PRESENT

Americans of Irish descent have ranked among our country's leading achievers since long before there was a United States. In the political and military efforts that established American independence, in fact, individuals of Irish heritage – Catholic and Protestant alike – were unusually active as both leaders and rank-and-file. And since then – despite the anti-Irish bias triggered by the mass influx of poor, mostly Catholic, famine victims in the 1830s and 1840s – Irish-Americans have earned fame and often fortune in virtually every field.

As with some other sections of this book, we make no pretense that this is the final word on the subject. Our space is far too limited to do justice to the thousands of Irish- Americans who have a good claim to be represented here. Nor do we claim that the 125-odd individuals covered below are *the* most important Irish-Americans.

Such lists, of course, always reflect opinion and arbitrary judgment. Most of us would agree that the names of John F. Kennedy, Charles Carroll of Carrollton, Eugene O'Neill, General Philip Sheridan, Herman "Babe" Ruth and a few others belong at or near the top in any selection of Irish-American "greats." But, pretty soon after these, the going gets a lot tougher. What criteria do you use?

Is a famous Irish-American architect more important than a leading singer? How do you measure fame or importance, anyway? And, in a society that recalls too little of its past – and where opinion is often shaped by those with a flair for promoting themselves or others – how closely does someone's fame parallel his or her historical importance? Is popularity or name- recognition a measure, since quantifying a person's importance is otherwise impossible?

Enough said! The distinguished Irish-Americans covered below are *among* the most important, living or dead. Collectively, their stories show the range and depth of the Irish contribution to America. (Note that John F. Kennedy, Ronald Reagan and 15 other U.S. presidents of Irish descent are covered in another chapter.):

BUSINESS, INDUSTRY AND FINANCE

ALEXANDER BROWN (1764-1834), a native of Ulster, emigrated from Belfast to Baltimore in 1800, where he soon became the largest American importer of Irish linens. He was active in trading a variety of commodities, but came to specialize in cotton exports to Liverpool.

Alexander Brown & Sons, the private mercantile and banking house Brown founded, is America's oldest investment banking firm. Brown entrusted each of his sons with a branch company, one of which survives as the prestigious New York-based firm, Brown Brothers Harriman. Alexander Brown was a major shareholder in the Bank of the United States and was instrumental in establishing the city waterworks of Baltimore and Mechanics Bank of Baltimore. He and one of his sons were also key figures in founding the Baltimore & Ohio Railroad in 1827, a major step in bringing railways to the United States. When he died, Brown was one of the nation's few millionaires.

MICHAEL CUDAHY (1841-1910) – One of the developers of the modern meatpacking industry, Cudahy was born in Callan, Ireland, and came to the United States with his family in 1849. He went to work as a meat packer in Milwaukee at age 14, and gradually worked his way up to management, then establishing his own firm. Cudahy's company pioneered the use of cold-storage facilities in packing plants. Since animals could now be slaughtered and frozen for later sale, his innovation revolutionized the industry by making possible for the first time the year-round marketing of livestock.

HENRY FORD (1863-1947) – A household name if ever there was one, Henry Ford was the son of Irish immigrants. The pioneering American automobile manufacturer was perhaps most famous for introducing mass-production techniques with the famous Ford Model T. This innovation made the automobile affordable to the average American for the first time, and helped unleash a far-reaching social and economic revolution. Ford's creation, the Ford Motor Company, ranks among the world's major industrial firms and has traditionally been second in the U.S. automotive market. Today it makes and markets not only cars but trucks, farm equipment, home appliances and aerospace vehicles and components.

WILLIAM RUSSELL GRACE (1832-1904) – Irish-American businessman, steamship line operator and public official. Born in County Cork, Grace emigrated to Peru, where he founded William R. Grace & Co., a shipping line, before relocating to the U.S. Thriving in his business pursuits, he ran successfully for mayor of New York in 1880. Grace was the first Roman Catholic to serve in that office, and a man known for his freedom from corruption.

WILLIAM RANDOLPH HEARST (1863-1951) – Legendary editor, publisher and political leader known for his grand style and autocratic manner. Hearst created the nation's largest newspaper chain, which has evolved into one of today's largest privately owned communications empires. He also served in Congress and found time to amass an impressive collection of art and antiquities, now housed at San Simeon, his palatial former estate in California. His life, achievements and methods inspired the classic film, *Citizen Kane*.

HOWARD R. HUGHES (1905-1976) – U.S. aviation pioneer and industrialist who owned one of the world's largest fortunes at the time of his death. A colorful, flamboyant playboy during his early career, Hughes became a reclusive, eccentric Midas during the last two decades of his life, prompting endless curiosity and speculation. Hughes Aircraft and Hughes Tool Company brought him billionaire status.

JOSEPH PATRICK KENNEDY (1888-1969) – Boston-born businessman and politician-statesman who sired three U.S. senators (John F., Robert F. and Edward M. Kennedy), the first of whom became 35th President of the United States. After amassing a fortune in the pre-Depression stock market and motion picture ventures, Kennedy was named chairman of the newly formed Securities and Exchange Commission (SEC) by President Franklin D. Roosevelt in 1934. He served as ambassador to Britain from 1937 to 1940.

SAMUEL S. McCLURE (1857-1949) – Emigrating from County Antrim as a child, McClure became an active journalist during college in Illinois. In 1884 he launched a literary syndicate – America's first – which within a few years was supplying newspapers with high-quality material by the leading U.S. and European writers of the day. *McClure's Magazine* (1893–approx. 1925), published exposes by leading social crusaders including Ida Tarbell and Lincoln Steffens. It became a leading force in reform journalism or – as some preferred to call it – "muckraking."

ANDREW W. MELLON (1855-1933) – After starting a successful lumber firm, Mellon joined the Pittsburgh bank his immigrant father had founded, rising to head it ten years later. An astute judge of business ventures, he backed the start-up and growth of Aluminum Company of America, Gulf Oil, Union Steel and other firms that came to rank among the nation's largest. Though a major capitalist and one of the country's wealthiest men, Mellon was almost unknown to the public until he was named Treasury Secretary by President Harding in 1921. He guided the nation's financial affairs during the boom years of the 'Twenties and into America's severest depression, leaving office with the advent of FDR and the New Deal. Before his death Mellon donated his huge art collection to the government together with a major endowment, making possible the establishment of the National Gallery of Art, Washington, DC.

THOMAS A. MURPHY (1915-) – Joining General Motors in 1938, Murphy rose steadily through the ranks of financial management. From 1974 to 1980 – a period of great challenge for the U.S. automobile industry – he served as chairman and chief executive of this, the nation's largest manufacturing firm.

THOMAS F. RYAN (1851-1928) – A financier and businessman of uncommon talent, Ryan began his career by establishing a brokerage firm in 1873. He went on to acquire the franchise for New York City's street railways, later consolidating the lines with August Belmont's subway interests. He organized the American Tobacco Company – dissolved in 1911 as an illegal monopoly – and held large interests in banks, railroads, insurance companies and natural-resource ventures. His middle name, aptly, was "Fortune."

ALEXANDER T. STEWART (1803-1876) – County Antrim-born Stewart pioneered the department-store concept in America. A.T. Stewart & Co., the great New York store he founded, was later acquired by the Wanamaker chain of Philadelphia and continued to operate until 1954. Stewart was reputedly the richest man in America at one time, and used part of his fortune to establish Garden City, New York, one of the country's first planned communities.

EDUCATION

JOHN R. GREGG (1867-1948) – Born in Rockcorry, County Monaghan, he emigrated to the U.S. in 1893. Here he eventually perfected the Gregg system of shorthand, the first practical, easily learnable form of shorthand writing, which helped make office operations tremendously more productive. Although its days seem numbered, Gregg shorthand is still taught and widely used in this age of dictating machines and automated word processors.

WILLIAM H. McGUFFEY (1800-1873) –During an academic career in which he taught languages and moral philosophy at the college level and served as president of Cincinnati College and Ohio University, McGuffey pursued a lifelong interest in public education. The result was his famous series of *Eclectic Readers*, used by generations of American elementary-school students. The six readers went through numerous revisions and expansions, eventually selling more than 120 million copies. "McGuffey's Readers" had a major influence on how Americans thought during the 19th century.

ENTERTAINMENT: MUSIC, FILMS, THEATRE AND BROADCAST

WALTER BRENNAN (1894-1974) – An actor who portrayed colorful old-timers in scores of Westerns, Brennan was named to the Cowboy Hall of Fame in 1970. He appeared in over 100 films, winning three Oscars as Best Supporting Actor. Brennan is perhaps best remembered as the crochety but lovable Grandpa McCoy, the role he created in the TV series, *The Real McCoys.*

ELLEN BURSTYN (1932-) – Born Edna Rae Gillooly to a middle-class Irish-Catholic family, this Detroit-reared actress hit her stride in the 1970s. In 1974 she had the rare distinction of winning both a Tony Award (for *Same Time, Next Year*) and an Oscar (for *Alice Doesn't Live Here Anymore*). Burstyn has also earned one Emmy nomination and three others for Oscars.

JAMES CAGNEY (1904-1986) – From his first tough-guy role in *Public Enemy*, no gangster film in the 1930s seemed complete without him. When gangsters went out of vogue with the end of Prohibition, Cagney sweetened up his on-camera image. In 1942, he won an Oscar as Best Actor for *Yankee Doodle Dandy*, a movie that immortalized the life and career of the Irish-American composer, George M. Cohan. His more recent film credits included *Ragtime* and *Terrible Joe Moran*. The American Film Institute bestowed its Life Achievement Award on Cagney in 1974.

HOAGY CARMICHAEL (1899-1981) – Born Hoagland Howard Carmichael, "Hoagy" was blessed with a multitude of talents. He is probably best remembered, however, as the song writer who gave us such numbers as "Stardust," "Lazy River," "Georgia on My Mind," "Lazy Bones," and "Heart and Soul." At least 50 of his songs, in fact, made it to the hit lists. Carmichael also sang, acted and excelled on the piano; he wrote music for the theatre, films, nightclub acts and his own TV show.

GEORGE M. COHAN (1878-1942) – Generally considered the father of American musical comedy, Cohan was a man of legendary versatility: actor, songwriter, playwright, director and producer. His patriotic World War I composition, "Over There," earned him a Congressional medal, and other songs like "You're a Grand Old Flag" and "Give My Regards to Broadway" also set Americans' toes a-tapping. Cohan's life and career were celebrated in the 1942 movie, *Yankee Doodle Dandy* as well as the Broadway show, *George M.*

HARRY L. ("BING") CROSBY (1904-1977) – One of America's best-loved entertainers, "Bing" was best known for his mellow, dreamy crooning. He gave us classic renditions of "Blue Skies," "Silent Night" and "White Christmas," with the last selling more copies than any other single ever released. Crosby made over 850 recordings and sold over 300 million records. He appeared in over 50 films — including the popular "Road" comedies with Bob Hope and Dorothy Lamour — and won an Oscar in 1944 for *Going My Way*. An avid golfer, Crosby established the Crosby National Pro-Am Golf Tournament.

THE DORSEY BROTHERS: JIMMY (1904-1956) **& TOMMY** (1905-1956) – As dance-band leaders, these brothers rode the crest of the swing craze during the big-band era of the 1930s and 1940s. With Jimmy playing saxophone and Tommy the trombone, they formed the first of their renowned jazz bands around 1920. Going their separate ways for 18 years, the Dorseys pursued successful careers as band leaders and in film and TV appearances. Reunited in 1953, they put together one final, popular orchestra.

FAYE DUNAWAY (1941-) – This glamorous actress zoomed to stardom after playing Bonnie Parker, the Depression-era bank robber, in the bloody and controversial film, *Bonnie and Clyde*. She won an Oscar for that role, and a second for her portrayal of a ruthless TV executive in the 1976 release, *Network*. Among Dunaway's other films are *Chinatown, Three Days of the Condor* and *Mommie Dearest*.

DANIEL D. EMMETT (1815-1904) – Born in Mount Vernon, Ohio, Emmett organized one of the first minstrel show troupes, a form of entertainment that became enormously popular during the 19th century. In 1859, he wrote the song, "Dixie," for the conclusion of a minstrel-show performance. The song became popular overnight, particularly in the South, and during the Civil War it became the unofficial national anthem of the Confederacy. It has remained a powerful symbol of traditional Southern culture and values.

EILEEN FARRELL (1920-) – Born to Irish-American parents active in vaudeville, singer Farrell launched her career in 1941 with popular songs for the Columbia Broadcasting Company. The range of her soprano voice and her dramatic flair, however, soon proved that she could tackle a far wider repertoire. She turned to classical music, touring the U.S. and Latin American with major symphony orchestras, and made her debut with New York's Metropolitan Opera in 1960.

JOHN FORD (1895-1973) – Born Sean O'Feeney in Maine, Ford directed over 130 films whose standards of excellence continue to inspire filmmakers today. Sweeping scenes of nature and an undercurrent of social concern characterize many of his works. Ford won Oscars for *The Informer, The Grapes of Wrath, How Green Was My Valley, The Battle of Midway* and *December Seventh.* He also received the American Film Institute's Life Achievement Award and the Presidential Medal of Freedom.

JACKIE GLEASON (1916-) – A rotund, irrepressible entertainer, Gleason became a cult figure for many Americans in his role as the bombastic but lovable Ralph Kramden in the TV series, *The Honeymooners.* He also starred in the *Cavalcade of Stars* series during the 1950s as well as earning the title, "Mr. Saturday Night" as host of the popular, long-running *Jackie Gleason Show.* Gleason also brought his talents to Broadway and the screen, appearing in such films as *Requiem for a Heavyweight, Smokey and the Bandit* and *The Hustler.* As conductor of the Jackie Gleason Orchestra, he recorded some 40 albums.

ARTHUR GODFREY (1903-1983) – Americans first took note of Godfrey in 1945, when he defied convention by daring to poke fun at the commercial sponsors of his CBS radio show. His mastery of the ad-lib and his chatty, informal style kept viewers and sponsors guessing at what he'd say next. Branching out from radio, Godfrey went on to become a well-known TV host on such shows as *Arthur Godfrey's Talent Scouts* and *The Arthur Godfrey Show.*

HELEN HAYES (1900-) – Justly known as "First Lady of the American Theatre," Hayes' acting career spans eight decades. Particularly notable among her stage credits were the title roles in *Mary of Scotland* and *Victoria Regina.* She also appeared in many films, earning Oscars for *Claudet* (1932) and *Airport* (1971). Hayes' other honors include an Emmy, the Medal of the City of New York and — perhaps the ultimate compliment for an actress — having a Broadway theatre named for her in 1955. Despite her active professional career, Hayes has also found time for major efforts on behalf of charitable causes.

VICTOR HERBERT (1859-1924) – Born in Dublin, Herbert earned his most lasting fame as a composer of comic opera. He began his career as a cellist, playing with major orchestras in Europe and New York before accepting an offer to become conductor of the Pittsburgh Symphony in 1898. In 1904, Herbert turned to composing full-time, and was soon delighting audiences with such operettas as *Babes in Toyland, Naughty*

Marietta and *Mlle. Modiste*, whose songs and music are still widely loved. The first American to compose an original score for a motion picture, Herbert also wrote two grand operas, *Natoma* and *Madeleine.*

EMMETT KELLY (1898-1979) – America's most famous pantomime clown, Kelly was the son of a staunchly patriotic Irish immigrant who named him for the Irish patriot, Robert Emmet. Kelly's reputation was built on characterizations marked by pathos rather than slapstick comedy. He first created a tattered hobo, "Weary Willie," as a cartoon character, then brought Willie to life in circus performances in Britain and the U.S. Most closely associated with Ringling Brothers Barnum and Bailey Circus, Kelly became a familiar face on TV, in nightclub acts and in such movies as *The Greatest Show on Earth.*

GENE KELLY (1912-) – One of the country's most popular dancers, Kelly pirouetted, flipped and tap-danced his way into American hearts in such musicals as *On the Town, An American in Paris* and *Singing in the Rain.* His virile dance moves – combining ballet, gymnastics, tap and modern dance – revolutionized film choreography and helped create an American style of dance. Over four decades, Kelly not only danced, but wore the hats of dramatic actor, singer, director, choreographer and producer.

GRACE KELLY (1929-1982) – Rarely has life yielded to Hollywood fantasy so much as in Grace Kelly's career. Though the family she was born into was prosperous, even wealthy, it had come very far very quickly. Her immigrant grandfather had established a bricklaying firm in Philadelphia, and her father had worked at the craft as well as helping manage the business. "Jack" Kelly had gone on, however, to win laurels as an Olympic rower, and brothers George and Walter had gained reputations as a playwright and a vaudeville performer, respectively. After her stage debut in 1948, Grace Kelly's career blossomed with a series of film roles. She starred in such movies as *Dial M for Murder, Rear Window, To Catch a Thief* and *High Noon,* and her performance in *The Country Girl* brought an Oscar in 1954. Not long afterwards, having caught the eye and heart of Monaco's Prince Ranier, she was drawn into a whirlwind romance that ended in a fairytale marriage and her transformation to Her Serene Highness, Princess Grace of Monaco. As a real-life princess, Kelly never forgot her Irish roots, and devoted herself to family, charities and cultural projects before her tragic, untimely death in an auto accident.

JOSHUA LOGAN (1908-) – After getting his start in college theatricals at Princeton, Logan spent most of his career behind the scenes as a writer, director or producer — and sometimes all three. His unusual combination of talents helped bring to life such legendary stage productions as *Mister Roberts, South Pacific* and *Fanny.* Logan's many film credits included *South Pacific, Camelot* and *Ensign Pulver.*

JOHN McCORMACK (1884-1945) – Probably the most famous of Irish tenors, McCormack was born at Athlone, County Westmeath. After winning a gold medal at age 18 in Dublin's National Irish Festival, he studied in Italy and went on to a series of operatic successes in leading European and U.S. cities. By the time he became a U.S. citizen in 1917, McCormack had given up operatic performances in favor of concerts. He was equally at home with classical arias and traditional Irish songs, and is fondly remembered for his moving renditions of the latter.

ED McMAHON (1923-) – Ed McMahon has been Johnny Carson's "Number Two" on *The Tonight Show* for 24 years. As Carson's sidekick and straightman, however, his inimitable "He-e-e-e-re's Johnny!!" introduction and distinctive belly laugh have made him as unforgettable as Carson himself. McMahon has also done numerous commercials, plugging everything from beer to Cheer; acted in several movies; and carved out a niche as a successful TV host and producer in his own right.

J. CARROLL NAISH (1900-1973) – Born on New York's Upper East Side, this Irish-American traced his Irish roots to the 13th century. In a career that took in stage, TV, radio and over 250 movies, Naish showed an unsurpassed mastery of languages and talent for mimicry. His skills enabled him to portray characters of many nationalities, earning him a reputation as "Hollywood's one-man United Nations."

JACK NICHOLSON (1937-) – Bit parts in B-films marked the early years of Nicholson's Hollywood career until his role in the 1969 release, *Easy Rider*, thrust him to the fore. He went on to win Oscars for such acclaimed films as *One Flew Over the Cuckoo's Nest* (1975) and *Terms of Endearment* (1983). Nicholson has also shown talent as a director and producer.

PAT O'BRIEN (1899-1983) – All four of his grandparents were Irish immigrants, so it will come as little surprise that Pat O'Brien spent most of his career playing the stereotypical Irish-American – rugged, friendly and loquacious. He won roles in over 100 movies, typically playing priests, policemen and soldiers. O'Brien is well-known also for his lead in the TV series, *Harrigan and Son*, as well as for his screen portrayals of the legendary Notre Dame football coach in *Knute Rockne – All-American*, and of Father Duffy, legendary chaplain of *The Fighting 69th.*

CARROLL O'CONNOR (1924-) – O'Connor made his reputation as Archie Bunker, the blue-collar bigot and bully known to millions from the controversial TV comedy, *All in the Family.* During the dozen years he ruled the airwaves as Archie, he won four Emmies and brought such explosive issues as integration right into America's living rooms. Born in New York City, O'Connor returned to the land of his ancestors to study at the National University of Ireland, and traveled the country on an acting tour.

MAUREEN O'HARA (1921-) – Born Maureen Fitzsimmons to a theatrical family in Dublin, O'Hara emigrated to the U.S. in 1939. The red-haired beauty, with her classic looks, was soon a sought-after actress, often as the heroine in swashbuckling adventure movies. Notable among her long list of credits are *How Green Was My Valley*, *The Quiet Man* and *Miracle on 34th Street.* In more recent years, she married an airline pilot who ran a Caribbean-based airline, then took over active management of the line following his death in an accident.

RYAN O'NEAL (1941-) – Starting with bit parts on TV in the 1960s, O'Neal landed a starring role in the popular series, *Peyton Place.* His creditable performances, boyish good looks and clean-cut image made him a natural choice for a co-lead as the Harvard preppie in the blockbuster 1970 film, *Love Story.* That role earned him an Oscar nomination and catapulted him to stardom. His roles since then have included *Paper Moon* (1973), in which his daughter, Tatum O'Neal, also played a leading part.

GREGORY PECK (1916-) – One of America's most distinguished film actors, Gregory Peck was born in San Diego, California, the son of Katerine Ashe, a native of Dingle, County Kerry. Between dozens of film roles — including *To Kill A Mockingbird*, which won him an Oscar, and *Keys of the Kingdom, The Yearling, Gentlemen's Agreement* and *Twelve O'Clock High*, for which he received Oscar nominations — Peck has kept up his connections in Ireland, living in Galway for a time in 1970. One of his earlier films, *Moby Dick*, was filmed in Ireland.

TYRONE POWER (1914-1958) – If ever acting was in someone's blood, it was in Tyrone Power's. The great-grandson of a noted Irish actor who had been a comedian at London's Drury Lane Theatre, Power also brought classic good looks and a swashbuckling flair to his roles.

Beginning with a stage company in Shakespearean repertory, Power went on to star in more than 40 movies. He was particularly sought after for historical romances such as *The Black Rose* and *Blood and Sand*.

ANTHONY RUDOLPH OAXACA QUINN (1915-) – For many people, Anthony Quinn will always be "Zorba the Greek," the role he created in the 1964 film and again, on Broadway, in 1983. Born in Mexico to a Mexican mother and an Irish father, his trademarks are his swarthy looks and the intensity he projects. Quinn has made over 175 films, winning Oscars for *Viva Zapata* and *Lust for Life*. *Requiem for a Heavyweight* and *The Shoes of the Fisherman* were other Quinn landmarks. He is less familiar, but nonetheless talented, as a writer and artist.

MICKEY ROONEY (1920-) – Born Joe Yule, Jr. into a family of vaudevillians, this short, baby-faced actor made his acting debut at age 3 by wandering onstage during a performance. In 1938, he launched the popular, long-running "Andy Hardy" film series and has since appeared in a number of other movies, including *Boys Town, The Bridges at Toko-Ri, Huckleberry Finn* and *Requiem for a Heavyweight*. Like his fellow child-actor, Jackie Cooper, Rooney reached a point where it seemed he was a has-been. Though he declared bankruptcy in 1963, he was always the irrepressible entertainer. Rooney made a successful comeback, highlighted beginning in 1979 by a lead role opposite Ann Miller in the long-running Broadway hit, *Sugar Babies*. He married actress Ava Gardner during World War II and has since remarried seven times.

ROBERT RYAN (1909- 1973) – Film actor Robert Ryan, typically cast as the tough, macho, yet intelligent type, came to acting by a roundabout route. Graduating from Dartmouth in the Depression year of 1932, Ryan studied with noted acting teachers but then pursued a long string of unrelated if often colorful jobs. By the time he broke into stage and film roles in the early 1940s, he had worked as a sandhog, seaman, salesman, miner, cowboy, gold prospector, photographer's model, WPA laborer, paving supervisor, loan collector and school supplies superintendent. If anything, these experiences gave him added credibility in his film career, whose highlights include *Flying Leathernecks, Berlin Express, Clash by Night, Bad Day at Black Rock, God's Little Acre, Knockout, The Longest Day* and *Billy Budd*. Ryan has also been active offstage, founding a private, nonsectarian school for children and heading the Southern California branch of the United World Federalists.

MACK SENNETT (1884-1960) – Born Michael Sinnott, Sennett was a pioneering director and producer of American motion pictures. Although he made about 1,000 films during his career, he earned his reputation with *The Keystone Cops* and other slapstick comedy classics of the silent-film era. Custard-pie fights and automobile chases were typical Sennett touches. Among the renowned comic actors he directed were Charlie Chaplin, Buster Keaton and W.C. Fields. A biography of Sennett, *King of Comedy*, appeared in 1954.

ED SULLIVAN (1902-1974) – Beginning his career in vaudeville and subsequently writing a syndicated Broadway gossip column, Ed Sullivan went on to become, in the opinion of many, the greatest showman of the century. In 1948 he launched his television career with the show, "Toast of the Town." This program evolved into "The Ed Sullivan Show," which ran until 1970. Over the years he used his variety shows to introduce an enormous range of talent to American viewers – from the Beatles to Nureyev, to name but two examples. Personally, Sullivan's style was characterized by a dead-pan expression and low-key presentation. Among many honors he received were four government citations for his extensive benefit work.

SPENCER TRACY (1900-1967) – As an "actor's actor" whose hallmark was his quiet reserve, Spencer Tracy drew crowds to American cinemas for more than 30 years. He co-starred in nine films with long-time friend Katherine Hepburn and was often cast as a tough-minded man facing formidable odds or as a strong father figure. Tracy won Oscars for his portrayal of a Portuguese-American fisherman in *Captains Courageous* (1937) and of Father Flanagan in *Boys Town* (1938). His other notable films include *The Old Man and the Sea, Inherit the Wind* and *Judgment at Nuremberg*.

FINE ARTS AND ARCHITECTURE

JAMES E. KELLY (1855-1933) – A New York-born artist, Kelly earned the title, "the sculptor of American history." Although relatively few recognize his name, Kelly's works are familiar to millions. They include *Sheridan's Ride* and *Paul Revere*; bronze busts of American military heroes, including Grant, Sherman, Sheridan and Admiral Dewey; and an equestrian statue of "Teddy" Roosevelt at San Juan Hill.

GEORGIA O'KEEFFE (1887-1986) – Deciding to become a painter at age 12 – "the only thing I could do that was nobody else's business" –

O'Keeffe remained a staunch individualist throughout her long and distinguished artistic career. At a time when working outside the home was unusual for a woman – let alone blazing trails in a virtually all-male field – O'Keeffe quickly became known for paintings that were strong, candid and colorful, offering fresh insights into their subjects. Her many paintings of desert scenes near her New Mexico home, and of natural objects such as flowers, shells and bones, have found their way into leading collections around the world and helped bring her prestigious awards as well as the admiration of her peers.

LOUIS H. SULLIVAN (1856-1924) – Boston-born Sullivan, son of an immigrant from County Cork, is considered the "father of modernism in architecture." He revolutionized the face of America's cities with his radical new building designs, including the Transportation Building for the World's Columbian Exposition of 1892-1893 and Chicago's Auditorium and Gage buildings. More than anyone, Sullivan created the modern sky-scraper. He broke with the classical tradition that had long governed archictectural design and created buildings "whose form followed their function." Frank Lloyd Wright, a later architectural giant, cited Sullivan as his chief inspiration.

HUMAN SERVICE

THOMAS ANTHONY DOOLEY III (1927-1961) – Tom Dooley gave up the chance for a lucrative medical practice in the United States to serve suffering thousands in Southeast Asia. His first experience of the region came as a Navy doctor in 1954, when he helped refugees fleeing Communist North Vietnam. Leaving the service in 1956, he began a medical mission in the jungle of neighboring Laos. The next year Dooley founded MEDICO (Medical International Cooperation Organization), which he used to channel money from his writing and speaking tours to establish hospitals. He set up two in Laos and three more in other Southeast Asian countries. When cancer ended Dooley's life and career at age 34, he had accomplished more than most men do in a normal lifetime, but far less than he had hoped. Congress voted him a posthumous gold medal for his humanitarian service. *Deliver Us from Evil*, Dooley's first book, recounts his Navy medical service in Vietnam.

FATHER EDWARD J. FLANAGAN (1886-1948) – A native of Ballymoe, County Roscommon, Flanagan came to the U.S. in 1904 and soon entered seminary. He continued his studies at the Gregorian University in Rome and the University of Innsbruck, Austria. Back in the

U.S., Flanagan was assigned a parish in Nebraska and soon took an interest in social service, founding a hostel for working men in Omaha. Soon his compassion turned him to helping disadvantaged boys who had broken the law, or came from broken homes. He began appearing at juvenile court hearings, insisting that "there is no such thing as a bad boy" and usually persuading the judge to give boy offenders into his care for "another chance." These activities led him in 1917 to establish Boys Town, U.S.A., a haven for boys of all religions and races. His work there was immortalized in the 1938 movie, *Boys Town*, starring Spencer Tracy and Mickey Rooney.

INVENTORS & PIONEERS OF TECHNOLOGY

MATTHEW B. BRADY (1822?-1896) – An American-born photographer and historian, Brady documented the Civil War in a superb series of photographs that captured its suffering and sacrifices for generations unborn. Taken by himself and the "photographic corps" he organized in 1861, the photographs proved a financial disaster but left a priceless legacy for artists and historians. Brady died tragically, his last years marked by bankruptcy and alcoholism.

CHARLES EDGAR DURYEA (1861-1938) – American-born automobile pioneer who, together with his younger brother, J. Frank Duryea (1869-1967), built the nation's first successful gasoline-powered automobile. The Duryea brothers, both Illinois natives, ushered the U.S. into the automotive age on September 21, 1893, with a one-cylinder, two-cycle vehicle first shown at Springfield, Massachusetts. In 1895 they founded the Duryea Motor Wagon Company, and that same year one of their automobiles won the nation's first gasoline-automobile race, from Chicago to Evanston, Illinois.

ROBERT FULTON (1765-1815) – Pennsylvania-born artist, civil engineer and inventor. After a successful period painting portraits, miniatures and landscapes, Fulton turned to designing canals, bridges and aqueducts, then to developing a semi-successful submarine mine and torpedo. Although he did not, in fact, invent the steamboat, his fame rests on his success in designing and building the *Clermont*, which in 1807 demonstrated that steam-powered navigation was commercially as well as technically feasible.

JOHN P. HOLLAND (1840?-1914) – County Clare-born Holland, who began his career as a schoolteacher in Ireland, went on to invent the first practicable submarine, demonstrating its potential as a major naval weapon. Holland had begun drawing plans for a submarine while in Ireland, but it was only after he came to the United States that he was able to build his first successful boat, the *Fenian Ram* (1881), with funds from the Irish republican group. Despite some support from U.S. naval officers, most of Holland's early offers to design submarine craft were rebuffed by the American naval establishment. He financed the *Holland*, launched in 1898, with his own money, and finally convinced the skeptics. The U.S. Navy ordered six more of this prototype; and others were built for Britain, Russia and Japan in the run-up to World War I. Holland also invented an escape device for use by craft that were disabled underwater.

STEPHEN H. HORGAN (1854-1941) – Horgan, who was born near Norfolk, Virginia, developed the process that newspapers still use to reproduce photographs on their pages. Fascinated by photography from childhood, he joined the New York *Daily Graphic* as a staff photographer. There he discovered how to use a line screen to convert black-and-white photographs – so-called continuous-tone art – into "halftones" suitable for printing. The *Graphic* published the first newspaper halftones in 1880. In 1893, Horgan became art director at the *New York Herald*, where he improved the halftone process so that newspapers could print photos using high-speed presses. He later worked on a process for transmitting color photographs by wire.

WILLIAM KELLY (1811-1888) – Born in Pittsburgh, the center of America's iron and steel industry, Kelly developed the basic air-blast process that has been used for decades to refine pig iron inexpensively into steel. He patented his discovery in 1857, after learning that an Englishman, Henry Bessemer, had already received a U.S. patent for a similar process. Technical and financial problems delayed the commercial use of Kelly's process until 1864, however. Two years later, the companies that owned his and Bessemer's patents decided to merge to avoid costly patent litigation, and began selling their product as "Bessemer Steel." Commonly known as the Bessemer process ever since, this conversion technique directs blasts of air through molten iron, which together with the iron's carbon content, creates the higher temperatures needed to change it into steel.

THOMAS E. MURRAY (1860-1929) – Trained as an engineer, Murray in the late 1880s became a technical adviser to Anthony Brady, who operated a number of utility companies. As general director of the New York and Brooklyn Edison companies, he consolidated and managed much of the system and also oversaw the design and construction of New York

City's main power plants as well as similar facilities throughout the nation. Murray's greatest legacy, however, was his inventive genius. He conceived useful new devices for a wide range of industries and received patents on over 1,100 – second only to Thomas Edison himself among American inventors.

JOURNALISM AND LITERATURE

JIMMY BRESLIN (1929-) – Known for his outspoken, colorful style, street-smart Breslin ranks among America's best-known and most widely read journalists and novelists. Readers first took notice of the Queens native while he was a sports writer for New York's now-defunct *Herald Tribune*; he has since come to be regarded as a key developer of "the new journalism." During the early 1960s, Breslin also began writing novels on the side, initially to help support his growing family. *The Gang That Couldn't Shoot Straight; World Without End, Amen; Forsaking All Others* and other Breslin books have been widely acclaimed. Breslin's award-winning syndicated column has a large, enthusiastic following; its subjects are far-ranging, from humorous profiles of his low-life cronies to impressionistic pieces on the events of the day. Much of his non-fiction writing shows a strong concern for those he sees as disadvantaged or oppressed. Breslin has also brought a convincing command of "the Queens [New York] English" to television as a network commentator. In a digression from his usual pursuits, he campaigned unsuccessfully in 1969 to become president of the City Council of New York, together with novelist Norman Mailer, his running mate, who lost a bid for the mayoralty. One critic has observed that, though the "bulky, rumpled" Breslin may have the appearance of a "slob" and the vocabulary of a "hood," he "writes like a man of wit, intelligence and sensitivity."

WILLIAM F. BUCKLEY, JR. (1925-) – American editor, writer, novelist and champion of conservative causes – a prolific and versatile talent, whether you love or hate his views and manner. Buckley first came to national attention with *God and Man at Yale* (1951), a book criticizing the alleged liberal tendencies of his alma mater. In 1955 he co-founded the conservative magazine, *National Review*, where he continues as editor-in-chief. Branching out into the electronic media, Buckley in 1966 launched his own TV program, *Firing Line*, a showcase for his often ascerbic wit and criticism. In recent years, he has shown a penchant for fiction with such novels as *Who's on First, Airborne* and *Saving the Queen*, among many.

JAMES T. FARRELL (1904-1979) – Farrell, the son of an Irish-born teamster, grew up in a rough neighborhood on Chicago's South Side. He incorporated his Chicago upbringing into his 1930s trilogy, *Studs Lonigan*, and his later five-novel series about Danny O'Neill.

FRANCIS SCOTT KEY FITZGERALD (1896-1940) -- "F. Scott," the "spokesman of the roaring twenties," ranks among America's most gifted writers. Born in St. Paul, Minnesota, and educated a Catholic in New Jersey, his life followed a course stamped by extremes -- from the heights of glamour, fame and success to the depths of desperation and despair, a pattern mirrored in many of his characters. Fitzgerald attended Princeton starting in 1913, but left before graduation to enlist in the army. Much of his writing chronicled the carefree, decadent younger generation of the "Jazz Age." His first novel, *This Side of Paradise* (1920), painted a picture of life among the typically privileged students at his beloved alma mater. *Paradise* propelled him to financial success and paved the way for his marriage to Zelda Sayre. Their life together began with a phase of gaiety and desperate fun-seeking, but gradually degenerated, with a retreat to Europe for several years. She suffered two breakdowns, never recovering; he took to heavy drinking. Along the way, however, F. Scott managed to produce *The Beautiful and the Damned* (1922); regular short stories for leading magazines; *The Great Gatsby* (1925), his masterpiece, which was highly acclaimed but a financial flop; and *Tender is the Night*, a critical failure. He spent his last years in the seclusion of a small Southern town and in Hollywood, writing movie scripts.

MARGARET MITCHELL (1900-1949) – For several years after college, Mitchell worked as a feature writer for the *Atlanta Journal*. Turning to fiction, she wrote *Gone With the Wind*, a romantic novel set in her native Atlanta during and after the Civil War. The book was an immediate success. It is thought, in fact, to be the best-selling work of fiction ever produced in America, having supplanted *Uncle Tom's Cabin*, the previous record-holder. *Gone With the Wind* received a Pulitzer Prize and also became perhaps the most popular motion picture of all time.

EDWARD R. MURROW (1908-1965) – One of the most influential personalities in 20th century American broadcast journalism, Murrow joined CBS as a radio reporter in 1935. Sent to Britain as a war correspondent with the coming of World War II, he became familiar to millions from his radio reports to America during the German "Blitz" bombing of the British capital. During the 1950s and 1960s, the chain-smoking Murrow became a familiar face on television in the *See It Now* and *Person to Person* series. Before his death from lung cancer, he served for a time as Director of the United States Information Agency (USIA).

FLANNERY O'CONNOR (1925-1964) – A novelist and short-story writer, O'Connor is remembered for unconventional works that are typically set in the rural South and deal with alienation and the relationship of individuals to God. *A Good Man Is Hard to Find, and Other Stories*, published in 1955, established her as a master of the short-story form. O'Connor's other works include a novel, *The Violent Bear It Away* (1960) and a collection of stories, *Everything That Rises Must Converge* (1965).

JOHN O'HARA (1905-1970) – Born into a wealthy Irish-American family in Pottsville, Pennsylvania, O'Hara abandoned plans to attend Yale after the death of his father. After traveling widely, he settled in New York, where he worked as a critic and reporter. This journalistic experience would be evident in his subsequent writing style. In the late 1920s, O'Hara began the writing for which he is remembered: a series of novels and short stories that mirror the social history of upwardly mobile Americans between the 1920s and the 1940s. In such novels as *Butterfield 8* (1935) and *From the Terrace* (1958), O'Hara showed his fascination with how class, money and sexuality affect Americans. The dialogue and detail that mark his writing form a valuable record of the decades he wrote about. One of O'Hara's novels, *Ten North Frederick*, won a National Book Award in 1955.

EUGENE G. O'NEILL (1888-1953) – Son of a touring actor known for his portrayal of the Count of Monte Cristo in a stage adaptation of Dumas' novel, Eugene O'Neill remains the foremost playwright America has produced. His plays typically explore the tormented dimensions of human relationships, especially man's struggle with God and religion. Many scholars have traced these themes to his insecure childhood, which was marked by constant moving around required by his father's theatrical engagements – and influenced by the "peasant Irish Catholicism" of his father and the more refined, mystical religiosity of his mother, who succumbed to drug addiction. The young O'Neill attended Princeton University briefly (1906-1907), a prelude to six years marked by work as a merchant seaman, a derelict's life on the waterfronts of three continents, alcoholic nightmares and an attempt at suicide. He would later see this period of adventure, danger and low-life as an invaluable education for his career as a dramatist. O'Neill's first play, the one-act *Bound East for Cardiff*, was produced in Provincetown, Massachusetts, in 1916, and restaged later that year as his New York debut. Four years later he brought his first full-length effort, *Beyond the Horizon*, to Broadway, following it with 20 long plays and several shorter ones between 1920 and 1943. Among his most powerful and enduring works are *Anna Christie; The Emperor Jones; Mourning Becomes Electra; The Iceman Cometh; Long Day's Journey into Night;* and *A Moon for the Misbegotten.* O'Neill won four Pulitzer prizes for drama; he was the first and, to date, is the only American playwright to win the Nobel Prize for Literature (1936). He spent his last years in a Boston hotel, withdrawn, unproductive and waiting for death – as tragic a figure as he had ever created for the stage.

ROBERT L. RIPLEY (1893-1949) – A newspaper sports cartoonist and feature artist, Ripley is best known for the famous *Believe It or Not!* series, which first appeared in 1918 and subsequently earned him a fortune. Still widely syndicated today, it has inspired radio programs, movie shorts, a television series and a chain of museums devoted to oddities.

ABRAM J. RYAN (1838-1886) – Ryan, a Roman Catholic priest who joined the Confederate Army as a chaplain in 1862, is often called "The Poet of the Confederacy." His verse celebrated the traditional values of the South as well as Catholic subjects.

MICKEY SPILLANE (1918-) – American-born novelist known for a series of mystery/detective stories featuring the hero, Mike Hammer, and agent Tigermane. *I, The Jury* (1942) was an early Spillane best-seller.

LABOR LEADERS

ELIZABETH GURLEY FLYNN (1890-1964) – American labor leader, the first woman to head the Communist Party in this country. Born in New Hampshire into a socialist family that moved to New York in 1900, Flynn began giving street-corner speeches for workers' rights at age 15. In 1906 she joined the radical labor group, the International Workers of the World (IWW), where she led several bloody strikes. She was a cofounder of the American Civil Liberties Union in 1920, and in 1937 she joined the U.S. Communist Party. Over the next two decades Flynn rose to head that organization and in 1955 went to prison for allegedly violating the Smith Act. This law, used to jail many Communist leaders during the strongly anticommunist 'Fifties, forbade preaching the violent overthrow of the U.S. government. Though the Supreme Court ruled in 1957 that teaching communism was not in itself illegal – and Flynn was released –she went into self-imposed exile in Moscow, dying there in 1964.

THOMAS W. ("TEDDY") GLEASON (1900-) – Brooklyn-born
Gleason went to work at age 15 as a longshoreman on the New York
docks, quickly showing leadership and organizing talent. From organizing
and negotiating posts at the local level, he became president of Local 1 of
the International Longshoremen's Association. In 1963 Gleason was
elected president of the ILA and also became a vice president of the AFL-
CIO. He remains active in labor and civic affairs.

GEORGE MEANY (1894-1980) – A gruff, formidable individual,
Meany was the labor movement's undisputed "power" for nearly three
decades. Born in New York, he began his career at 16 as an apprentice
plumber. Meany soon became active in union management, and by 1952,
had been elected president of the American Federation of Labor (AFL).
Three years later, in 1955, he was instrumental in merging that group with
the Congress of Industrial Organizations (CIO), forming a national labor
organization of unprecedented size and strength. Meany presided over the
united organization until his retirement in 1979. As head of the AFL-CIO,
he worked vigorously to reduce corruption in the labor movement, and
was a key mover in expelling the powerful Teamsters Union from the
organization in 1957, after serious charges of unethical conduct were
brought against its leaders. Meany also tried to strengthen U.S. labor's
stand against Communism, both at home and abroad, and he strongly
backed the Vietnam War from start to finish.

PETER JAMES McGUIRE (1852-1906) – Peter McGuire is best
remembered today as the "Father of Labor Day," but his contributions to
the welfare of American workers were much broader. Born in New York
City, McGuire left school at 11 to help support his family, while
continuing his education at night. During the late 1870s he worked as an
organizer for the Social Democratic party, also sponsoring legislation in
Missouri that established one of the country's first bureaus of labor
statistics. After a time as deputy commissioner in the Missouri bureau, he
returned to his trade, furniture making. McGuire organized the St. Louis
carpenters and then became the driving force behind a national convention
of carpenters' unions that resulted in formation of the United Brotherhood
of Carpenters and Joiners (UBC). As chief administrator of the UBC and
editor of its newspaper, *The Carpenter*, McGuire issued the call for a
conference of national labor union leaders in Chicago, which led to the
creation in 1881 of the Federation of Organized Trades and Labor Unions
of the United States and Canada. Moving the UBC's headquarters to New
York, McGuire became an active champion of the eight-hour day; was a
leader of the May Day demonstrations of 1886 and 1890; and led the
movement that ultimately resulted in enactment of the national Labor Day

holiday in 1894. McGuire was one of the founders of the American Federation of Labor (AFL) in 1886, and served as first secretary, and a vice president, of that organization.

TERENCE VINCENT POWDERLY (1849-1924) – Pioneering labor leader. Powderly joined the Knights of Labor in 1874, rising to head the organization five years later. During the 1880s, with K of L membership over 700,000, Powderly was the nation's most powerful union leader. He served for a time as mayor of Scranton, Pennsylvania, and in 1897 was appointed Commissioner General of Immigration by President McKinley.

MICHAEL JOSEPH QUILL (1905-1966) – Born in Kilgarvan, County Kerry, Mike Quill became a volunteer in the Irish Republican Army and served in the Rebellion of 1919-1923. He came to New York in 1926 and, after several jobs, became a gateman with the Interborough Rapid Transit Company. In 1934 Quill was one of the founders of the Transport Workers Union of America (TWUA), which elected him its president and full-time organizer the following year. In the following decades, he was active in local and national union affairs, becoming president of the new International Transport Workers Union after it affiliated with the Congress of Industrial Organizations (CIO) in 1937. Quill also served, off and on, as a member of the New York City Council. In 1965 he led a strike against New York's bus and subway lines that paralyzed the city for 12 days. Refusing a court order to end the strike, he was sent to prison. There he suffered a heart attack that probably hastened his death the following January. Quill had generally followed the Communist line early in his career, but he ultimately became strongly anti-Communist and worked to eliminate Communist influence in the U.S. labor movement.

MILITARY SERVICE

JOHN BARRY (1745-1803) – American Revolutionary naval officer whom many consider the "Father of the U.S. Navy." Born in Tacumshane, Ireland, Barry emigrated to Philadelphia and became a shipmaster. When the Revolution erupted, the Continental Congress commissioned him and gave him command of several ships which became the nucleus of the American fleet. At his death, Commodore Barry was the Navy's senior officer.

PATRICK R. CLEBURNE (1828-1864) – A native of Cork, Cleburne was one of several Irish-born soldiers who held high rank in the South during the Civil War. His skill and courage earned him the rank of major-general, and his military exploits along the Mississippi won him the sobriquet, "Stonewall Jackson of the West." Cleburne was killed in action after winning commendations for valor at Shiloh, Chickamauga and Missionary Ridge.

WILLIAM J. DONOVAN (1883-1959) – Soldier, politician and statesman, Donovan is best remembered as founder of the OSS (Office of Strategic Services), World War II predecessor of the CIA. He first came to national attention during World War I, when his heroic exploits as colonel of the "Fighting 69th," the famous New York Irish-American regiment, earned him the Medal of Honor and the nickname, "Wild Bill." After the Second World War, Donovan became active in New York Republican politics and served briefly as ambassador to Thailand.

FRANCIS P. DUFFY (1871-1932) – American army chaplain, famed for his service with the men of the 69th Regiment ("The Fighting 69th"), New York National Guard during World War I. The actor Pat O'Brien immortalized Father Duffy in a movie about his life, and his memorial stands in New York City's Times Square.

JAMES M. GAVIN (1907-) – Born in Brooklyn and raised in an adoptive family in Pennsylvania, Gavin enlisted in the army at age 17 and won appointment to West Point the next year. By the eve of Pearl Harbor he had earned the rank of major. While teaching tactics at West Point, moreover, Gavin had been impressed with the effectiveness of the blitzkrieg tactics the German army had used against Poland and the Anglo-French allies. He signed up for parachute training, feeling sure that this rapid, mobile technique would play an important role in the conflict America was about to enter. After commanding a parachute regiment dropped to support the Allied invasion of Sicily, Gavin was made deputy to Gen. Matthew Ridgway, inheriting command of the renowned 82nd Airborne Division from him in August 1944. He thus became the youngest division commander of the war. As a temporary major-general later that year, Gavin played a crucial role in halting the German advance during the Battle of the Bulge. He held successive field and staff commands after the war, retiring in 1958. Gavin went on to join the international consulting firm, Arthur D. Little, rising from vice president to chairman in two years. He served as U.S. ambassador to France during the first years of the Kennedy administration.

COLIN P. KELLY (1915-1941) – Captain Kelly, a U.S. army air force officer, became one of America's first World War II heroes when he crash-dived his crippled bomber into a Japanese battleship off the Phillipines three days after Pearl Harbor. The battleship was destroyed, and for his courageous self-sacrifice, Kelly was posthumously awarded the Distinguished Service Cross.

WILLIAM D. LEAHY (1875-1959) – Born in Hampton, Iowa, Leahy attended the U.S. Naval Academy, followed by service in the Phillipines during the Spanish-American War; with U.S. occupation forces in Nicaragua; and during World War I. Between the wars he headed the Navy Bureau of Ordnance and served as Chief of Naval Operations, retiring as an admiral in 1939. When the Germans overran France in 1940 and established a puppet government at Vichy, Leahy was appointed ambassador to this sensitive capital. Recalled to active duty in 1942 with the rank of fleet admiral, Leahy served as Chief of Staff to Franklin Roosevelt until the President's death, and continued in the post under Harry Truman, retiring in 1949.

ALFRED THAYER MAHAN (1840-1914) – A U.S. naval officer and historian, Mahan was the son of a professor at West Point, the U.S. Military academy. He attended the U.S. Naval Academy, Annapolis, and served with the Union Navy during the Civil War. By 1884, he had compiled a sufficiently impressive reputation to be invited to lecture on naval history and tactics at the Naval War College. He taught there for several years, basing his lectures on his extensive study of naval history from ancient times to the 19th century. Far more influential were Mahan's three books: *The Influence of Sea Power upon History, 1660-1783* (1890); *The Influence of Sea Power upon the French Revolution and Empire, 1793-1812* (1892); and *The Interest of America in Sea Power, Present and Future* (1897). The first two showed convincingly how British political and economic supremacy from the 17th through the early 19th centuries had resulted largely from her commercial and military sea power. The last helped shape America's development as a major naval power after the Spanish-American War, and also influenced naval thinking around the world.

ANTHONY McAULIFFE (1898-1975) –A U.S. Army officer, McAuliffe found himself commanding American airborne troops who were desperately defending the key Belgian town of Bastogne against superior German forces during the Battle of the Bulge (Winter, 1944-1945). Confronted with a German ultimatum demanding his surrender, General

McAuliffe offered a one-word reply: "Nuts!" His terse, no-nonsense response made McAuliffe an instant legend, symbolizing dogged defiance and courage in the face of overwhelming odds.

RICHARD MONTGOMERY (1738-1775) – A native of Swords, County Dublin, Montgomery was named a brigadier general in the revolutionary army after the colonies declared their independence from Britain. He served as second-in-command of the American expeditionary force that attempted to invade Canada, and was killed during the Seige of Quebec.

AUDIE MURPHY (1924-1971) – A U.S. war hero and movie actor, Murphy won the Medal of Honor in 1945 for killing some 240 German soldiers. This and other brave feats helped make the modest young man the most decorated U.S. soldier of World War II. After the war, he played himself in a movie about his life and war exploits, launching a film career which included starring roles in *The Red Badge of Courage, To Hell and Back* and a series of low-budget Westerns. Murphy died in an airplane crash.

PHILIP J. SHERIDAN (1831-1888) – A native of County Sligo (some sources say he was born in the U.S.) and from an Irish-Catholic family, Sheridan ranked among the foremost Union generals during the Civil War. His brilliant leadership won several battles for the North, and he played a key role in forcing Robert E. Lee's final surrender at Appomattox. After notable service on the western frontier, Sheridan was named commander-in-chief of the U.S. Army in 1884 and became a full general shortly before his death.

JOHN SULLIVAN (1740-1795) – Born to immigrant parents at Somersworth, New Hampshire, Sullivan began his career as a successful lawyer. In 1774, a major in the New Hampshire militia, he was sent as a delegate to the Continental Congress. Sullivan became a brigadier general in 1775 and for a time commanded Continental forces in the northern colonies. Promoted to major-general in 1776, he was captured at the Battle of Long Island but soon released in a prisoner exchange. He served with distinction at the crucial battles of Trenton and Princeton, then resigned in late 1779 in ill health. Recovering his health, Sullivan served again as a New Hampshire delegate to the Continental Congress and, during the Confederation period, was governor of his state for three years.

POLITICS AND PUBLIC SERVICE

WILLIAM G. BRENNAN (1906-) – Born in Newark, New Jersey, Brennan became a judge in the state's Superior Court in 1949. His distinguished record there earned him national attention, and in 1956 he was named an associate justice of the United States Supreme Court. On the nation's highest court, Brennan has been a consistent champion of individual liberties and civil rights, often leading the Court's now-dwindling liberal faction.

EDMUND GERALD ("JERRY") BROWN, JR. (1938-) – A San Francisco native like his father, Governor Edmund G. ("Pat") Brown, Jerry Brown went off to seminary after high school. In 1960, perhaps influenced by the excitement of John F. Kennedy's presidential campaign, he dropped plans to enter the priesthood and matriculated at Berkeley, followed by law study at Yale. After briefly practicing law in Los Angeles, Brown was elected California secretary of state in 1970, and subsequently served as governor from 1975 to 1983. Though his ambitions went further, Brown was unsuccessful in two bids for the Democratic presidential nomination (1976 and 1980), and lost his race for the U.S. Senate in 1982. His political style combined the natural campaigning ability of his father with a flair for the unorthodox and a certain unpredictability.

JAMES F. BYRNES (1879-1972) – South Carolina-born Byrnes was one of few individuals who have served at high levels in all three branches of the Federal government as well as in state posts. The Charleston native had little formal schooling as a boy but, like Lincoln and others before him, entered the legal profession after reading law on his own. In 1911 Byrnes was elected a Democratic member of the U.S. House of Representatives from South Carolina. He served there until 1925 followed, beginning in 1931, by a decade in the Senate. In 1941, Franklin Roosevelt named Byrnes to the Supreme Court, persuading him the next year to move to the executive branch. Byrnes held major agency posts during World War II, heading the Office of Economic Stabilization and the Office of War Mobilization. He was named Secretary of State in 1945, showing increasing firmness in the face of Soviet violations of the Yalta agreements and Allied-Soviet friction in Germany. Leaving Washington, Byrnes returned to his native state to serve as governor from 1951 to 1955.

THOMAS G. CORCORAN (1900-) – "Tommy the Cork," as he came to be called, took a law degree at Harvard and practiced what might have become a conventional law career until 1932. Having befriended influential New York Democrats, he followed Franklin Roosevelt to Washington. The official posts he was named to were modest-sounding: special assistant to the Attorney General; special counsel to the Reconstruction Finance Corporation; assistant to the Secretary of the Treasury. But these positions belied his influential role as a confidante of Roosevelt and a major shaper of New Deal legislation, including the 1933 Securities Act, the Securities Exchange Act (1934) and the Public Utilities Holding Company Act (1935).

RICHARD JOSEPH DALEY (1902-1976) – Though he never held public office beyond the local level, Richard Daley became one of the nation's most powerful Democratic leaders. The future Chicago mayor was born on that city's West Side and received his law degree from De Paul University. Daley was elected to the Illinois legislature in 1936 and became a close associate of Governor Adlai Stevenson, serving the future Democratic presidential candidate as a legislative adviser. After serving as clerk of Cook County and county Democratic chairman during the early 1950s, he was elected mayor of Chicago in 1955, winning reelection by decisive margins every four years through 1975. As mayor, Daley reduced traditional political graft, made reforms in the police and fire departments and helped rejuvenate the city's economy. At the same time, he built a masterful political machine that could deliver votes to order: "Last of the Bosses," some called him. He was Democratic leader of Illinois as well as Chicago, and provided support that proved crucial to the presidential nominations of Adlai Stevenson, John F. Kennedy, Hubert Humphrey and Jimmy Carter. Daley attracted widespread criticism after the Democratic party held its 1968 national convention in Chicago. Chicago police clashed with demonstrators who opposed the Vietnam war, and hundreds of demonstrators, police and journalists were hurt. Four years later the convention refused to recognize Daley and his delegates, opting for delegates it contended were more representative of Illinois Democrats.

SIR THOMAS DONGAN (1634-1715) – A colonial governor of New York, Dongan was the first Catholic governor in the American colonies. He was born in Castletown Kildrought (Celbridge), County Kildare, son of a member of the Irish parliament, Sir John Dongan. When Charles II was executed in 1649, Dongan went into exile in France, subsequently becoming colonel of an Irish regiment. He returned to England in 1678 and went to Tangiers as lieutenant governor. In 1682, Dongan was appointed governor of the now-bankrupt colony of New York. Though he served for only six years, he achieved much. Dongan set what are substantially the current boundaries of New York State, after conferring with officials from Connecticut, Pennsylvania and Canada; developed a sensible Indian policy that kept the powerful Iroquois on England's side; set up a post office; and granted charters to the cities of New York and Albany. Most notable, however, was his Charter of Liberties, an abortive attempt to establish parity between the New York provincial legislature and Parliament; to guarantee religious freedom; and to uphold the principle of no taxation without representation as well as a number of other principles far ahead of their time. Dongan was replaced in 1688, and returned to England in 1691, later succeeding his brother as earl of Limerick.

JAMES A. FARLEY (1888-1976) – During a successful business career in New York, Farley also cultivated friendships with leading New York Democrats, including Franklin D. Roosevelt. He was named chairman of the Democratic National Committee in 1932, managing Roosevelt's first three presidential campaigns. A close political adviser to FDR, he also served as Postmaster General from 1932 to 1940.

THE KENNEDY BROTHERS – Of the four sons born to Joseph Patrick Kennedy (See "Business, Industry and Finance") and Rose Fitzgerald Kennedy, three were destined for prominent careers in national Democratic politics. The Kennedys trained their children to compete and achieve from childhood, beginning with Joseph P. Kennedy, Jr. (1915-1944), their eldest son. Joe, Jr's death in a secret World War II air mission quashed the plans his wealthy and influential father had made to launch him on what many expected would have been a brilliant political career. The details of the Kennedy family's subsequent fortunes are familiar enough to require no retelling. Briefly, however, Joe's death thrust the mantle of family destiny onto **JOHN FITZGERALD KENNEDY** (1917-1963), who, after heroic Navy service in the South Pacific, won election to Congress from Massachusetts in 1946; subsequently served as U.S. Senator; and in 1961 became the first Roman Catholic U.S. president. Following his assassination in 1963, JFK's younger brother, **ROBERT FRANCIS KENNEDY** (1925-1968), came to the fore. RFK or Bobby, as he was known, had been his brother's closest political adviser and attorney general in his cabinet. He left the Johnson administration in 1964; ran successfully for the Senate, representing New York; and was himself assassinated in 1968 during a campaign for the Democratic presidential nomination. **EDWARD MOORE KENNEDY** (1932-), the last representative of his generation among the Kennedy males, has represented Massachusetts in the Senate since 1962. Perhaps the Senate's most prominent liberal, Teddy has served as Democratic whip (assistant leader) and as chairman of the Senate Judiciary Committee. After a 1969 incident in which the car he was driving plunged off a bridge on Chappaquiddick Island, Massachusetts, drowning the young woman with him, serious questions were raised about Kennedy's role in the matter and his subsequent handling of it. Charges of a cover-up, which have continued to this day, made Kennedy defer his plans to run for the presidential nomination; he failed in a 1980 bid. One is hard-pressed to name an American family that has been so widely loved and admired – or, so controversial.

MIKE MANSFIELD (1903-) – As majority leader in the U.S. Senate, this Montana Democrat served in that post longer than any other person (1961-1977). Michael Joseph Mansfield, born in New York City and reared in Montana, left school at 14 to join the Navy during World War I. Then, enlisting in the Army, he served there and in the Marine Corps until 1922. He worked as a miner and mining engineer for the rest of the 1920s, then earned bachelor's and master's degrees from Montana State University despite the fact that he had never attended high school. After teaching Hispanic and Far Eastern history there, he entered Congress in 1943, moving up to the Senate ten years later. He left his Senate post in 1977 to become U.S. ambassador to Japan, and proved so effective that he continued to serve there under Ronald Reagan.

EUGENE McCARTHY (1916-) – A Minnesota native who began his career in high school and college classrooms, McCarthy put teaching aside in the late 1940s to enter Democratic politics. He was elected to Congress from Minnesota in 1949, moving up to the Senate in 1959. McCarthy's opposition to the Vietnam conflict won him strong backing, particularly among college students, and propelled him into a bid for the Democratic presidential nomination in 1968. Although he ultimately lost the nomination, his primary successes helped persuade Robert Kennedy to enter the race and also put pressure on Lyndon Johnson to abandon a bid for a second term. McCarthy ran as an independent presidential candidate in 1976, and afterwards returned to his first loves: teaching, lecturing and writing poetry.

JOSEPH RAYMOND McCARTHY (1908-1957) – Controversial Senator from Wisconsin (1947-1957), famous for the campaign he launched in 1950 to expose alleged Communist penetration of the U.S. State Department and other government agencies. His anti-Communist crusade, which many came to see as a self-serving political gambit, was centered on the hearings he conducted as chairman of the Senate's Permanent Subcommittee on Investigations. The so-called McCarthy

Hearings, televised in 1954, tainted the reputations of many public officials, some justly, most unfairly. In the end, however, they also showed the Senator up as a demagogue in the eyes of most Americans.

ROBERT S. McNAMARA (1916-) – San Francisco-born McNamara attended the University of California, then Harvard Business School, where he taught from 1940-1943. He was an army air force officer during the war, afterwards joining Ford Motor Company as one of a high-powered group of young managers called the "Whiz Kids." In 1960, barely a month after being named president of Ford, McNamara was lured to Washington to become Secretary of Defense in the Kennedy administration. He remained in the post through most of the Johnson years. McNamara's influence went far beyond defense matters, however; he advised both presidents on economic and foreign affairs as well. At the Pentagon, McNamara tried to introduce more scientific budgeting methods, bringing systems analysis and other scientific methods to bear on management of the enormous Defense Department budget. As the cabinet officer directly responsible for the armed forces, McNamara became closely identified with the administration's Vietnam policy; some took to calling the conflict "McNamara's War." By 1967, however, he had come to doubt the wisdom or practicality of a military solution in Vietnam and similar situations, and resigned from the cabinet that same year. In 1968 McNamara was appointed head of the International Bank for Reconstruction and Development (the so-called World Bank), where he served until 1981. In that job, he urged the more prosperous nations of the world to fund accelerated economic development in the Third World as the best long-term means to world peace and stability.

DANIEL P. MOYNIHAN (1927-) – Born in Tulsa, Oklahoma, Moynihan grew up in the tough Hell's Kitchen area of Manhattan, graduating from Tufts University with both bachelor's and doctoral degrees. He quickly gained a reputation for expertise on urban problems and minority groups, and wrote influential books on immigration, the antipoverty program and black family life. After teaching at Harvard and M.I.T., Moynihan was lured to Washington as an adviser to President Nixon, then returned to Cambridge until his appointment as U.S. Ambassador to India from 1973 to 1975. Over the next year, he served as U.S. Ambassador to the United Nations, winning high visibility for his outspoken attacks on those who criticized the administration's policies. Democrat Moynihan has represented New York in the U.S. Senate since 1977.

SANDRA DAY O'CONNOR (1930-) – The first woman ever appointed to the United States Supreme Court (1981), Mrs. O'Connor is descended on her father's side from the O'Deas ("Day" is a corruption). Born in El Paso, Texas, she graduated third in her class at Stanford University Law School, where a classmate was fellow Supreme Court Justice William Rehnquist. O'Connor practiced law in California and Arizona until 1965, when she became assistant attorney-general of the state. Then she served, in succession, as a member of the Arizona Senate; Superior Court Judge, Maricopa County; and a member of the Arizona Court of Appeals. Since her appointment to the highest U.S. court by President Reagan, O'Connor has written moderate to conservative opinions on most cases, although on many issues she has disregarded political ideology.

THOMAS P. ("TIP") O'NEILL (1912-) – Speaker of the U.S. House of Representatives from 1977 to 1986, this Massachusetts Democrat was elected to the state's House of Representatives in 1936, the same year he graduated from Boston College. O'Neill was named leader of the Democratic minority in 1947, rising the next year to become House speaker. Winning election to the U.S. House of Representatives in 1952, he began a course that paralleled his state political career. He was named majority whip (assistant leader) in 1971, majority leader in 1973 and Speaker in 1977. Among O'Neill's major accomplishments were his successful leadership of a fight to have all votes in the House publicly recorded, and his early opposition to the Vietnam conflict.

ALFRED EMANUEL SMITH (1873-1944) – A child of New York's Lower East Side, where he attended the school of St. James Church, Smith became active in city politics at 22. Starting within the Tammany Hall organization, he won election to the state legislature in 1903. The governorship of New York State followed in 1919, and in 1924 Smith was an unsuccessful candidate for the Democratic presidential nomination. With the backing of Governor Franklin Delano Roosevelt, Smith tried again in 1928. This time the so-called "Happy Warrior" won nomination but was defeated at the polls by Herbert Hoover, who benefitted from continuing anti-Catholic prejudice and Smith's stand on prohibition.

JAMES J. WALKER (1881-1946) – Universally known as Jimmy, Walker was born to Irish immigrants in New York's Greenwich Village. After college and law school, he worked briefly on Broadway, writing songs and later marrying a theatrical singer. Entering politics, he was elected to the New York State Assembly in 1909 and, with Al Smith's backing, to the State Senate. He became mayor of New York in 1925, founding the Department of Sanitation, consolidating the city's hospitals and improving its parks and playgrounds, among other achievements. Handsome, debonair and fun-loving, Walker became a popular symbol of the "Roaring 'Twenties." After his 1929 reelection, however, he came under increasing fire, and state legislators brought 15 charges of illegal, improper conduct against him, including questions about large, unexplained sums in his bank account. Walker resigned in 1932, went into "exile" in Europe and then returned to the U.S. in 1935 to pursue a business career.

RELIGION

JOHN CARROLL (1735-1815) – Maryland-born Carroll, member of one of the leading Catholic families that settled the colony under Lord Baltimore, studied for the priesthood in France. After his order, the Jesuits, was suppressed in 1773, he returned to America. Carroll was consecrated America's first Catholic bishop in 1790, and became Archbishop of Baltimore in 1808. He was instrumental in founding Georgetown University, the nation's oldest Catholic institution of higher learning, in 1789.

RICHARD J. CUSHING (1895-1970) – Richard Cardinal Cushing became familiar to tens of millions of Americans when he prayed at the inaugural cermony for John F. Kennedy in 1961 and officiated at the funeral Mass for the slain president nearly three years later. Born in South Boston, Cushing studied at Boston College and St. John's Seminary before his ordination in 1921. He was soon assigned to the Boston office of the Society for the Propagation of the Faith, where his gifts as a public speaker helped to raise large sums for mission work. Together with Mother Katherine Drexel, he also worked to aid poor blacks in the Roxbury area. Appointed auxiliary bishop of Boston in 1939, Cushing was raised to archbishop five years later, making him, at age 49, the youngest Roman Catholic archbishop in the world. His energetic pursuit of social justice led him to found the Missionary Order of St. James, which sends clergy from the Boston archdiocese on assignments to Latin America. He also played an active role in civic, relief and juvenile programs, earning a reputation as Boston's "most pervasive social force." Cushing was elevated to cardinal by Pope John XXIII in 1958. For many years he was a close friend of the Kennedy family.

JOHN JOSEPH HUGHES (1797-1864) – Hughes, a native of County Tyrone, served as first Archbishop of New York and began construction of St. Patrick's Cathedral, which he did not live to see finished. Emigrating to America at 21, Hughes worked as a laborer and seminary gardener in Chambersburg, Pennsylvania, beginning study for the priesthood there in 1820. He was ordained in 1826 for the Philadelphia diocese, and was consecrated coadjutor bishop of New York in 1838. He succeeded to the bishopric in 1842 and became archbishop in 1842 with creation of the Archdiocese of New York. Hughes set in motion the construction of a new cathedral for the archdiocese in 1858. As leader of New York's Catholic community, Hughes opposed abolition while criticizing slavery; encouraged Irish immigrants to remain in the cities, under Church guidance, instead of moving West; promoted the growth of parochial schools; and checked the growing control of local church affairs by laymen.

FRANCIS MAKEMIE (1658?-1708) – The "Founder of American Presbyterianism" was born in Rathmelton, County Donegal, and pursued a business career before emigrating to the colonies. Here he was ordained into the Presbyterian ministry, afterwards travelling widely in the colonies and the West Indies, preaching and founding many churches. In 1706 Makemie founded the Presbytery of Philadelphia, the first in America, which united scattered churches in Maryland, Pennsylvania, New York and Virginia. The following year, not long before his death, he was arrested in New York and prosecuted for preaching without a license. His subsequent acquittal was considered a major victory for religious toleration in America.

JOHN McCLOSKEY (1810-1885) – The first American cardinal of the Roman Catholic Church, McCloskey was born in Brooklyn, New York, the son of immigrants from County Derry. He received a private school education in New York and, after studies at Mount St. Mary's College, Emmitsburg, Maryland, followed by seminary, was ordained a priest in 1834. McCloskey studied in Rome for two years, returning to New York in 1837, where he was assigned to St. Joseph's Church. In 1841 he was appointed first president of St. John's College (now Fordham University), but returned to parochial duties after a year. Soon afterward, on the recommendation of New York Bishop John Joseph Hughes, McCloskey was appointed titular bishop of Axiere and coadjutor of New York. In 1847, he was transferred to Albany, where he remained for 17 years and built many churches and related institutions, including the Cathedral of the Immaculate Conception. McCloskey succeeded Hughes as archbishop of New York on the latter's death in 1864 and in 1875 became the first American cardinal. He completed the construction of St. Patrick's Cathedral, begun by Hughes, and officiated at its dedication in 1879.

FULTON J. SHEEN (1895-1979) – One of the best-known, most eloquent spokesmen for Catholic theology in modern times, Sheen was born Peter Sheen in El Paso, Illinois. He was ordained in 1919, then studied philosophy at the Catholic University of Louvain, Belgium. Returning to the U.S. in 1926, he began a quarter-century teaching career at Catholic University of America, and also published the first of 50 books, *God and Intelligence in Modern Philosophy*. The Church had long recognized Sheen's persuasive powers — he had given talks on radio's *Catholic Hour* since 1930. In 1950 he was named director of the Society for the Propagation of the Faith in the United States, where he used his talents in raising funds for mission work abroad. During the 1950s, he also became a familiar TV personality with his program, *Life is Worth Living*. But Sheen was not only effective with mass audiences; he acquired a reputation as a proselytizer, converting a number of well-known Americans including Clare Booth Luce. Sheen was named bishop of Rochester, New York, in 1966 and titular archbishop of Newport in 1969, but to many's surprise, never received a cardinal's hat.

FRANCIS CARDINAL SPELLMAN (1889-1967) – Spellman, a native of Whitman, Massachusetts, earned his B.A. at Fordham and took holy orders in 1916. After service in Boston, he was assigned to the Papal Secretariat at Rome from 1925 to 1932. Returning to the U.S., Spellman served as auxiliary bishop of Boston before being named Archbishop of New York in 1939 and elevated to cardinal in 1946. Spellman served as apostolic vicar to the U.S. armed forces, making several wartime visits to battle zones. Thanks to his wide acquaintance with church leaders throughout the world, he also took on several missions as an envoy for presidents Roosevelt and Truman.

SPORTS

CHARLES ALBERT COMISKEY (1858-1931) – An American baseball player and manager, Comiskey founded the Chicago White Sox in 1900. The Baseball Hall of Fame recognized his outstanding achievements by inducting him into its membership in 1939. The White Sox' home stadium, Comiskey Park, also honors him.

JAMES ("JIMMY") CONNORS (1952-) – The American tennis star first attracted wide notice by winning the men's singles at Wimbledon in 1974. Ranked #1 internationally in 1978, Connors has remained among the top echelon of contenders in a more competitive field.

JAMES JOHN ("GENTLEMAN JIM") CORBETT (1866-1933) –
An American boxer, Corbett was born in San Francisco. In 1892 he won
the first heavyweight title to be fought with gloves by defeating fellow
Irish-American John L. Sullivan. Corbett lost the title to Bob Fitzsimmons
in 1897.

WILLIAM H. ("JACK") DEMPSEY (1895-1983) – One of the
century's greatest boxers, Dempsey became known as "the Manassa
Mauler" after his Colorado birthplace. He defeated Jess Willard for the
world heavyweight title in 1919, finally losing it to Gene Tunney in 1926.
Dempsey was elected to the Boxing Hall of Fame in 1954.

HOWARD EDWARD ("RED") GRANGE (1903-) – One of the
most outstanding football players of all time, Grange earned the nickname,
"The Galloping Ghost," after scoring five touchdowns (four on long runs)
for Illinois against the University of Michigan in 1924. This and other
feats earned him All-American ranking. Grange turned pro in 1925,
playing for the Chicago Bears, the New York Yankees, and again with the
Bears. He retired after the 1934 NFL season, eventually working as a
radio and television sports commentator. "Red" Grange was elected to the
Football Hall of Fame in 1963.

WILLIAM BENJAMIN ("BEN") HOGAN (1912-) – Hogan, one
of the immortals of U.S. golf, won four U.S. Open competitions (1948,
1950, 1951, 1953); two PGA titles (1946, 1948); two Masters
tournaments (1951, 1953); and the British Open (1953).

CONNIE MACK (1862-1956) – Among American baseball's greatest
managers of all time, Mack was born Cornelius McGillicuddy in
Brookfield, Massachusetts. As manager of the Philadelphia A's (Athletics)
from 1901 to 1950, he achieved the highest win record in baseball history
– 3,776 games. Mack was inducted into the Baseball Hall of Fame in
1937.

JOHN McENROE (1959-) – Known as much for his on-court temper
tantrums as for his skill with a racquet, the Queens, New York-born tennis
star rose to prominence with first-place finishes in the U.S. Open singles
championships in 1979, 1980 and 1981. He also took top honors at
Wimbledon in 1981.

HERMAN ("BABE") RUTH (1895-1948) – Dubbed "the Sultan of
Swat" and "The Babe," the legendary New York Yankee outfielder is
probably best remembered for the record he set in hitting home runs – 714

over 22 seasons. He achieved a lifetime batting average of .342. "Babe" Ruth is arguably the best-known American sports star – ever.

SAMUEL JACKSON ("SAM") SNEAD (1912-) – An American golf star, Snead has won a record 84 professional tournaments. He is also the only pro to have won competitions over a span of six decades. "Slammin' Sam" Snead was elected to the PGA Hall of Fame in 1953.

JOHN L. SULLIVAN (1858-1918) – Perhaps the first American boxer to achieve wide recognition, Sullivan fought bare-knuckled from 1878 until his 1892 match with James J. Corbett, when he adopted gloves. Corbett knocked out the long-time champion in the 21st round of their heavyweight match.

NOBEL PRIZE WINNERS
OF IRISH BIRTH OR HERITAGE *

As a smallish nation only independent in her own right for several decades, Ireland has been preoccupied with political questions and with working to improve the basic living conditions of her people. Even so, in the heady arena of international achievement symbolized by the Nobel Prize competition, those of Irish birth have won an impressive degree of recognition. Winners of Irish heritage have, many would say, given Ireland an even larger claim to the world's respect.

For Peace

Sean MacBride (Ireland), 1974
Mairead Corrigan and **Betty Williams**
    (Britain/Northern Ireland), 1976

For Economics

James Tobin (United States), 1981

For Literature

William Butler Yeats (Ireland), 1923
George Bernard Shaw (Britain), 1925
Eugene O'Neill (United States), 1936
Samuel Beckett (Ireland), 1969
Patrick White (Australia), 1973

For Physiology or Medicine

William P. Murphy (United States), 1934
Allan M. Cormack (United States), 1979

―――――――――

* Country of citizenship shown in parentheses.

For Chemistry

Richard L.M. Synge (Britain), 1953
Robert S. Mulliken (United States), 1966
Stanford Moore (United States), 1972

For Physics

Robert A. Millikan (United States), 1923
Ernest T.S. Walton (Ireland), 1951

IRISH OLYMPIC ACHIEVEMENTS:
AN UNDERSTATED RECORD

Since Ireland first fielded an Olympic team under its own flag in 1924, Irishmen have officially been credited with four gold, five silver and seven bronze medals. Not a bad record for a nation of three to four million souls. Ireland's official gold medalists are:

   1928 - **Patrick O'Callaghan** – Gold medal, 16 lb. Hammer Throw
   1932 - **Patrick O'Callaghan** – Gold medal, 16 lb. Hammer Throw
   1932 - **Robert Tisdall** – Gold medal, 400m Hurdles
   1956 - **Ron Delaney** – Gold medal, 1500m Run

But the real Irish Olympic achievement is far greater. From the first modern Games, in 1896, until 1924, residents of what is now the Republic competed officially under the British flag — and regularly won distinction. Moreover, from 1896 until the latest Summer Games in Los Angeles (1984), Irish emigrants and their descendants have taken home medals to the United States, Britain, Australia, South Africa and Canada. Most such gold medal winners, though by no means all, are listed below.

Ireland's contribution to the Games has gone beyond the sphere of competition. An Irish citizen, Lord Killanin, served as President of the International Olympic Committee from 1972 to 1980, a critical period in Olympic history. Faced with political, nationalistic and commercial controversies that threatened to subvert the Games' original spirit, Killanin was widely praised for his quiet, effective diplomacy in addressing these problems. When he decided, despite protests, to stand aside in 1980, he was unanimously elected Honorary Life President of the IOC, on which he has served since 1952.

   1896 - **John Pius Boland**, Britain - (2) Gold medals, Lawn Tennis
           Thomas Burke, U.S. - Gold medals, 100m and 400m Dash
           James B. Connolly, U.S. - Gold medal, Triple Jump

   1900 - **John Flanagan**, U.S. - Gold medal, Hammer Throw

   1904 - **John Flanagan**, U.S. - Gold medal, Hammer Throw
           Martin Sheridan, U.S. - Gold medal, Discus
           Thomas Kiely, Britain - Gold medal, All-round
                                   Competition (10 events)

1906 - **Con Leahy**, Britain - Gold medal, Running High Jump
       Martin Sheridan, U.S. - Gold medals in 16 lb. Shot Put
                                   and Discus
       P.G. O'Connor, Britain - Gold medal, Triple Jump

1908 - **Reginald Walker**, South Africa - Gold medal, 100m Dash
       Timothy Ahearne, Britain - Gold medal, Triple Jump
       Martin Sheridan, U.S. - Gold medals in Discus and
                                   Greek-style Discus
       John Flanagan, U.S. - Gold medal, 16 lb. Hammer Throw

1912 - **Kenneth McArthur**, South Africa - Gold medal, Marathon
       Frederick Kelly, U.S. - Gold medal, 110m Hurdles
       Matt McGrath, U.S. - Gold medal, 16 lb. Hammer Throw

1920 - **Patrick Ryan**, U.S. - Gold medal, 16 lb. Hammer Throw
       Jack Kelly, Sr., U.S. - Gold medal, Single Sculls
       Edward Eagan, U.S. - Gold medal, Boxing (Lt. Hvywt.)

1924 - **Daniel Kinsey**, U.S. - Gold medal, 110m Hurdles

1928 - **Helen Meany**, U.S. - Gold medal, Women's Springboard
                                Dive

1932 - **Edward Flynn**, U.S. - Gold medal, Boxing (Lt. Wltrwt.)

1952- **Parry O'Brien**, U.S. - Gold medal, 16 lb. Shot Put
      Patricia McCormick, U.S. - Gold medal, Women's Spring-
                                     board and Platform Dives

1956 - **Parry O'Brien**, U.S. - Gold medal, 16 lb. Shot Put
       Patricia McCormick, U.S. - Gold medal, Women's
                                      Springboard and Platform Dives
       Harold Connolly, U.S. - Gold medal, 16 lb. Hammer
                                   Throw

1964 - **Ian O'Brien**, Australia - Gold medal, 200m Breaststroke

1968 - **Bill Toomey**, U.S. - Gold medal, Decathlon

1976 - **John Walker,** New Zealand - Gold medal, 1500m Run

1980 - **Michelle Ford,** Australia - Gold medal, Women's 200m
Freestyle Swimming

1984 - **Mary Meagher,** U.S. - Gold medal, Women's 100m and
200m Butterfly
Michael O'Brien, U.S. - Gold medal, 1500m Freestyle
Swimming
Rick Carey, U.S. - Gold medals, 100m and 200m
Backstroke

IRISH NAMES UPON OUR LAND

Irishmen were active in settling this country and pushing it westward from the days of the earliest English colonies. So it's not surprising that Irish family and place names are common throughout the "Lower 48."

In 1914, for example, two scholars estimated that there were 65 places in the U.S. named after people whose names began with the Irish prefix "O," and more than 1,000 that commemorated the "Macs."

They found 253 counties and about 7,000 other places named after Irish places or families. Among these were 24 Dublins, 21 Waterfords, 18 Belfasts, 16 Tyrones, 10 Limericks, nine Antrims, eight Sligos, seven Derrys, six Corks and five Kildares. (Many of these have apparently been swallowed up by other communities; only some 13 Dublins remain today, for example.)

Places named for prominent Irishmen and Irish-Americans as well as lesser-known countrymen are beyond counting. The Carrolls of Maryland, for example, live on in the names of many communities, as do the famous Irish-American generals, Philip Kearny and Philip Sheridan. Irish patriots who never set foot in America are likewise remembered, as Charles Stewart Parnell is in the name of an Arkansas community.

For good measure, New York claims a community named Erin and Missouri's towns include one called St. Patrick. Towns named Shamrock can be found in North Carolina and Oklahoma, and Pennsylvania has a Shamrock Station.

Below is a state-by-state listing of places that bear the names of places in Ireland. We have not even attempted to enumerate the places that bear Irish (family) surnames, since they are so many and, in any case, sometimes difficult to distinguish:

ALABAMA – Ardmore; Carlowville; Shannon

ARKANSAS – Belfast; Shannon

CALIFORNIA – Boyle; Dublin; Shandon

COLORADO – Sligo; Tyrone

FLORIDA – Mayo

GEORGIA – Auburn; Dublin; Shannon; Tyrone

IDAHO – Rathdrum

ILLINOIS – Auburn; Munster; Shannon

INDIANA – Bandon; Clare; Dublin; Greencastle; Munster

IOWA – Clare; Curlew; Shannon City

KANSAS – Boyle; Longford

KENTUCKY – Boyle County; Dublin

LOUISIANA – Antrim; Clare; Derry; Sligo

MAINE – Belfast; Carlow Island; Clontarf; Limerick

MARYLAND – Ardmore; Baltimore; Dublin; Dundalk; Mayo

MASSACHUSETTS – Auburn

MICHIGAN – Antrim; Boyne City; Clare; Darragh; Dublin; New Baltimore; Roscommon; Wexford County

MINNESOTA – Avoca; Clontarf; Kilkenny; Lismore

MISSISSIPPI – Boyle; Dublin; Shannon

NEW HAMPSHIRE – Antrim; Derry; Dublin; Londonderry

NEW MEXICO –Derry; Tyrone

NEW YORK – Auburn; Avoca; Belfast; Galway; Tyrone; Ulster County

NORTH CAROLINA – Dublin; Mayo River; Shannon

NORTH DAKOTA – Bantry; Donnybrook; Kenmare

OHIO – Belfast; Dublin; Londonderry

OKLAHOMA – Ardmore; Kildare; Tyrone

PENNSYLVANIA – Antrim; Ardmore; Armagh; Castle Shannon; Colrain Township; Derry; Donegal; Dublin; Dunmore; Fermanagh Township; New Derry; Sligo; Tyrone

SOUTH CAROLINA –Mayo; Shannontown

SOUTH DAKOTA – Ardmore

TENNESSEE – Ardmore; Belfast

TEXAS – Donnybrook Place; Dublin; Ireland; Kildare

VERMONT – Londonderry

VIRGINIA – Dublin; Dungannon; Dunmore County; Kinsale; Mayo; Stormont

WASHINGTON – Curlew; Lake Shannon

WEST VIRGINIA – Dunmore; Ireland; Killarney; Tralee

WISCONSIN – Kildare; New Munster

WYOMING – Tipperary

WHERE IRELAND RANKS
AMONG THE NATIONS

- 110th in area, with 26,600 square miles. (Between Sierra Leone and Sri Lanka, formerly Ceylon.)

- 101st in population, with 3,533,000 inhabitants in the 26 counties of the Republic. (Between Sierra Leone and Libya.)

- 61st in number of years as an independent nation-state.

- 57th richest, based on *per capita* income.

- Spent $205 million for defense in 1980, compared, for example, with the United States' $126.4 billion, the Soviet Union's $114 billion, Britain's $19 billion and Malta's $ll million.

- Ranked in the lower-middle group of nations in population growth, registering a 1.5 percent yearly increase from 1975 to 1980. Comparative figures include Italy, .3 percent; India, 2.2 percent; Canada, 1.1 percent; United States, 1.0 percent; Britain, .1 percent; Germany (East and West), .0 percent.

- Registered 6.3 marriages per 1,000 inhabitants in 1980, compared with 10.5 for the United States, 7.7 for Britain, 6.3 for Finland and .7 for Mozambique.

- 58 percent of its population lives in cities (1980), compared with 77 percent in the United States, 91 percent in Britain, 85 percent in West Germany, 69 percent in Italy and 5 percent in Nepal.

- Ranked fourth in the percentage of bachelors, ages 45 to 49, with 28.3 percent. Figures for other countries included 5.6 in the United States; .2 percent in South Korea; 2.4 percent in Japan; and 10.1 percent in England and Wales.

- Supported an average household of 4.0 people, compared with 2.0 in the United States, 2.7 in Britain, 3.0 in Italy and 6.0 in Nigeria.

- Ranked fifth in the ratio of children of high-school age attending school.

- Ranked first in average calories consumed daily by each inhabitant; tenth in *per capita* meat consumption; sixth in daily protein consumption; and seventh in milk consumption.

- Ranked 14th on the Physical Quality of Life Index, tied with Japan and Iceland, among others, at 98 percent. By comparison, the United States scores 96 percent; Britain, 95 percent; Soviet Union, 90 percent; and Ethiopia, 20 percent. (This index is a composite rating that combines a nation's average life expectancy, its infant mortality rate and its literacy rate.)

- Highest and lowest recorded temperatures (Dublin) – Highest: 86 degrees F. Lowest: 8 degrees F.

The rankings above are based on officially reported statistical, demographic and other data from various countries and international organizations, and may be found in fuller form in George Thomas Kurian, *The New Book of World Rankings* (New York: Facts on File, 1984.) Most of the data are current as of censuses and surveys taken in 1980.

BEFORE THE KENNEDYS:
THE CARROLLS OF MARYLAND,
AMERICA'S FIRST IRISH-CATHOLIC
DYNASTY

Had George Washington declined to serve a second term, the United States might have had an Irish-Catholic president in 1792 – some 169 years before John F. Kennedy moved into the White House.*

As Washington neared the end of his first term, many doubted that he wished to continue in office, even if he were physically able. The general's party, the Federalists, met to decide whom they might turn to if Washington stepped aside. Their choice was Charles Carroll of Carrollton. Carroll, one of the most respected Americans of his day, came from one of Maryland's oldest Irish-Catholic families. He was, in fact, one of the Signers of the Declaration of Independence. When he died in 1832 at age 95, he would be the last survivor of that group.

American Beginnings

Carroll's grandfather, also named Charles, had come to Maryland in 1688 as attorney general for Charles Calvert, the third Lord Baltimore. Although the family's former status in Ireland is uncertain, his grandson's biographers would later claim that they were descended from "the old Irish princely family of the Carrolls of Ely O'Carroll, in Kings County (now County Offaly)."

As it turned out, the immigrant Carroll would serve only briefly as attorney general. Lord Baltimore, a Catholic nobleman, had inherited the colony, which his grandfather, Charles, first Lord Baltimore, had received in 1632 under a royal charter that gave him the right to rule essentially as he wished. His wish had been to establish religious freedom for Catholic and Protestant alike. Unfortunately for the Calverts and the cause of religious toleration, the family lost control of Maryland in 1689. Word came from England that the Catholic James II had been defeated at the Battle of the Boyne and that William and Mary, his Protestant son-in-law and daughter, had ascended the throne. But no orders had yet arrived from Lord Baltimore instructing the colonists to honor the new monarchs.

------

* This, at least, is the claim made by John Corry in *Golden Clan: The Murrays, the McDonnells and the Irish American Aristocracy* (Boston: Houghton Mifflin, 1977). Mr. Corry is a columnist for *The New York Times*.

George Calvert's supposed disloyalty to the throne led to a Protestant takeover in Maryland. The leaders of the colony's religious majority seized power and asked London to send a royal governor. This done, Maryland remained a crown colony until 1715, when Benedict Calvert, fourth Lord Baltimore, regained the family's rights by becoming a Protestant and convincing George I of his loyalty.

In any case, the Carrolls and other Maryland Catholics were now subject to many of the injustices their fellow Catholics in Ireland and England had been suffering under the so-called Penal Laws. They were barred from voting, from holding office, from worshiping openly and even from having their children educated as Catholics. Nothing, though, kept them from making money, and Charles Carroll the immigrant proceeded to build a substantial fortune in land and tobacco.

The immigrant's son – called Charles Carroll of Annapolis to distinguish him from his father – managed to improve so much on his father's estate that many guessed he had made himself the richest man in the colonies. But despite his material good fortune, anti-Catholic discrimination left him a bitter man.

Charles the Signer

Though Catholic education was outlawed, Charles Carroll of Annapolis saw to his son's Catholic upbringing. The boy was taught first by Jesuits in the "underground" school at Bohemia Manor, Maryland. Later he was sent abroad to school – to France for several years, followed by law studies in England. When he returned to Maryland at the age of 28, he planned not to practice law but to manage Carrollton Manor, the 10,000-acre estate in Frederick County his father had given him.

In 1768, four years after his return, Carroll married his cousin, Mary Darnall. But he was not to continue the life of a country gentleman. When Parliament had imposed the Stamp Act in 1765, he shared the growing discontent among American colonists. His studies had convinced him that such laws were unconstitutional.

The event that launched Carroll into public life, however, was the governor's insistence, in 1773, that he – and not the Maryland legislature – had the right to set fees for crown officers and salaries for clergy of the established church. A letter defending the governor's position was published in the *Maryland Gazette* by one of his supporters, Daniel Dulaney – who signed himself "First Citizen." Carroll wrote a brilliantly argued reply published over the name "Second Citizen."

As the political repartee continued, Carroll won the respect and admiration of many Marylanders. He took an increasingly active role in politics, backing measures to boycott English imports in 1774 and joining in the work of the Annapolis Committee of Correspondence, the first Maryland Convention and other revolutionary bodies.

Nurturing the New Nation

In 1776 Carroll was elected a delegate to the Maryland Convention, which was considering whether to join the other colonies in moving to separate from England. His efforts were instrumental in the resolution's passage. Confident of his abilities, the convention elected him one of the colony's representatives to the Continental Congress that was soon to meet in Philadelphia. On August 2, Charles Carroll of Carrollton added his name to the Declaration of Independence.

Henceforth Carroll took a leading role in both Maryland and national affairs. As one of the leading drafters of the Maryland Constitution, he made clear his opposition to proposals to confiscate British property and other measures that seemed as unjust as the English laws that had angered so many colonists.

In Congress, where he served from 1776 to 1778, Carroll was active on the Board of War and other vital committees. His business background provided good experience for helping make sure that the Continental forces had the money and materiel they needed to resist the armed might of Britain.

After the war ended, Carroll declined to serve as a delegate to the national convention that drafted the Constitution between 1787 and 1789. He did, however, speak in favor of the document's ratification. Already a member of the Maryland Senate since the mid-1770s, Carroll was elected to the United States Senate when it was established in 1789. In 1792, when it became legally impossible to hold both state and federal office at the same time, he chose to remain in the Maryland Senate, where he served for several more years.

After leaving politics, Carroll turned his energies to managing his substantial properties, which included 70,000 to 80,000 acres in Maryland, Pennsylvania and New York. He became an active member of the Potomac Company, which hoped to build a canal to Ohio and the West, and of its successor, the Chesapeake & Ohio Canal Company (1823). Carroll was also a founding director of the Baltimore & Ohio Railroad, whose cornerstone he laid in 1828.

When he died at Baltimore in 1832, Charles Carroll of Carrollton was the last surviving signer of the Declaration of Independence. He was also reputed to be the wealthiest man in America.

All in the Family

Carroll was to have distinguished descendants as well as forebears. His daughter, Mrs. Richard Caton, set out to make her mark as a society figure. Decades before Jennie Jerome of New York married Lord Randolph Churchill and Nancy Langhorne of Virginia married Viscount Astor, Mrs. Caton aspired to have European titles in the family. She succeeded, in fact, in marrying off all three daughters to English peers. The first became the Duchess of Leeds, the second the Marchioness of Wellesley, and the third the Baroness Stafford. London society hailed the girls as "the American graces." Mrs. Caton went on to found the first great resort frequented by America's social elite – at White Sulphur Springs, Virginia.

John Lee Carroll (1830-1911), a great-grandson of the Signer, also studied law and later embarked on a political career. Like his distinguished forebear, he served as president of the Maryland Senate. From there he went on to become governor of the state in 1875, filling the post ably during a time of economic depression and labor unrest. His cousin, Samuel Sprigg Carroll (1832-1893), attended West Point and fought with distinction in the Civil War, twice suffering wounds and rising to become a brigadier-general of volunteers.

Bishop John and the Other Carrolls

The achievements of Charles Carroll of Carrollton and those of his fathers and descendents are impressive by themselves. If we add in the record of the other Carrolls of Maryland, however, the story becomes even more remarkable. The Carrolls of colonial Maryland were descended from two 17th-century immigrants: Charles Carroll (discussed above) and Kean Carroll, cousins who shared a common ancestor in Ireland. Just as Charles of Carrollton was to become the most distinguished member of the first branch, so his cousin, friend and schoolmate, John Carroll, would become the most eminent representative of the other Carrolls. John Carroll was to be the first Roman Catholic bishop in the United States – and the first archbishop.

Born in Upper Marlboro, Maryland, in 1735, John Carroll attended the illegal Jesuit academy at Bohemia Manor (see section entitled, "Irish-American Landmarks") together with young Charles Carroll of Carrollton. Later both boys were dispatched by their families to Flanders, where they continued their studies at St. Omer.

Carroll became a novice in the Jesuit foundation at Walten, France, in 1753, and was ordained in the late 1760s. When the Jesuits were suppressed by the Pope in 1773, he returned to Maryland and established a mission church in his mother's house at Rock Creek, in the area of what is now Washington, D.C. When the Continental Congress decided to send a delegation to French Canada in 1776 to appeal for support of the revolution, John Carroll was persuaded to join Benjamin Franklin, Samuel Chase and his cousin, Charles Carroll, in this unsuccessful effort.

Building an American Church

Returning to matters spiritual, Carroll joined with several other priests in appealing to Rome for permission to continue their missions in Maryland. They also asked for one among them to be named their superior; Carroll was named prefect-apostolic and charged with nurturing the infant church throughout the 13 states. That same year, 1784, he published *An Address to the Roman Catholics of the United States of North America*. In this pamphlet – the first work ever published by a Catholic in this country – Carroll defended his faith against attacks made by the Reverend Charles Wharton, a distant cousin and a former Jesuit who had become an Episcopalian clergyman.

Moving to Baltimore in 1786, John Carroll became active in a variety of new pursuits. He was named head of the Library Company and of the trustees of Baltimore College; and also became a trustee of St. John's College, Annapolis, and a co-founder of the Maryland Historical Society. Most notably, he was appointed Bishop of Baltimore in 1791 – the first American bishop of the first American see. He journeyed to England for the installation.

As bishop, Carroll laid the foundations of the nation's Catholic educational system. He had already been the moving force in establishing Georgetown College (founded in 1789; now Georgetown University), the nation's first Catholic institution of higher learning. Now he brought members of many European orders to the United States to establish and operate new institutions: Sulpicians, Trappists, Jesuits, Dominicans, Carmelites and others.

Carroll also began planning and raising money to build a cathedral. Though he laid the cornerstone in 1806, the building was not finished until several years after his death. But Baltimore's Basilica of the Assumption, designed by Benjamin Latrobe, came to be widely considered the most beautiful church in the country.

In 1808, Baltimore was elevated to an archdiocese, which encompassed four new dioceses: Boston, New York, Philadelphia and Bardstown, Kentucky (Louisville). Carroll, now an archbishop, effectively selected his four new bishops and actively counseled them in overseeing their dioceses. By the year of his death, 1815, he had placed American Catholicism on firm foundations, free of foreign influences and poised for dramatic growth with the coming influx of hundreds of thousands of immigrants from Ireland and elsewhere.

Daniel Carroll (1733-1796), educated in Flanders like his younger brother, Archbishop John Carroll, and Charles Carroll of Carrollton, married Elizabeth Carroll of Duddington, apparently a first cousin of Charles. He then settled into the lifestyle of a country gentleman until the Revolution, when he represented Maryland in the Continental Congress from 1780 to 1784. Daniel Carroll was the only Roman Catholic to sign the Articles of Confederation. When the Constitutional Convention of 1787-1789 was convened, he served as a delegate from Maryland. He played a major role in influencing his state to vote for ratification of the new charter, rebutting the anti-Federalist arguments of Samuel Chase, another Maryland delegate.

Elected senator from Maryland to the First Congress of the United States, Daniel Carroll was appointed in 1791 to a three-man commission charged with laying out a site for the new capital at Washington, D.C. The Carroll family owned large amounts of land in what was to become the District of Columbia. Daniel Carroll left the government in 1795 and died the following year at Rock Creek, his home just outside the capital.

The experience of the Carrolls of Maryland may not be typical of Irish-Americans in general, either then or now. Yet they proved, to a considerable degree, what able Americans might aspire to achieve – whether of Irish or other heritages.

IRISH-AMERICAN FESTIVALS:
A DIRECTORY

Arizona

PHOENIX IRISH FEIS
St. Gregory Parish Grounds
3434 North 18th Avenue
Phoenix, AZ

Late October. Saturday/Sunday. Competition in traditional music and
dancing events. Irish food and drink. Irish crafts and other imports on
sale. CONTACT: Write P. Casey, 526 East Dunlap Street, Phoenix, AZ
85020; or phone John Corcoran, Chairman, at (602) 939-1183.

California

GRAND NATIONAL IRISH FAIR
& MUSIC FESTIVAL
The Rose Bowl
Pasadena, CA

Mid-June. Saturday/Sunday. Features continuous entertainment on
several stages, with showbands, traditional musicians and music groups
from the U.S. and Ireland. Also: pipe bands; parades; Gaelic sports;
traditional food. CONTACT: Irish Fair Foundation, P.O. Box 341,
Pasadena, CA 91102. (818) 843-3644 or (714) 523- 5784.

IRISH FESTIVAL WEEK
San Francisco, CA

Mid-October. One week. Celebrates Ireland's culture, heritage and
traditions with performances of dances, music and drama as well as art
shows and the crowning of "Miss Ireland." CONTACT: San Francisco
Convention and Visitors Bureau, Hallidie Plaza, 900 Market Street, San
Francisco, CA 94102. (415) 974-6900.

Connecticut

GREATER HARTFORD IRISH FESTIVAL
The Irish American Home
132 Glastonbury Street
Glastonbury, CT

Late July. Friday through Sunday. Irish entertainers and show bands;
"Miss Irish Festival" competition; children's games and rides; craft exhibits
and demonstrations; Irish imports; food and drink. CONTACT: Call (203)
289-5705.

NEW HAVEN FEIS
Bowen Field
New Haven, CT

Last Sunday in June. Competitions in music, dancing, art, Gaelic
language and singing. Also: concert featuring big-name Irish bands;
football and hurling matches. Food and drink. CONTACT: Jim McCabe,
Feis Secretary, Irish American Community Center, P.O. Box 1184, New
Haven, CT 06505. (203) 269-0371 (evenings/weekends).

Delaware

ANNUAL FEIS
Concord High School Grounds
Wilmington, DE

Mid-August. Sunday. Competition in Irish dance, music, arts, crafts,
poetry, essays and other feis events for all age levels. Irish soda bread and
other food and drink. Celebration of Mass. CONTACT: Irish Culture
Club of Delaware, P.O. Box 9326, Wilmington, DE 19809. (302) 762-
1538.

Illinois

CHICAGO IRISH FEST
Olive Park (Lakefront, near Navy Pier)
Chicago, IL

Early August. Saturday/Sunday. Co-sponsored by the Chicago Gaelic
Athletic Association (GAA) and the Irish American Heritage Center.

Features leading Irish music groups from Ireland and the U.S. as well as local talent from the Chicago Irish Musicians Association; traditional dancers; Irish imports; Irish, American and multi-ethnic food and drink. CONTACT: Irish American Heritage Center, 4626 North Knox Avenue, Chicago, IL 60630. (312) 282-7035.

CHICAGO FEIS
DuPage County Fairgrounds
Wheaton, IL

May/June. One day. Competition in traditional dance events. CONTACT: Harry Costelloe, President, Chicago Feis Society on (312) 636-8560.

Kentucky

IRISH HERITAGE WEEKEND
Riverfront Plaza on the Belvedere
Louisville, KY

Late June. Saturday/Sunday. One of a series of Heritage Weekends, each highlighting three or four nationality groups. The Irish event offers traditional music; stepdancers; Irish ballads; Irish imports on sale; cultural exhibits; and Irish food and drink. CONTACT: The Heritage Corporation, 1 Riverfront Plaza, Louisville, KY 40202. (502) 566-5068.

Maryland

IRISH FESTIVAL WEEKEND
Harborplace
Baltimore, MD

Mid-September. Friday through Sunday. Traditional ceili music groups. Mid-Atlantic Stepdancing Competition. Irish craftmaking demonstrations. Irish storyteller. Crafts and imports on sale. Irish food and drink. CONTACT: Mike O'Shea, O'Shea Lumber Company, P.O. Box 299, Cockeysville, MD 21030. (301) 666-1200 days; (301) 329-6280 evenings and weekends.

ANNUAL IRISH DANCE COMPETITION
Glen Echo Park
McArthur Boulevard
Glen Echo, MD

Saturday of Memorial Day Weekend. The program for this feis includes competition in traditional dancing and music events as well as selected arts and crafts. CONTACT: Irish Dance Festival of Northern Virginia, c/o Mr. Ben Malcom, P.O. Box 71, Merrifield, VA 22116. (703) 591-5191.

IRISH FOLK FESTIVAL
Glen Echo Park
McArthur Boulevard
Glen Echo, MD

Sunday of Memorial Day Weekend. Starts with a Gaelic Mass at noon. Then comes a day of Irish dancing, singing, instrumental music and other entertainment as well as demonstrations of traditional crafts. Clowns, magicians and games are provided for the younger set. Concludes with an evening ceili. CONTACT: Michael Denney, 7408 Flower Avenue, Takoma Park, MD 20012. (301) 279-1496.

Massachusetts

FITCHBURG IRISH FESTIVAL
Wallace Civic Center
John Fitch Highway
Fitchburg, MA

Mid-July. Sunday. Traditional music; stepdancers; Irish-English Mass; Irish films; Irish imports; food and drink specialties. CONTACT: Irish Festival Committee, P.O. Box 236, Fitchburg, MA 01420.

NEW ENGLAND IRISH FESTIVAL
Sullivan Stadium -- Route 1
Foxboro, MA

Late June. Saturday/Sunday. Music, singing and dancing groups. Pipe bands. Stepdancing. Ceili. Celtic arts and crafts exhibit. Authentic Irish cottage recreation. Irish marketplace. CONTACT: Coordinator, New England Irish Festival, Sullivan Stadium, Route 1, Foxboro, MA 02035. (617) 262-1776 (9-5 weekdays).

CELTIC IRISH FESTIVAL
Holyoke, MA

Mid-August. Friday through Sunday. The program includes solo and group performances of traditional and folk music for instruments and voice; Irish dancing and showband music; Irish football; Irish crafts and imports; movies provided by the Irish Consulate; and genealogical help from specialists for those interested in tracing their Irish roots. CONTACT: Holyoke St. Patrick Irish Festival Committee, P.O. Box 871, Holyoke, MA 01040. (413) 533-0909.

Michigan

IRISH FESTIVAL OF DETROIT
Waterfront Plaza – Downtown
Detroit, MI

Early June. Friday through Sunday. One of a series of ethnic heritage weekends in downtown Detroit. Features celebrity entertainers and groups from Ireland; traditional Irish musicians and stepdancers; ceili dancing; movies about Ireland; cultural exhibits; demonstrations of traditional crafts; Irish drama performances; an Irish storyteller; Irish imports on sale; and Irish food and drink. CONTACT: Irish Festival of Detroit, Inc., c/o Chris Murray, Chairman, The Gaelic League & Irish American Club of Detroit, 2068 Michigan Avenue, Detroit, MI 48216. (313) 963-8895.

DETROIT INTERNATIONAL FEIS
Ford Field
Livonia, MI

Mid-June. A day of competition in traditional Irish music, dancing, oratory, poetry and other events. 1986 marks this festival's 24th year. CONTACT: Ken Kuhns, Feis Chairman on (313) 281-6809.

New Jersey

IRISH FEIS AND SCOTTISH GAMES FESTIVAL
Freehold Raceway
Freehold, NJ

Mid-July. One day. Features Irish ballads, stepdancing, Irish band music
and pipe band competition as well as such Irish field sports as Gaelic
football and soccer. CONTACT: Information Office, Freehold Raceway,
Freehold, NJ 07728. (201) 462-3800.

IRISH FESTIVAL
Garden State Arts Center
Holmdell, NJ

Last Sunday in June. One of a series of ethnic festivals held at the Arts
Center each year. Opens with a pipe band competition at 9 am, followed
by an 11:00 Mass. The afternoon line-up includes singers, musicians, folk
dancers, harpists, stepdancers and celebrities. CONTACT: Irish Festival,
c/o Garden State Arts Center, Garden State Parkway, Woodbridge, NJ
07095. (201) 442- 8600 ext. 221.

IRISH FESTIVAL
Action Park
Vernon, NJ

Early August. Saturday/Sunday. Held at a commercially operated theme
park, this festival features Irish showbands and folk singers; Irish dancing;
and pipe bands. CONTACT: Irish Festival, P.O. Box 848, McAfee, NJ
07428. (201) 827-2000.

New York

EMPIRE STATE IRISH FESTIVAL
The Plaza
Albany, NY

Early August. Thursday. A day-long event co-sponsored by the Ancient
Order of Hibernians and New York State. Features continuous music by
"name" Irish bands as well as continuous ceili dancing. Also: stepdancers;

pipe bands; harpists; Irish imports; food and drink. CONTACT: Mike Hession, Irish Festival Coordinator, Capital District Council, AOH, 12 Buchanan Street, Albany, NY 12206. (518) 489-3144.

THE GREAT IRISH FAIR
Coney Island
Brooklyn, NY

First weekend after Labor Day. Friday through Sunday. A well- attended event co-sponsored since 1981 by the Ancient Order of Hibernians and the Brooklyn Borough President's Office. This festival features music, dancing and sports competition, including show-band and traditional Irish music performed by celebrity entertainers; stepdancing and ceili performances; races in currachs, a traditional boat of the west of Ireland; and Gaelic sports competition matching an Irish championship team with an all-star team from the New York Gaelic Athletic Association. Also: demonstrations of traditional arts and crafts; sale of Irish imports; games and rides for children; and Irish-style food and drink. CONTACT: Mary Henry, 37 Joval Court, Brooklyn, NY 11229. (718) 468-3931.

GREENE COUNTY IRISH FESTIVAL
East Durham, NY

Memorial Day Weekend. Saturday through Monday. Leading Irish show bands, traditional music groups. Bagpipers. Stepdancers. Working craftsmen and artists. Games. Children's entertainment/animal farm/pony ride. Imported Irish gifts. Irish food and drink. CONTACT: East Durham Vacationland Association, Box 67, East Durham, NY 12423. (518) 634-7100.

INTERNATIONAL CELTIC FESTIVAL
Hunter, NY

Late August. Friday through Sunday. A celebration of Irish, Welsh and Scottish cultures and their common Celtic origins. Events include pipe band competitions, Highland games, dancing competitions, singing groups. CONTACT: Exposition Planners, Bridge Street, Hunter, NY 12442. (518) 263-3800.

LEEDS IRISH FESTIVAL
Hunter, NY

Labor Day Weekend. Saturday through Monday. Program highlights
include show bands, bagpiping, traditional music and dancing and
children's games. Irish food, drink and imports are on sale. CONTACT:
Leeds Irish Festival, P.O. Box 6, Leeds, NY 12451. (518) 943-9820 or
943-9814.

BUFFALO IRISH FESTIVAL
Weimar's Grove
Broadway and Bowen Roads
Lancaster, NY

Late August. Friday through Sunday. Started in 1983, this festival
features traditional Irish entertainment by leading U.S. and Canadian
musical groups; ceili and stepdancing; solo bagpipers; singers; free
consultations with a specialist in Irish genealogy; a children's entertainment
area; food and drink; and booths selling Irish imports. CONTACT: Kevin
Townsell, Coordinator, Buffalo Irish Festival, c/o The Shannon Pub,
4230 Genesee Street, Buffalo, NY 14225. (716) 632-8400.

IRISH TRADITIONAL MUSIC FESTIVAL
Snug Harbor Cultural Center
Staten Island, NY

Late June/early July. Saturday or Sunday. A festival highlighting
traditional music, song and dance. Includes performances by big-name
Irish entertainers and others from Ireland and the U.S. Ceili instruction is
held throughout the day, both for beginners and for experienced dancers.
Also: workshops in various instruments (harp, flute, tin whistle, etc.) and
singing techniques. A children's area offers song, dance and games. Irish
food and drink are on sale. A ceili follows in the evening. CONTACT:
Irish Arts Center, 553 West 51st Street, New York, NY 10019. (212) 757-
3318.

UNITED IRISH COUNTIES ASSOCIATION FEIS
St. Joseph's Seminary
Yonkers, NY

Early June. Sunday. This may be the nation's largest Irish festival and, in any event — after 54 years — is almost certainly its oldest. 250 competitions cover such categories as Irish music; harp playing; pipe bands; Irish language; poetry; oratory; art and Celtic design; and needlecrafts. CONTACT: United Irish Counties Assn. of New York, 326 West 48th Street, New York, NY 10036. (212) 265-4226.

Ohio

IRISH CULTURAL FESTIVAL OF CLEVELAND
7863 York Road
Parma, OH

First weekend in August. Friday through Sunday. Features singers, showbands and traditional Irish musical groups; ceili and stepdancing exhibitions; Irish drama; Gaelic football and camogie; storyteller; and folklore demonstrations. Also: ceili workshops; demonstrations of traditional arts and crafts; booths selling Irish imports. Noon Mass on Sunday. CONTACT: John O'Brien, Irish Festival Chairman, 14708 Westland Avenue, Cleveland, OH 44111. (216) 251-0711.

Pennsylvania

IRISH JUBILEE AND CELTIC FESTIVAL
Rocky Park Glen
Avoca, PA

Late August. Friday through Sunday. A full schedule of traditional and popular Irish music, dancing and entertainment. Sunday Mass in Gaelic. CONTACT: Rocky Park Glen, P.O. Box 37, Avoca, PA 18641-0037. (717) 457-7401 or 655-5500.

TRADITIONAL IRISH MUSIC AND DANCE FESTIVAL
Fischer's Pool
Lansdale, PA

Mid-September. One day. CONTACT: The Philadelphia Ceili Group, Attn.: Robin Cook, Room 2, The Irish Center/Commodore Barry Club, 6815 Emlen Street, Philadelphia, PA 19119. (215) 849-8899.

IRISH FESTIVAL AT MONTAGE MOUNTAIN
Exit 51 – Route 81
Scranton, PA

Memorial Day Weekend. Saturday through Monday. Leading Irish entertainers: singers, instrumentalists and groups. Stepdancers. Imported gifts on sale. Irish food and drink. Gaelic Mass at noon Sunday. CONTACT: Irish Cultural Society, P.O. Box 573, Scranton, PA 18501. (717) 961-0143 or 347-4609; or, Montage Ski Resort: (717) 969-7669.

IRISH DAYS
Coal Street Park
Wilkes-Barre, PA

First *full* three-day weekend *following* July 4th. Friday through Sunday. Entertainment line-up for this weather-sheltered festival includes show bands and traditional Irish music groups; stepdancing and ceili; pipe bands; Irish storyteller; cultural exhibits; and a children's playland. Also: Irish imports on sale; Irish-style food and drink. Mass in Gaelic on Sunday. CONTACT: George Horn, Irish Days Chairman, The Donegal Society of Wilkes-Barre, P.O. Box 184, Wilkes-Barre, PA 18701. (717) 822- 7376.

Rhode Island

IRISH HERITAGE MONTH
Newport, RI

March. A month-long line-up of Irish-related festivities sponsored by the Newport Tourism & Convention Authority. Features a ceremony reenacting the Lighting of the Fire of Tara; a rugby tournament; an Irish market place, offering imported crafts and gift items; performances by musicians, dancers and singers; and an annual St. Patrick's Day parade on March 17th. CONTACT: Phone 800-343-4511 for a free Irish Heritage Month calendar and other information.

Texas

NORTH TEXAS IRISH FESTIVAL
The Embarcadero and Adjacent Buildings
Fair Park
Dallas, TX

Early March. Saturday/Sunday. An indoor festival featuring "name" Irish entertainers; traditional Irish musical groups; stepdancing exhibitions; Texas Rose of Tralee competition; Irish stew cook-off; Irish food and drink; and arts and crafts booths. CONTACT: North Texas Irish Festival, P.O. Box 4474, Dallas, TX 75208. (214) 942-6687.

SOUTHERN UNITED STATES FEIS
(Exact location varies)
Houston, TX

February. One day. Competition in traditional dancing and music events. Cultural exhibits. Irish food and drink. Ceili in evening. CONTACT: EIRE (Emerald Isle Renaissant Enthusiasts), 4135 Martinshire Drive, Houston, TX 77025. (713) 664-3460.

SAN ANTONIO IRISH FEIS
Fiesta Plaza Mall
San Antonio, TX

June. One day. Competition in traditional dancing, music and speaking events. Live entertainment. Irish imports. Irish food and drink. A ceili follows the competitions. CONTACT: Colm O'Maoileidigh, P.O. Box 438, Helotes, TX 78023. (512) 695-9357.

SOUTH TEXAS IRISH FESTIVAL
La Villita Plaza
San Antonio, TX

March. Friday through Sunday, the weekend before St. Patrick's Day.
Live Irish music. Stepdancing exhibitions. Irish food and drink.
CONTACT: Fr. Bill Davis, St. Mary's Church, 202 North St. Mary's
Street, San Antonio, TX 78205. (512) 226-8381.

TEXAS FOLKLIFE FESTIVAL
Festival Grounds
Institute of Texan Cultures
San Antonio, TX

First weekend in August. Thursday through Sunday. This festival
celebrates many of Texas' nationality groups, each in a separate area. The
Irish section features a thatched cottage with an exhibit on the Irish cultural
heritage of Texas. Also: ceili bands; stepdancing performances; Irish
storyteller; and bagpipers. Food and refreshments. CONTACT: Patrick
Dowd, Harp & Shamrock Society, 19843 Encino Brook, San Antonio,
TX 78259. (512) 497-8435.

Wisconsin

IRISH FEST
Summerfest Grounds, Lakeside
Milwaukee, WI

Mid-August. Friday through Sunday. One of America's biggest Irish
events, with an exceptional line-up of Irish bands and entertainers, plus
stepdancers; Irish drama; children's theater; cultural exhibits; Irish
marketplace; wandering performers; Gaelic football and rugby; pipe bands;
ceili dancing; clan reunions; parades; contests; and a bake-off.
CONTACT: Greater Milwaukee Visitors and Convention Bureau, 756
North Milwaukee Street, Milwaukee, WI 53202; (414) 273-3950. Or:
Irish Fest, Box 599, Milwaukee, WI 53201; (414) 466-6640.

VERSES STIRRING AND SENTIMENTAL

Ireland's National Anthem: "The Soldier's Song"
("Amhran na bhFiann")

First published in 1912, "The Soldier's Song" was adopted as the official national anthem in July 1926. It is nearly always sung in Gaelic. Peadar Kearney, who wrote the words, also wrote the music together with Patrick Heaney. Here are the lyrics in English:

VERSE 1:   We'll sing a song, a soldier's song,
                  With cheering, rousing chorus,
                  As round our blazing fires we throng,
                  The starry heavens o'er us;

                  Impatient for the coming fight,
                  And as we wait for the morning's light,
                  Here in the silence of the night,
                  We'll chant a soldier's song.

CHORUS: Soldiers are we, whose lives are pledged to Ireland;
                  Some have come from a land beyond the wave,
                  Sworn to be free, no more our ancient sireland,
                  Shall shelter the despot or the slave.

                  Tonight we man the bearna bacghail,
                  In Erin's cause, come woe or weal;
                  'Mid cannons' roar and rifles' peal,
                  We'll chant a soldier's song.

VERSE 2:   In valley green, on towering crag,
                  Our fathers fought before us,
                  And conquered 'neath the same old flag,
                  That's proudly floating o'er us;

                  We're children of a fighting race,
                  That never yet has known disgrace,
                  And as we march, the foe to face,
                  We'll chant a soldier's song.

(CHORUS)

VERSE 3:   Sons of the Gael! Men of the Pale!
The long watched day is breaking;
The serried ranks of Inisfail,
Shall set the Tyrant quaking.

Our camp fires now are burning low,
See in the east a silv'ry glow,
Out yonder waits the Saxon foe,
So chant a soldier's song.

(CHORUS)

A Favorite of Yesteryear: Kathleen Mavourneen

Kathleen Mavourneen! the grey dawn is breaking,
The horn of the hunter is heard on the hill;
The lark from her light wing the bright dew is shaking,
Kathleen Mavourneen! What, slumbering still?
Oh! Hast thou forgotten how soon we must sever?
Oh! Hast thou forgotten this day we must part?
It may be for years, and it may be forever,
Oh! Why art thou silent, thou voice of my heart?
It may be for years, and it may be forever,
Then why art thou silent, Kathleen Mavourneen?

Kathleen Mavourneen! awake from thy slumbers,
The blue mountains glow in the sun's golden light,
Ah! where is the spell that once hung on thy numbers,
Arise in thy beauty, thou star of my light.
Mavourneen, Mavourneen, my sad tears are falling,
To think that from Erin and thee I must part;
It may be for years, and it may be forever,
Then why art thou silent, thou voice of my heart?
It may be for years, and it may be forever;
Then why art thou silent, Kathleen Mavourneen?

The Potato

Sublime potatoes! that from Antrim's shore
To famous Kerry, form the poor man's store;
Agreeing well with every place and state –
The peasant's noggin, or the rich man's plate.
Much prized when smoking from the teeming pot,
Or in turf-embers roasted crisp and hot.
Welcome, although you be our only dish;
Welcome, companion to flesh, fowl, or fish;
But to the real gourmands, the learned few,
Most welcome, steaming in an Irish stew.

By Thomas Crofton Crocker
(1798-1854), who collected
many traditional Irish airs
and stories, editing and
publishing some himself and
sending others to Thomas
Moore, famous for his *Collected
Melodies.*

The Irish Colonel

Said the king to the colonel,
"The complaints are eternal,
That you Irish give more trouble
Than any other corps,"

Said the colonel to the king,
"This complaint is no new thing,
Sire, your enemies have made it
A hundred times before."

By Sir Arthur Conan Doyle
(1859-1930), the creator of
Sherlock Holmes, in tribute
to the fighting record of
Irish troops in the British
army.

The Shandon Bells

With deep affection, and recollection
I often think of those Shandon bells,
Whose sound so wild would, in the days of my childhood,
Fling round my cradle their magic spells.
On this I ponder, where'er I wander,
And thus grow fonder, sweet Cork, of thee,
With thy bells of Shandon, that sound so grand on
The pleasant waters of the River Lee.

I've heard bells chiming, full many a clime in,
Tolling sublime in Cathedral shrine,
While at a glib rate, brass tongues would vibrate –
But all their music spoke naught like thine;
For memory dwelling, on each proud swelling,
Of the belfry knelling, its bold notes free,
Made the bells of Shandon, sound far more grand on,
The pleasant waters of the River Lee.

I've heard bells tolling, Old "Adrian's Mole" in,
Their thunder rolling from the Vatican,
And cymbals glorious, swinging uproarious,
In the gorgeous turrets of Notre Dame;
But their sounds were sweeter, than the dome of Peter,
Flings o'er the Tiber, pealing solemnly; –
Oh! the bells of Shandon sound far more grand on,
The pleasant waters of the River Lee.

There's a bell in Moscow, while a tower and kiosk o!
In Saint Sophia the Turkman gets,
And loud in air, calls men to prayer,
From the tapering summit, of tall minarets.
Such empty phantom, I freely grant them;
But there is an anthem, more dear to me, –
'Tis the bells of Shandon, that sound so grand on,
The pleasant waters of the River Lee.

Traditional song

The Rising of the Moon A.D. 1798
(Traditionally sung to "The Wearing of the Green")

"Oh, then, tell me, Shawn O'Ferrall,
Tell me why you hurry so?"
"Hush! ma bouchal, hush, and listen;"
And his cheeks were all a-glow;
"I bear orders from the Captain –
Get you ready quick and soon;
"For the pikes must be together
At the risin' of the moon."

"Oh, then, tell me, Shawn O'Ferrall,
Where the gath'rin' is to be?"
"In the ould spot by the river,
Right well known to you and me;
One more word – for signal token
Whistle up the marchin' tune,
With your pike upon your shoulder,
By the risin' of the moon."

Out from many a mud-wall cabin
Eyes were watchin' thro' that night;
Many a manly chest was throbbing
For the blessed warning light.
Murmurs passed along the valleys,
Like the banshee's lonely croon,
And a thousand blades were flashing
At the risin' of the moon.

There, beside the singing river,
That dark mass of men was seen –
Far above the shining weapons
Hung their own beloved "Green;"
"Death to ev'ry foe and traitor!
Forward! strike the marchin' tune,
And hurrah, my boys, for freedom!
'Tis the risin' of the moon."

Well they fought for poor Old Ireland,
And full bitter was their fate;
(Oh! what glorious pride and sorrow
Fill the name of 'Ninety-Eight!)
Yet, thank God, e'en still are beating
Hearts in manhood's burning noon,
Who would follow in their footsteps
At the risin' of the moon!

John Keegan Casey
(1846-1870)

The Harp That Once Through Tara's Halls

The harp that once through Tara's halls
The soul of music shed,
Now hangs as mute on Tara's walls
As if that soul were fled.
So sleeps the pride of former days
So glory's trill is o'er,
And hearts, that once beat high for praise
Now feel that pulse no more.

No more to chiefs and ladies bright
The harp of Tara swells,
The chord alone, that breaks at night
Its tale of ruin tells.
Thus freedom now so seldom wakes
The only throb she gives,
Is when some heart indignant breaks
To show that she still lives.

From *Irish Melodies*, collected
by Thomas Moore (1779-1852).

Believe Me, If All Those Endearing Young Charms

Believe me, if all those endearing young charms
Which I gaze on so fondly today,
Were to change by tomorrow and fleet in my arms
Like the fairy gifts fading away,
Thou would'st still be adored as this moment thou art,
Let thy loveliness fade as it will,
And around the dear ruin each wish of my heart
Would entwine itself verdantly still!

It is not while beauty and youth are thine own
And thy cheeks unprofaned by a tear,
That the fervor and faith of a soul can be known
To which time will but make thee more dear!
No, the heart that has truly lov'd never forgets,
But as truly loves on to the close;
As the sunflower turns on her god, when he sets,
The same look which she turn'd when he rose!

From *Irish Melodies*, collected
by Thomas Moore (1779-1852)

Mary from Dungloe

Oh then fare thee well, sweet Donegal,
The Rosses and Gweedore
I'm crossing the main ocean
Where the foaming billows roar
It breaks my heart from you to part
Where I spent many happy days
Farewell to kind relations
I am bound for Amerikay.

Oh then Mary you're my heart's delight
My pride and only care
It was your cruel father
Would not let me stay here
But absence makes the heart grow fond
And when I am over the main
May the Lord protect my darling girl
'Till I return again.

And I wish I was in sweet Dungloe
And seated on the grass
And by my side a bottle of wine
And on my knee a lass
I'd call for liquor of the best
And I'd pay before I'd go
And I'd roll my Mary in my arms
In the town of sweet Dungloe.

Traditional ballad by
Colm O'Loughlainn

IRELAND & IRISH AMERICA
IN THE MOVIES

They've been making movies about Ireland, the Irish and their American cousins for nearly as long as there have been movies to make. *How Molly Malone Made Good*, one of the earliest efforts, came to the screen in 1915. A small flood of other silent films followed in the 1920s, including *My Wild Irish Rose* (1922), *Irish Luck* (1925), *The Callahans and the Murphys* (1927) and *Blarney* (1928).

Most of these early releases, like silent-era movies in general, were clearly products of an infant industry undergoing growing pains. The few copies that remain in film archives today are curiosity pieces or grist for scholarly histories. By the 1930s, however, the advent of "talkies" had, by and large, brought with it new actors, better scripts and more sophisticated production techniques.

Though "Irish" films have never been immune to bad directing, bad acting, bad scripts and other ills – even to the present day – many have benefitted from the best talent available. *The Informer*, still a television staple around St. Patrick's Day, marked one of the best early efforts by John Ford, the distinguished Irish-American director, bringing him an Oscar in 1935 – and a second for its writer, Dudley Nichols.

The Informer and a selection of other films made since the 1930s are summarized below. Many of these titles can be rented or bought in videocassette format:

The Informer (U.S. RKO. 1935. 91 min.) Nominated for Best Picture. Starring Victor McLaglen. A simple-minded hanger-on betrays an IRA leader to earn a payoff that will help him emigrate. He finds that he can escape neither the wrath of his former comrades nor the pangs of his own conscience.

Beloved Enemy (U.S. Samuel Goldwyn or United Artists. 1936. 90 min.) Starring Brian Aherne, Merle Oberon, David Niven. Amid the turmoil of the 1921 Irish rebellion, the rebel leader steals the heart of a British officer's fiancee.

The Plough and the Stars (U.S. RKO. 1936. 72 min.) Directed by John Ford. Starring Barbara Stanwyck, Preston Foster, Barry Fitzgerald, Arthur Shields, Una O'Connor, Bonita Granville. Screen version of the Sean O'Casey play but, despite the cast, not a match for the original. In 1916 Dublin, amid "The Troubles," a man's marriage is threatened when he is appointed to command the nationalist forces.

Parnell (U.S. MGM. 1937. 96 min.) Starring Clark Gable, Myrna Loy, Edmund Gwenn, Donald Crisp. Charles Stewart Parnell, the champion of Irish nationalism during the late 19th century, finds his career tragically destroyed when he becomes romantically involved with a married woman.

The Fighting 69th (U.S. Warner Brothers. 1940. 89 min.) Starring James Cagney, Pat O'Brien, George Brent, Jeffrey Lynn, Alan Hale, Frank McHugh. Serving with the famous Irish-American regiment in the muddy trenches of World War I France, a cocky recruit surprises his buddies with heroism that costs him his life.

Going My Way (U.S. Paramount. 1940. 130 min.) Awarded Best Picture. Starring Bing Crosby, Barry Fitzgerald, Rise Stevens, Frank McHugh. Bing plays a young priest sent out to serve a tough New York parish under the watchful eye of its tightwad rector.

Hungry Hill (Britain. GFD/Two Cities. 1946. 92 min.) Starring Margaret Lockwood, Dennis Price, Cecil Parker, Michael Denison, Siobhan McKenna, Dan O'Herlihy. Three generations of an Irish family are trapped in an ongoing feud.

Captain Boycott (Britain. GFD/Individual/Universal. 1947. 93 min.) Starring Stewart Granger, Kathleen Ryan, Alistair Sim, Robert Donat, Cecil Parker, Noel Purcell, Niall MacGinnis. Hard-pressed Irish tenant farmers, squeezed to the limit and threatened with eviction, organize to resist oppressive landlords and their agents.

My Wild Irish Rose (U.S. Warner Brothers. 1947. 101 min.) Starring Dennis Morgan, Arlene Dahl, Andrea King, Alan Hale, George Tobias. A middling period musical that follows Irish tenor Chauncey Olcott through a roller-coaster relationship with Lillian Russell.

The Luck of the Irish (U.S. Twentieth Century Fox. 1947/1948. 99 min.) Starring Tyrone Power, Cecil Kellaway, Anne Baxter, Lee J. Cobb and Jayne Meadows. A New York journalist visiting Ireland meets a leprechaun, whose efforts to be helpful only complicate his love life.

Fighting Father Dunne (U.S. Warner Brothers. 1948. 93 min.) Starring Pat O'Brien, Darryl Hickman, Una O'Connor. A priest works to help poor boys amid the squalor and violence of an urban slum.

Top o' the Morning (U.S. Paramount. 1949. 100 min.) Starring
Bing Crosby, Barry Fitzgerald, Anne Blythe and Hume Cronin. The
Blarney Stone disappears, and investigations follow.

The Fighting O'Flynn (U.S. United Artists. 1949. 94 min.)
Starring Douglas Fairbanks, Jr., Helena Carter and Richard Greene. In
the waning years of the 18th century, an impoverished young adventurer
foils Napoleon's plans to invade Ireland. The premise of this film will
occasion understandable ambivalence among many.

The Quiet Man (U.S. Republic/Argosy. 1952. 129 min.) Nominated
for Best Picture. Starring John Wayne, Maureen O'Hara, Barry
Fitzgerald, Victor McLaglen, Ward Bond. A former boxer returns from
America to Ireland in search of a peaceful retirement and a wife. A
boisterous comedy full of Irish wit and color.

Captain Lightfoot (U.S. Universal. 1955. 92 min.) Starring Rock
Hudson, Barbara Rush, Jeff Morrow, Kathleen Ryan. A rebel struggles
against injustice and foreign rule in 19th-century Ireland. Not an award
winner.

The Search for Bridey Murphy (U.S. Paramount. 1956. 84 min.)
Starring Teresa Wright, Louis Hayward, Kenneth Tobey, Richard
Anderson. A Colorado businessman whose hobby is hypnotism
persuades a woman neighbor to let him transport her back into her
previous existence as a long-dead Irish peasant. The tension builds when
she seems unable to return from her previous life.

The Last Hurrah (U.S. Columbia. 1958. 125 min.) Directed by John
Ford. Starring Spencer Tracy, Jeffrey Hunter, Diane Foster, Pat O'Brien,
Basil Rathbone, Donald Crisp. As Frank Skeffington, the veteran Irish-
American political boss of a New England town, Spencer Tracy takes to
the campaign trail in a final reelection bid. Humorous touches and a
variety of well-acted characters complement Tracy's performance.

Darby O'Gill and the Little People (U.S. Disney. 1959.) A blend
of animation with real characters and sets, starring Albert Sharpe, Janet
Munro, Sean Connery and Jimmy O'Dea. An Irish storyteller on the verge
of losing his job falls down a well into the realm of the little people. There
he ultimately wins the right to have three wishes granted. Blarney-soaked
but charming family fare, with good special effects.

Shake Hands with the Devil (Ireland. United Artists/Troy/
Pennebaker. 1959. 110 min.) Starring James Cagney, Glynis Johns,
Don Murray, Dana Wynter, Michael Redgrave, Sybil Thorndike, Cyril
Cusack and Richard Harris. A surgeon in 1921 Dublin leads a double life
as secret leader of the IRA and grows attached to violence for its own sake
rather than as a means to an end.

Studs Lonigan (U.S. 1960. 95 min.) A young Irish-American,
without great prospects, grows up amid the fast-paced, sometimes violent
surroundings of 1920s Chicago. Based on the novel by James T. Farrell.

The Night Fighters (Allied Artists. 1960. 90 min.) Original title: *A
Terrible Beauty*. Starring Robert Mitchum, Anne Heywood, Dan
O'Herlihy, Cyril Cusack and Richard Harris. As World War II erupts, the
IRA revives its activities in a northern Irish village.

The Girl with Green Eyes (Britain. United Artists. 1963. 91 min.)
Starring Rita Tushingham, Peter Finch and Lynn Redgrave. Incisive
drama of relationship between a naive Dublin shopgirl and a worldly-wise
writer. Good location scenes strengthen the film.

Young Cassidy (Britain. MGM/Sextant. 1964. 110 min.) Starring
Rod Taylor, Maggie Smith, Edith Evans, Flora Robson, Michael
Redgrave, Julie Christie, Jack McGowran, Sian Phillips, T.P. McKenna.
The early Dublin years of Irish playwright Sean O'Casey on film.

The Fighting Prince of Donegal (Britain. Walt Disney. 1966. 104
min.) Starring Peter McEnery, Susan Hampshire, Tom Adams, Gordon
Jackson and Andrew Keir. An Irish chieftain fights the encroachments of
Elizabeth I's lieutenants in the 16th century.

Ulysses (Britain. Walter Reade. 1967. 132 min.) Starring Maurice
Roeves, Milo O'Shea, Barbara Jefford and T.P. McKenna. Based on
James Joyce's classic novel, this film follows a young poet and a Jewish
journalist through 24 hours of adventures in Dublin. It was considered
extreme at the time for its off-color language, and the critics were generally
uncharitable.

Finian's Rainbow (U.S. Warner Brothers/Seven Arts. 1968. 140
min.) Starring Fred Astaire, Petula Clark, Tommy Steele and Keenan
Wynn. A leprechaun attempts to find and bring back a pot of gold taken to
America by an old wanderer. Not up to the standards of the 1947
Broadway hit.

The Molly Maguires (U.S. Paramount/Tamm. 1970. 123 minutes.)
Starring Richard Harris, Sean Connery, Samantha Eggar, Frank Finlay
and Anthony Zerbe. A detective infiltrates a secret society dedicated to
fighting the oppressive system imposed on Pennsylvania coal miners in the
1870s and exposes its leaders. Based on a true story, many of whose
characters were Irish-American.

Quackser Fortune Has a Cousin in The Bronx (U.S. UMC
Pictures. 1970. 90 min.) Starring Gene Wilder, Margot Kidder, Eileen
Colgan and Seamus Ford. An Irish layabout strikes up an acquaintance
with an American student.

Ryan's Daughter (MGM/Faraway. 1970. 206 min.) Starring Sarah
Miles, Robert Mitchum, John Mills, Trevor Howard and Leo McKern. In
1916 Ireland, a rural schoolmaster's wife falls in love with a British
officer.

Barry Lyndon (1975/1976) Director: Stanley Kubrick. Starring Ryan
O'Neal, Marisa Berenson, Patrick Magee, Hardy Kruger. Thackeray's
novel brought to life in one of the most visually stunning movies ever
made. An Irish peasant rises from obscurity to wealth and position during
the period of the Seven Years War between England and France.

The Outsider (1978/1979.) Starring Sterling Hayden, Craig Wasson.
A young American Vietnam veteran joins the IRA.

Cal (1984. 140 min.) Starring John Lynch and Helen Mirren. A
Protestant policeman's widow and a Catholic youth fall in love amid the
violence of present-day Northern Ireland.

IRISH-AMERICAN LANDMARKS:
A SHORT DIRECTORY

To do justice to the subject of Irish-American landmarks could easily require a book in itself. Right now, in fact, a book is being written solely about New York City's Irish-American landmarks.

We attempt here to cover a number of the more important, though "more important" is always, naturally, a matter of judgment. Collectively, the landmarks described below illustrate some essential aspects of the Irish-American experience, including immigration; building the nation; military service and sacrifice; political life; the Irish-American religious heritage; and achieving the American Dream.

California

MILL VALLEY: The Reed Sawmill Restoration. This Marin County landmark, across the Golden Gate from San Francisco, played a key role in the birth of the "Empire City of the Pacific." Built in the 1840s by John Reed, a Dublin native and first non-Spanish settler of the Marin area, the sawmill was working when the so-called 'Forty-Niners descended on California after James Marshall discovered gold at Sutter's Mill. Tens of thousands – a large percentage of Irish birth or parentage – arrived at San Francisco and, almost overnight, erected a city of tents and shacks. It was Reed's mill that supplied the lumber to build the first permanent structures. Meanwhile, another Dubliner, Jasper O'Farrell, had planned and laid out the city that has long been called one of the most beautiful on the continent. He named his vast estate outside San Francisco, Annaly, after a territory once ruled by the O'Farrells in County Longford. Reed's sawmill has been preserved as a landmark, and is open to the public. O'Farrell is commemorated in the name of one of San Francisco's major streets.

SAN FRANCISCO: Robert Emmet Statue, Golden Gate Park.
Erected to commemorate the great Irish patriot who was executed in 1803 for leading an uprising, the statue has long been a popular site for Irish-American speeches and events. Each year Emmet's eloquent and prophetic "Speech from the Dock" is read here as a memorial.

SAN FRANCISCO: St. Patrick's Church, 756 Mission Street.
This has been called "the most Irish church on the continent." The present structure, built of brick with a slender tower and steeple, is the fourth

erected by the parish since it was established in 1851 by Father Maginnis, then the only English-speaking priest in San Francisco. The church interior is faced with translucent green Connemara marble, brought from Ireland, and Caen stone. The crucifix and vestments were inspired by Irish designs of the sixth and eighth centuries. A series of stained-glass windows tells the stories of various Irish saints, each a patron of or closely associated with one of the 32 counties.

SAN FRANCISCO: The Former James Flood Mansion, corner of California and Mason Streets, Nob Hill. Nob Hill looks down, figuratively and literally, on most of San Francisco. It was here that much of the city's elite chose to build imposing mansions in the late 1800s. Irish-Americans formed a disproportionate share of these self-made men. While their experience was scarcely typical of their fellow immigrants from Ireland, scores of shrewd, able and lucky men with names like O'Brien, Fair, Brown and Downey found in the West a chance to build fortunes in mining, building and contracting, transportation and other fields. James C. Flood was one of the "Irish-American Big Four" – four immigrants who bought out Henry Comstock's interest in a Nevada silver strike for $11,000 before he realized that the "Comstock Lode" held hundreds of millions in silver and gold. Flood spent $1.5 million in the 1860s to build a massive mansion atop Nob Hill. The brass railing in front of the house ran for two blocks and reportedly required a full-time worker to keep it polished and bright. Flood's was the only house on the hill to survive the San Francisco Fire of 1906. You can still see it today – if you settle for an outside view. It is now occupied by the exclusive Pacific Union Club.

District of Columbia

WASHINGTON: Georgetown University, Georgetown. This world-famous Jesuit institution, founded in 1789 by soon-to-be-Bishop John Carroll and other leading Irish-American Catholics, was the country's first Catholic institution of higher learning. (Note: Other well-known institutions with Irish-Catholic roots include Boston and Holy Cross colleges, Boston, MA; Seton Hall University, South Orange, NJ; Fordham University and Iona College, The Bronx, NY; and Villanova University, Villanova, PA. Despite the fact that its teams are called "the Fighting Irish," however, Notre Dame University, at South Bend, IN, owes its founding as much to Franco-Americans as to Irish-Americans. Princeton University, Princeton, NJ, grew largely out of efforts by Irish-Americans of Ulster Presbyterian origins, who helped found it in 1746 to serve the Middle colonies and also to counter the theological liberalism of Harvard and Yale.)

Illinois

CHICAGO: Old St. Patrick's Church, 718 West Adams. If you believe in miracles, there may be one in the fact that this church still stands. During the Great Fire of 1871, most of the city center – and its churches – were destroyed. The flames devastated everything around St. Patrick's as well, even the adjoining buildings, but stopped abruptly at the church steps. Dedicated on Christmas Day, 1856, and built in the Romanesque style, St. Patrick's is Chicago's oldest standing church – and perhaps its oldest public building. Two towers, one Gothic, the other Byzantine, were added later to symbolize the meeting of East and West in the ethnically mixed area surrounding the church. St. Patrick's is especially known for its stained-glass windows. Designed by Chicago artist Thomas O'Shaughnessy in 1911, the nave windows depict the major saints of Ireland, including Patrick, Brigid, Finbarr, Colman, Brendan, Columbanus, and Columkille (Columba). Most celebrated, however, is O'Shaughnessy's McSwiney Memorial Window, honoring the revolutionary Lord Mayor of Cork who died after a hunger strike in 1920. It is a triptych representing Faith, Hope and Charity and containing 150,000 separate pieces of glass in a seemingly unlimited palette of pastels. Throughout the church, decorative touches taken from the *Book of Kells* and ancient Celtic design motifs abound.

Maryland

BALTIMORE: Babe Ruth Birthplace Shrine and Museum, 216 Emory Street. Herman "Babe" Ruth, dubbed the "Sultan of Swat" for his legendary skill with a baseball bat, is one of scores of Irish-American sports figures whose names have become household words over the past century or so. But no sports figure – of any heritage – has ever been so widely recognized or admired as the legendary New York Yankee outfielder. The Museum, which is open Wednesday through Sunday, 10:30-5:00, houses an assortment of Ruth memorabilia.

BALTIMORE: Basilica of the Assumption, Cathedral and Mulberry Streets. Designed by Benjamin Latrobe, this was the first Catholic cathedral built in the United States. In 1806, the year the cornerstone was laid by John Carroll, more than half the nation's Catholics lived in Maryland. Carroll, the nation's first Catholic bishop (and archbishop) and a member of one of the oldest and most distinguished Irish-American families, did not live to see the project completed. The War of 1812 and other problems delayed construction, and it was 1821 before the Classical Revival-style structure was opened to worshippers. Because of its seniority among U.S. cathedrals, the Basilica is sometimes called "the Holy See of the United States." Pope Pius XI designated it a minor basilica in 1936, recognizing its special historical importance. The basilica is laid out in a cruciform pattern with a vaulted, domed interior. Among the prelates buried in the crypt beneath the altar are Archbishop John Carroll and James Cardinal Gibbons. The basilica is open to visitors between 6:30 AM and 3:30 PM daily.

WARWICK: St. Francis Xavier/Old Bohemia Mission.
Established in 1704, this church on Maryland's Eastern Shore was one of the earliest permanent Catholic foundations in the colonies. Jesuits also operated an academy here starting in 1745. Among its pupils were both John Carroll, the nation's first bishop, and his cousin, Charles Carroll of Carrollton, a Signer of the Declaration of Independence. Although the school was illegal, and closed after a few years, the gracious Georgian-style building that housed it still stands at the site. The former rectory now contains a museum, and in the adjoining cemetery can be seen the gravestones of many early parishioners. Mass is celebrated at the church at 4 PM on the third Sunday of April, May, September and October. The rectory and museum are open, 12:00 to 3:00 PM, on Sundays during the summer.

Massachusetts

BOSTON: St. Stephen's Church, 401 Hanover Street. Located in what is now the largely Italian North End, St. Stephen's was originally built for a Protestant congregation and known as New North Church. It was designed in 1804 by Charles Bulfinch, the great Boston architect. (Five years earlier Bulfinch had donated the design for Boston's first Catholic church, the original Church of the Holy Cross, on a site nearby.) In 1862 New North Church was sold to St. Stephen's parish and soon became the parish church for many of Boston's leading Irish families. The Fitzgeralds – who gave the city a mayor and, through marriage with the Kennedys, three U.S. senators and a president – worshipped here. And here they baptized the infant Rose Fitzgerald (Kennedy). Of several Boston churches designed by Bulfinch, only St. Stephen's still stands. The rest have gone the way of the original Church of the Holy Cross – a close architectural cousin of St. Stephen's – which was demolished in 1875 when its parish moved into the present Cathedral of the Holy Cross. In 1965, then-Cardinal Cushing had St. Stephen's restored to its original condition. In the course of the project, workers uncovered copper nails and sheathing that had been fabricated over 160 years earlier in Paul Revere's forge. Revere also cast the church's large tower bell.

BOSTON: John Boyle O'Reilly Memorial, The Fenway.

Boston abounds with mementos of this 19th-century Irish-born journalist and poet, who became owner and editor of *The Boston Pilot* in 1876. He not only made the *Pilot* the most influential and respected Irish-American journal of its day but won many admirers through his public speaking, his poetry and his outspoken championship of oppressed groups, including blacks and Jews as well as his fellow Irish and Irish-Americans. In addition to the Fenway memorial, Boston has a John Boyle O'Reilly Plaza; and Brookline's Holy Rood Cemetery contains his funeral monument. O'Reilly's home, now a private residence, still stands in Charlestown, and his summer home, at Hull, is now the public library.

BROOKLINE: Kennedy National Historic Site, 83 Beals

Street. Birthplace of the 35th U.S. President, the first Irish-American Catholic to attain that office. Joseph and Rose Kennedy lived here from 1915 until 1921, when the needs of their growing family forced them to move to a larger house nearby. JFK's birthplace is furnished as it was during those years and also contains a collection of Kennedy family memorabilia. Maps are available showing other local sites associated with the family. Open daily, 10 AM to 4:30 PM. (President Kennedy is buried, of course, in Arlington National Cemetery, Arlington, VA. Most of his official papers as well as exhibits relating to his life and career are housed in the Kennedy Memorial Library, University of Massachusetts Campus, Boston, MA.)

COHASSET: The *St. John* Memorial, Cohasset Central

Cemetery. In 1849, the *St. John*, a two-masted ship bringing Famine immigrants from Galway and County Clare, foundered in a storm on the Grampuses, some hidden rocks about a mile off the port town of Cohasset. Only 20-odd souls survived and, of the 99 who drowned, 45 were never identified. Henry David Thoreau visited Cohasset several days after the wreck and wrote movingly of what he saw in the first chapter of his book, *Cape Cod*. In 1914, the Ladies Ancient Order of Hibernians erected a 20-foot Celtic cross to the memory of the nameless victims of the *St. John* disaster. The cemetery is private; you may need permission to enter.

Michigan

**DEARBORN: Henry Ford Birthplace, Greenfield Village,
20900 Oakwood Boulevard.** Ford, the son of Famine immigrants
from County Cork, pioneered standardization and mass-production
techniques in the infant U.S. automobile industry, enabling the average
American to afford a car for the first time. Relocated here by Ford, who
brought together at Greenfield Village homes and buildings linked with
many famous Americans, the Ford Birthplace is open seven days a week.

New York

GREENE COUNTY: Cairo and East Durham. Set amid the
northern Catskill Mountains of New York State, these Greene County
resort communities have been a summer and holiday retreat for Irish-
Americans for half a century. Hotels and guest houses bearing names
from every corner of Ireland stand along the wooded roads, and at least
three Irish festivals are held in the area each summer. The local chamber of
commerce bills Greene County as "Ireland's 33rd county."

NEW YORK: The New York Port of Entry. The experience of
millions of immigrants from Ireland and elsewhere can be relived, to some
degree, by visiting the former immigration facilities and associated
museums in Lower Manhattan and New York Harbor: (a) South Street
Seaport, South Street, New York, which provides an idealized picture of
the scene awaiting Irish immigrants who landed from the Liverpool packets
that docked along South Street until 1856; (b) Castle Clinton National
Monument, Battery Park, where immigrants were processed between 1855
and 1889; (c) Ellis Island National Monument (formerly the United States
Immigration Station), where most immigrants were processed between the
early 1890s and 1954. (Immigrants from Ireland formed the second-
largest group to come through the station; in fact, a 15-year-old colleen
from County Cork was the first person officially processed after Ellis
Island opened on January 2, 1894.) Ellis Island is open in season and can
be reached via the Liberty Island Ferry from Battery Park; (d) the museums
of immigration on Liberty and Ellis islands, which are being greatly
expanded; and (e) The American Museum of Immigration, 15 Pine Street,
New York.

**NEW YORK: Old St. Patrick's Cathedral, Corner of Mott and
Prince Streets.** New York's second-oldest Catholic church, Old St.
Patrick's was begun in 1809 – a year after the Diocese of New York was

established – and completed in 1815. Its architect was Joseph Mangin, who co-designed New York's City Hall during the same period. Although little survives of the original church after an 1868 fire, experts consider St. Patrick's the second-oldest example of Gothic Revival architecture in the United States. Old St. Patrick's became a cathedral in 1850 and remained the seat of the Archdiocese of New York until 1879, when the more familiar structure uptown was dedicated. It was here, in 1875, that John McCloskey was installed as the first American cardinal. An adjoining cemetery contains the graves of many well-known parishioners. Others are buried in catacombs below the church.

NEW YORK: St. Patrick's Cathedral, Fifth Avenue at 50th Street. Built over a 21-year period, 1858 to 1879, "St. Pat's" was begun by the Right Reverend John Joseph Hughes, New York's first Catholic archbishop, and dedicated by John Cardinal McCloskey, America's first cardinal. A truly magnificent symbol of the country's wealthiest archdiocese, the cathedral was largely modelled after the Cathedral of Cologne, West Germany. The cathedral interior is 306 feet long and 108 feet high; its twin spires soar 330 feet above the street. From its very name, to its central role in New York's annual St. Patrick's Day Parade, to the heritage of its resident archbishops and much of its congregation, St. Patrick's has always been closely associated with New York's Irish community.

NEW YORK: St. James Church, 23 Oliver Street. St. James Parish was first organized in the mid-1820s by Fr. Felix Varela, a refugee Cuban priest, who arranged to purchase nearby Christ Church from its Episcopalian congregation. When fire destroyed this structure several years later, the parish bought a new site adjacent to James Street, and renamed itself in honor of St. James. The present building was completed in 1836-1837 and with its colonnaded front reflects the Greek Revival style so popular during the early 1800s. From the beginning, the parish was largely Irish-born, drawing many members from Five Points, a crowded slum on the other side of Chatham Square where newly arrived immigrants often settled. In 1836, the same year it opened its new building, the parish also witnessed a landmark event in Irish-American history, the founding of the Ancient Order of Hibernians in America (AOH). During the late 1870s, Al Smith – later governor of New York and the first Catholic nominated for President by a major party – attended the parish elementary school.

ROME: Old Erie Canal State Park, State Routes 5 and 46.
Here, as at some other points between Albany and Buffalo, surviving

sections of the original Erie Canal can be seen. Built largely by immigrant Irish muscle working for Irish-born contractors, the historic waterway was completed in 1825. It helped open America's interior to large-scale settlement and trade for the first time. And this, in turn, helped make New York City the nation's leading port. New York Governor DeWitt Clinton, whose brainchild the canal was, had an Irish-born grandfather himself. From the early years of the 19th century and into the 20th, not only canals but countless other public works were, more often than not, the fruit of Irish-American efforts: railroads, such as the Baltimore & Ohio and the Union Pacific; bridges, including that engineering marvel of its day, the Brooklyn Bridge; and the subway systems of New York, Boston and other great cities, to give just some examples.

Pennsylvania

GETTYSBURG: Gettysburg National Military Park. Here in the summer of 1863 a Confederate army under General Robert E. Lee sought a dramatic breakthrough victory on Northern soil. Instead, in three days of savage fighting, Northern forces commanded by Irish-American George G. Meade turned back the attempt, helping hasten the South's final surrender at Appomattox. For both sides, however, Gettysburg was a costly battle, paid for in 7,000 lives and 45,000 wounded and missing. Irish-Americans fought courageously on both sides, but the largest and most famous unit in which they fought as a group was the Union's Irish Brigade, organized by Colonel Michael Corcoran, a County Sligo native. The brigade had already suffered heavy losses at Bull Run, Fredericksburg, Antietam and Chancellorsville as well as lesser-known clashes. But so many were killed or wounded at Gettysburg that it ceased to exist thereafter. The courage and sacrifice of those who served in the Brigade is commemorated at Gettysburg in a poignant monument: a mourning wolfhound at the base of a Celtic cross. Park rangers will direct you to the monument.

READING: Daniel Boone Homestead, north of Baumstown, seven miles east of Reading. A descendant, like Davy Crockett, of 18th century immigrants from Donegal via Derry, Daniel Boone became a symbol of the first large-scale Irish settlements in America. Most of those who formed the so-called Ulster migration were Protestants driven from Ireland by economic hardship. Once in America, many drifted to the western frontier, where land was abundant and government minimal. The early phase of America's push westward is in large measure a story of hardy pioneers of Irish and Scots-Irish stock. (NOTE: The latter term only emerged in the early 1800s, when many whose forebears had arrived earlier from Ireland found it useful to distinguish themselves from the impoverished Catholic masses whose arrival was triggering prejudice against anything Irish among many Americans.) Daniel Boone was born in this house in 1734, when Reading was on the edge of the frontier. He was given his first rifle at age 10, and had become an expert at living in the wilds by the time the Boones moved south to North Carolina in 1750. The stone homestead has been restored to reflect life in the early 19th century; there are also a blacksmith shop, a smokehouse and other buildings. Open daily, 9:30 AM to 4:30 PM, except Sunday, 1:00 to 4:30.

Rhode Island

PROVIDENCE: George M. Cohan Birthplace, 536 Wickenden Street. Famous for such patriotic songs as "Yankee Doodle Dandy" and "Grand Old Flag," George Michael Cohan (1878-1942) was a giant of the American musical theater. He was not only a composer and dramatist, but was widely praised for his acting and song-and-dance routines as well. During a theatrical career that spanned over half a century, he had a hand (or voice) in scores of popular productions. Cohan's success inspired many younger Irish-Americans to enter the world of entertainment.

Texas

HOUSTON: The Dick Dowling Memorial, Hermann Park. This memorial commemorates the courage and fighting skill of a handful of Irish-born Houstonians who fought and won the Battle of Sabine Pass, a dramatic Confederate Civil War victory. On September 8, 1863, 42 members of the Jeff Davis Guards manned six cannon behind a simple earthworks at Sabine Pass, where the Sabine and Neches rivers empty into the Gulf of Mexico near Port Arthur. Nearly all the men were County Galway natives, like their commander, 25-year-old Lt. Richard W. ("Dick") Dowling. Offshore, a Union expedition of 20 ships prepared to disembark an invasion force of 5,000 troops. When the three Union gunboats moved inshore to "soften up" the defenses, however, the Davis Guards turned the tables. With just three or four shots, they put the first Federal gunboat out of action and then quickly disabled the second. The surrender of the second gunboat ended the battle, which had lasted only 45 minutes. The remaining Union ships sailed back to New Orleans, giving the expedition's commander, General Franklin, the honor of being the first American general to lose a fleet to shore batteries alone.

Wyoming

CODY: Cody Birthplace/Buffalo Bill Historical Center, 720 Sheridan Avenue. Son of an Irish immigrant, "Buffalo Bill" Cody came to symbolize the exploits of Americans in taming the Western frontier. He excelled as a scout and a hunter, and later became a world-famous showman, entertaining hordes with his "Wild West" troupe. The Cody Birthplace contains a fascinating collection of memorabilia. Within blocks, you may also visit the Whitney Gallery of Western Art; the Plains Indian Museum; and Buffalo Bill Village & Western Exhibits, a recreated town of the early West. All facilities are open daily, 7 AM to 10 PM, June through August.

THE OLD 32: THE HISTORICAL COUNTIES OF IRELAND

If you're an American, you're not just an American, of course. You're also a Texan, a Californian, a Minnesotan, a Vermonter or whatever. And so, too, if your roots lie in Ireland – or almost anywhere else.

Nations are usually too large and abstract to monopolize our loyalties. So for those of Irish heritage, traditional family ties remain important, as often do links to the native towns or villages of parents or grandparents. But the Irish have a special place in their hearts for their home counties – one or more of the 32 traditional divisions that have existed on the island for centuries.

Traditional county ties remain strong among many Irish Americans. Wherever there are large numbers of Americans with Irish roots, there are likely to be one or more local county clubs or societies. In some larger U.S. cities, such as New York, Boston, Chicago and Los Angeles, virtually all of Ireland's 32 counties are represented by local organizations under an umbrella group called "The United Irish Counties Association" or a similar name.

Considering the importance of county associations, we have brought together here – for the first time, so far as we can tell – sketches of all 32 counties, grouped alphabetically under their respective provinces. PLEASE NOTE:

1. The lists of "Notable Natives" under each county have been compiled using a variety of secondary sources, but mainly from Henry Boylan, *The Dictionary of Irish Biography* (New York: Barnes & Noble, 1978) and Brian de Breffny, General Editor, *Ireland: A Cultural Encyclopedia* (New York: Facts on File, 1983). We found several cases where an individual was claimed by more than one county, and have tried conscientiously to resolve such conflicts where possible.

2. Similarly, listings of annual events and festivals in each county have been compiled from official information supplied by the Irish Tourist Board, and supplemented from other sources. In a few cases we found conflicting information on the timing or location of a given event. Although we have tried to list only events that are held in the same place and at approximately the same time each year, the dates and locations are always subject to change. In some cases, moreover, an event may be cancelled, especially if it has been running regular deficits for some time. So we strongly urge you to contact the Irish Tourist Board for up-to-date details before you make travel plans around an event listed here.

Ireland's 32 Counties

Reprinted by courtesy of the Geography Department, Trinity College, Dublin, Ireland.

3. National and County Newspapers – For readers who may wish to sub-
scribe to one or more Irish newspapers, we have listed the main newspapers serving each county as well as the Dublin and Belfast newspapers. The latter are widely read far beyond these cities. To obtain a
sample issue before subscribing, we suggest you contact one of the
sources listed in the *Green Pages* section of this book under "Newspapers & Magazines – Imported – News Dealers." If your sample issue
doesn't contain information for overseas subscribers, request a copy
of *Newspapers* (Information Sheet No. 4) from the Irish Tourist Board
and then write or phone the newspaper for details. Information on
newspapers from all 32 counties is included in *Benn's Press Directory*,
available in many libraries. Lastly, you may call one of the several
U.S. consular offices maintained by Ireland or the United Kingdom,
depending on where the paper you're interested in is published.

PROVINCE OF CONNACHT (CONNAUGHT)

GALWAY
County town: Galway
Area: 2,293 sq.mi.
Notable natives: Lady Augusta Gregory (1852-1932), writer, dramatist
and nationalist, who was a leader of the Irish Revival and the Irish
theatre movement; Padraic O'Conaire (1883-1928), a leading short-
story writer of the early 20th-century Irish literary revival; Father
Tom Burke (1830-1883), Irish civil rights champion; Liam
O'Flaherty (1896-), novelist whose works include *Thy Neighbor's
Wife*, the prize-winning *The Informer* (1925), which was made into
the classic film of the same name, and *Insurrection* (1950); Robert
O'Hara Burke (1820-1861), first white man to cross Australia from
south to north; Colonel Thomas Blood (1618-1680), adventurer who
succeeded in stealing the Crown Jewels from the Tower of London in
1671 and, after his capture, was pardoned by Charles II out of admiration for his daring; Patrick Ford (1837-1913), founder of the recently defunct Irish-American newspaper, *Irish World*, who in his day
was, according to Michael Davitt, "the most powerful support on the
American continent of the struggle in Ireland;" Edward Martyn (1859-
1924), dramatist and co-founder of the Irish Literary Theatre (now
the Abbey Theatre), which produced his best play, *The Heather
Field*, in 1899.

Places of Interest: Galway Town, a port that still retains a certain
Mediterranean flavor, a legacy of centuries of trading with Venice,
Spain and other countries since the Middle Ages; the Church of St.
Nicholas, Galway, where Columbus is said to have prayed during a
supposed stopover at Galway on his first voyage of discovery;
Galway City Museum; the Aran Islands, 30 miles offshore and home
to Gaelic-speaking fisherfolk and weavers; the Brown and Alcock
monument, which marks the landing site of the first transatlantic
flight in 1919, eight years before Lindbergh's 1927 solo; Connemara, a district that is home to Connemara ponies, Ireland's only
native horse breed, and to the Connemara Gaeltacht, one of Ireland's
largest Gaelic-speaking areas; Coole Park, Gort, where Lady Gregory once hosted such literary stars as Shaw, Synge, O'Casey and
Yeats in her grand house, now destroyed – and whose wooded glens
figure in many Yeats poems; Kilkieran, a pretty Gaelic-speaking
harbor village whose main industry is seaweed harvesting; the fishing
village of Claddagh, where the famous rings of this name were first
made; Connemara Marble Factory, Moycullen, where you can watch
craftsmen cutting, grinding and polishing marble quarried nearby.

Events: Clarinbridge Oyster Festival, Clarinbridge (September); Connemara Pony Show (August); Galway International Motor Rally
(February); Galway Races (July); Great October Fair, Ballinasloe,
said to be the world's oldest horse fair; the Claddagh Festival
(August); Galway Horse Show (June/July); Feis Ceoil an Iarthair
(autumn), a festival of traditional song, dance and storytelling; the
Galway Salmon Run (June-July), when you can see the noble fish
lining up to jump Galway Town's salmon weir on their way to
upstream spawning grounds.

Newspapers: *Connacht Sentinel* (weekly); *Connacht Tribune* (weekly);
Herald & Western Advertiser (weekly).

LEITRIM
County town: Carrick-on-Shannon
Area: 589 sq.mi.
Notable natives: Sean McDiarmada (1886-1916), leader of the 1916
Easter Rebellion; Wilhemina Geddes (1887-1955), stained-glass
designer, who created notable windows in England, Canada and
Belgium as well as Ireland; Susan Langstaff Mitchell (1866-1926),
writer remembered for her religious poetry (*The Living Chalice and
Other Poems*) and her verses satirizing notable Irish literary and

public figures, many of whom she entertained as one of Dublin's leading hostesses; Thomas H. Parke (1857-1893), surgeon who accompanied Henry M. Stanley on his Congo basin explorations and was credited with keeping the expedition from disaster.

Places of interest: Carrick-on-Shannon, a center for river cruising and coarse fishing; O'Rourke's Table, a rock plateau that offers memorable views of Lough Gill and its islands, including Innisfree, which W.B. Yeats immortalized in verse; Prince Connell's Grave, the name given locally to a splendid prehistoric gallery grave dating from between 2000 and 1500 B.C.; Sheebeg, a hill overlooking the village of Keshcarrigan that is topped by a prehistoric mound reputed to contain the grave of the legendary hero, Finn McCool.

Events: Wild Rose Festival (August); Festival of the Shannon (July)

Newspapers: *Leitrim Observer* (weekly)

Miscellaneous: By the way, it's pronounced LEE-trim.

MAYO
County town: Castlebar
Area: 2,084 sq.mi.
Notable natives: Michael Davitt (1846-1906), founder of the Irish Land League; George Moore (1853-1933), playwright, short-story writer and novelist (*The Brook Kerith, Heloise and Abelard*) associated with Yeats, Lady Gregory, etc. in the Irish literary revival and founding of the Abbey Theatre; William O'Dwyer (1890-1964), Mayor of New York, 1946-1950, and U.S. Ambassador to Mexico, 1950-1952; Admiral William Brown (1777-1857), who emigrated to South America, where he founded the Argentine navy; Paul O'Dwyer (1907-), New York lawyer and politician.

Places of interest: Knock, whose Shrine of Our Lady of Knock rivals Lourdes and Fatima as a pilgrimage site: the village's new basilica, designed to seat 20,000, is Ireland's largest church – and the community recently got its own international airport as well!; Croagh Patrick, on whose peak St. Patrick is said to have fasted for 40 days, and where he supposedly banished the snakes from Ireland; Cong, the town where *The Quiet Man* was filmed; Westport, Mayo's most attractive town, which was laid out in the 18th century and was once a center for linen making; Westport House, Westport, a classical gem filled with collections of portraits, silver and Waterford glass; the Nephin Beg mountains, Ireland's most desolate and least-inhabited area; Ballintober Abbey (13th century), the only royal abbey in Ireland or Britain still operating after 750 years; Achill, Ireland's largest island, which is worth visiting to take in 2,200-foot Slievemore mountain and awesome oceanside drives above seas that thrash the rocks far below.

Events: Croagh Patrick Pilgrimage (last Sunday in July); International Sea Angling Festival, Westport (June); Castlebar International Song Contest (October); Westport Horse Show (June); Claremorris Ham Fair & Festival (July); Ballina Salmon Festival (July); Rock Music Festival, Castlebar (July); Ballina Agricultural & Industrial Show (August).

Newspapers: *Connacht Telegraph* (weekly); *Western Journal* (weekly); *Western People* (weekly); *Mayo News* (weekly); *Mayo Post* (weekly).

ROSCOMMON
County town: Roscommon
Area: 951 sq.mi.
Notable natives: Father Edward J. Flanagan (1886-1948), founder of Boys Town, U.S.A., Omaha, NB; Douglas Hyde (1860-1949), poet, scholar, playwright, translator, first president of the Gaelic League and first President of Ireland, 1937-1945; John G. Downey (1826-1894), Civil War governor of California and first Los Angeles land developer; Arthur Murphy (1727-1805), actor, journalist and lawyer, best known for the plays he wrote, including comedies and farces such as *Three Weeks After Marriage* and *The Way to Keep Him* as well as tragedies such as *Zenobia* and *The Orphan of China*; Padraig O Caoimh (1897-1964), General Secretary of the Gaelic Athletic Association, 1929-1964, a period during which the GAA became Ireland's largest and most powerful sporting organization; John E. Lawe (1923-), International Transport Workers Union president, 1985-present.

Places of interest: Strokestown Craft Centre; Horse Market, Athleague; Clonalis House, Castlerea, a Victorian mansion where state documents, original Irish manuscripts and priceless books are exhibited.

Events: O'Carolan Harp and Traditional Music Festival, Keadue (early August); Boyle Gala Coarse Fishing Festival, Boyle (May).

Newspapers: *Roscommon Champion* (weekly); *Roscommon Herald* (weekly)

SLIGO

County town: Sligo
Area: 694 sq.mi.
Notable natives: Michael Corcoran (1827-1863), who commanded the "Fighting 69th" New York Militia at the start of the Civil War and later recruited the Irish Brigade; Patrick Collins (1910-), self-taught painter of landscapes and figures, whose works are represented in all of Ireland's major collections; Thomas Rice Henn (1901-1974), Yeatsian scholar who organized and subsequently directed the Yeats International Summer School held annually in Sligo Town; William Higgins (1763?-1825), chemist who is said to have first formulated the atomic theory, which refuted the centuries-old Phlogiston theory explaining chemical phenomena.

Places of interest: The Yeats Memorial Museum; Yeats' grave, Drumcliff churchyard, and many other places associated with W.B. Yeats and his poetry; the County Museum, Sligo, with its Municipal Art Gallery, which has an excellent collection of modern Irish art; the impressive ruins of Sligo Abbey, a 13th-century Dominican friary; flat-topped Ben Bulben, the famous 1,730-foot-high mountain that looms above Yeats' grave at Drumcliff, and on whose summit you will find unusual arctic and alpine plants; Strandhill, a seaside resort whose beaches attract large numbers of surfers; Knockarea, a 1,078-foot hill on whose summit stands a stone cairn reputed to be the burial place of Maeve of Connacht, an ancient Irish warrior-queen; Lough Gill, which can be toured using shoreside roads, or on a three-hour boat cruise that leaves from Doorly Park, Sligo Town; Lissadell House, once home to the Gore-Booth family, with its noted sisters: Eva, the poetess, and Constance – later Countess Markievicz – who played a leading role in the 1916 rising and later in Irish politics.

Events: Yeats International Summer School, Sligo (August); Enniscrone International Sea Angling Festival (August); Sligo Fleadh Cheoil, a traditional music festival and fiddlers competition (June); Folk Festival, Ballisdare (August); Michael Coleman Commemoration, Riverside, honoring a legendary Sligo-born traditional fiddler

(September); Sligo Feisanna, Sligo (March/April); Sligo Midsummer Festival (June); Sligo Triathlon Competition (June).

Newspapers: *Sligo Champion* (weekly)

PROVINCE OF LEINSTER

CARLOW
County town: Carlow
Area: 346 sq.mi.
Notable natives: Pierce Butler (1744-1822), signer of the U.S. Constitution and U.S. Senator from South Carolina; Peter F. Collier (1846-1909), American publisher who founded *Collier's* magazine (3.2 million circulation at its peak) and pioneered subscription publishing with *The Harvard Classics* and other series; Patrick F. Moran (1830-1911), Archbishop of Sydney and first Australian cardinal, who championed Australian federation and Irish home rule; William Dargan (1799-1867), who built 600 miles of Irish railway – including Ireland's first line, from Dublin to Port Laoghaire – as well as the Ulster Canal; Myles Keogh (1840-1876), who fought with Papal forces against Garibaldi's army, then emigrated to the U.S., where he rose to lieutenant colonel in the Union Army, later commanding a troop of the 7th Cavalry at the Battle of the Little Big Horn, where he died; Kevin Barry (1902-1920), medical student who was captured while taking part in an IRA arms raid, and whose subsequent execution at age 18 became a *cause celebre* that attracted scores of fellow students to the outlawed group and inspired a popular ballad.

Places of interest: County Museum, Carlow; Browne's Hill, near Carlow town, the site of a prehistoric dolmen, or stone structure, which experts claim is up to 5,000 years old and has Ireland's, and perhaps Europe's, largest capstone: 5 feet thick, 20 feet square and 100 tons in weight.

Newspapers: *Nationalist & Leinster Times* (weekly)

Miscellaneous: One of Ireland's smallest counties, Carlow sent relatively few emigrants to the United States.

DUBLIN
County borough: Dublin
Area: 356 sq.mi.
Notable natives: As the seat of Ireland's metropolis and cultural center, County Dublin has long produced a disproportionately large number of people who have gone on to play leading roles in Ireland, the United States, Britain and other countries: Maureen O'Hara (1921-), Irish-American film actress; Victor Herbert (1859-1924), Irish-American composer of such beloved operettas as *Babes in Toyland* and *Naughty Marietta*; John Dowland (1562-1626), composer and lutenist, the foremost lute player of his day, whose songs were tremendously popular then and are still performed; Augustus Saint-Gaudens (1848-1907), world-famous American sculptor, born of a French father and an Irish mother; Eamonn Kevin Roche (1922-), prolific, distinguished Irish-American architect; Catherine McAuley (1778-1841), foundress of the Order of Mercy, largest religious congregation in the English-speaking world; Edmund Burke (1729-1797), British statesman and political writer, widely considered the father of modern political conservatism; Robert Emmet (1778-1803), eloquent patriot executed for his role in the abortive 1803 rising; Henry Grattan (1746-1820), statesman, orator and premature champion of Catholic emancipation; Theobald Wolfe Tone (1763-1798), revolutionary nationalist who founded the United Irishmen and was executed for his role in aiding the French expedition landed in 1798 to foment an anti-British rising; Patrick Pearse (1879-1916), poet, president of the 1916 Provisional Government and martyr of the Easter Rising; Arthur Griffith (1872-1922), founder of the *United Irishman* and of Sinn Fein and later president of the Dail; Cornelius Ryan (1920-1974), Irish-American war correspondent who went on to write such best-selling World War II chronicles as *The Longest Day, The Last Battle* and *A Bridge Too Far;* Richard Montgomery (1736-1775), American revolutionary general; the Anglo-Irish cleric and satirist, Jonathan Swift (1667-1745), author of *Gulliver's Travels*; Brendan Behan (1923-1964), the noted dramatist and writer; Bram Stoker (1847-1912), author of the chilling Gothic masterpiece, *Dracula*; James Joyce (1882-1941), author of *The Dubliners, Portrait of the Artist as a Young Man* and the monumental *Ulysses*; playwrights Samuel Beckett (1906-), Sean O'Casey (1880-1964), and Richard Brinsley Sheridan (1751-1816); Irish-American playwright Dion Boucicault (1820-1890), whose works include *The Colleen Bawn* and *The Shaughraun*; George Bernard Shaw (1856-1950), whose brilliant plays typically dealt with such themes as war (*Arms and the Man*), religion (*St. Joan*), prostitution (*Mrs. Warren's*

Profession) and economics; Oscar Wilde (1854-1900), known as much for his general wit as for such plays as *The Importance of Being Earnest* and *Lady Windermere's Fan,* and for a novel, *The Picture of Dorian Gray*; poet and playwright William Butler Yeats (1865-1939) whose genius and love of Ireland are legendary; and dramatist John Millington Synge (1871-1909), whose *Riders to the Sea* and *Shadow of the Glen* are marked by masterly use of the language of Irish fishermen and country folk.

Places of interest: Trinity College, Dublin (TCD), with its Library, which houses the *Book of Kells* and other Irish cultural treasures; Kilmainham Jail Museum; The Royal Hospital (1680s), Kilmainham, which is widely considered the most important 17th century building in Ireland and is certainly its first full-scale example of neoclassical architecture; the National Museum of Ireland, which has opened a new exhibit hall next to its main building devoted to early medieval Dublin and featuring recently unearthed Viking artifacts; Phoenix Park, one of Europe's largest and most beautiful urban green spaces; The Abbey Theatre, most prestigious and important of Dublin theatres; Dublin Castle, dating from the early 1200s, which was once the residence of English viceroys in Ireland as well as housing a prison for important prisoners; Christ Church Cathedral; St. Patrick's Cathedral; The Custom House (1791), Dublin's finest public building – in fact, one of Europe's finest; The Martello Tower, Sandycove, James Joyce's workplace-retreat; Dun Laoghaire, the port of Dublin and Ireland's main port-of-entry, with vessels sailing regularly to and from Britain; Guinness' Brewery, a 60-acre complex just south of the River Liffey, whose water is wondrously transformed here – and where you can also visit the Guinness Museum; Malahide Castle (14th century), which houses much of the National Portrait Collection; Hugh Lane Municipal Gallery of Art; the Chester Beatty Gallery of Oriental Art; National Botanical Gardens, Glasnevin, where 20,000 plant varieties grow under glass and outdoors; Howth Castle, renowned for its rhododendron gardens, which contain more than 2,000 varieties of the flowering shrub.

Events: Dublin Arts Festival (March); Dublin Horse Show, perhaps the year's premier social and sporting occasion (August); All-Ireland Hurling Final (September); All-Ireland Football Final (September); Major horse-racing events (May through September); Dublin Festival of 20th Century Music (June); An Fleadh Nua: Traditional Music and Dancing (June); Dublin Spring Show and Industries Fair (May); Irish International Boat Show and Fisheries Exhibitions (February);

Dublin Theatre Festival (October); Holiday and Leisure Fair (February); Antique Dealers Fair (August); Spring Season of International Grand Opera (April); Dublin Indoor International Horse Show (November); Polo Games, All-Ireland Polo Club, Phoenix Park (three times weekly, May through mid-September).

Newspapers: *Evening Herald* (daily); *Evening Press* (daily); *Irish Independent* (daily); *The Irish Press* (daily); *The Irish Times* (daily); *The Sunday Independent* (Sunday); *The Sunday World* (Sunday); *The Sunday Press* (Sunday); *Catholic Standard* (weekly); *Inniu/Today* (weekly); *Irish Oifigiuil/Dublin Gazette* (twice weekly); *Bray People* (weekly).

KILDARE
County town: Naas
Area: 654 sq.mi.
Notable natives: Arthur Guinness (1725-1803), founder of the Guinness Brewery; Sir Thomas Dongan (1634-1715), first Roman Catholic governor of (colonial) New York, 1682-1688, during the reigns of Charles II and James II, and later Earl of Limerick; Sir Ernest Shackleton (1874-1922), Antarctic explorer who nearly reached the South Pole in 1907; St. Laurence O'Toole (1132-1180), Archbishop of Dublin, who led resistance to the Anglo-Norman invasion; Richard Power (1928-1970), novelist in English and Gaelic (*Land of Youth, The Hungry Grass*); John Devoy (1842-1928), Fenian organizer exiled for his activities in Ireland, who settled in the U.S. where he became the preeminent leader of Clan na Gael and raised considerable sums for the cause of Irish independence.

Places of interest: The National Stud Farm and Irish Horse Museum, Tully; Castletown House, Celbridge, one of Europe's finest Georgian houses and headquarters of the Irish Georgian Society (demonstrations of 18th-century dancing are held on Sundays); Curragh Racecourse, center of Irish horse-racing and home of such famed flat races as the Irish Sweeps Derby, the Irish St. Leger and the Irish Oaks; St. Patrick's College, Maynooth, Ireland's premier Roman Catholic seminary, established during the 1790s (the College also houses the Ecclesiastical Museum); Naas and Punchestown, sites of popular racecourses; Cathedral of St. Brigid, Kildare, which has been much rebuilt but still has medieval remains; the Canal and Transport Museum, Robertstown; Irish Pewter Ltd., Timolin-

Moone, where you can watch pewter being made and buy pewter items at the mill's shop.

Events: Robertstown Grand Canal Fiesta (August); Freshwater Angling Gala Week, Prosperous (May); Festival of Great Irish Houses, Castletown House, Celbridge (June).

Newspapers: *Leinster Leader* (weekly)

KILKENNY
County town: Kilkenny
Area: 796 sq.mi.
Notable natives: James Hoban (1758-1831), architect of The White House, Washington, DC; Edmund Ignatius Rice (1762-1844), founder of the Irish Christian Brothers, a teaching order active in many countries; Michael Cudahy (1841-1910), founder of Cudahy Packing Company, whose innovations revolutionized the U.S. meatpacking industry; George Berkeley (1685-1753), Anglican bishop and religious philosopher, whose ideas have had a major impact on subsequent European philosophers; Mildred Anne Butler (1858-1941), painter known for her watercolors, which were unappreciated for years because they remained in the family's home; Thomas Kilroy (1934-), dramatist whose plays include *Death and Resurrection of Mr. Roche, The O'Neill* and *Tea, Sex and Shakespeare*; John O'Donovan (1809-1861), scholar of Irish antiquity, whose greatest achievements were his translations of *The Annals of the Kingdom of Ireland by the Four Masters* and *The Martyrology of Donegal*, and his role in founding the Irish Archaelogical Society; James Archer (1550?-1617/1624), Jesuit educator and missionary, who served as first rector of the Irish College at Salamanca, Spain, and also worked as an "underground" missioner in Ireland, narrowly escaping capture by Crown forces on many occasions; Henry Flood (1732-1791), statesman and orator, who led the nationalist opposition in the Irish House of Commons and was judged the finest speaker of his day; John Locke (1847-1889), Irish-American writer of poems and short stories, including "Morning on the Irish Coast," which expresses an exile's feelings on returning to Ireland.

Places of interest: Dunmore Cave, an enormous underground wonder; Edmund Rice Birthplace, Westcourt, Callan; Rothe House Museum, Kilkenny, an Elizabethan town house with a museum displaying archaeological relics from the area; Simon Pearce Glass, Bennettsbridge, where you can watch demonstrations of the ancient craft of glassblowing; Kilkenny Castle, a Butler family stronghold from Anglo-Norman times until 1935, which retains three of its four towers and houses a nicely restored art gallery in one wing; Jerpoint Abbey, built as a Cistercian house in the 13th century, which includes a church and a partly restored cloister with impressive, larger-than-life statues of medieval knights and church leaders.

Events: Kilkenny Beer Festival (May); Kilkenny Arts Week (late August/early September); Kilkenny Roots Weekend (April).

Newspapers: *Kilkenny People* (twice weekly)

LAOIS (LEIX)
County town: Portlaoise
Area: 664 sq.mi.
Notable natives: Richard Milhous (18th century?), great-great-grandfather of President Richard Milhous Nixon; Thomas Prior (1682-1751), founder of the Royal Dublin Society (now the RDS), which works to promote agriculture, manufacturing, the arts and sciences; James Fintan Lalor (1807-1849), United Irishmen activist who worked to promote land reform and tenant rights; Frank Power (1858-1884), war correspondent who, as acting British consul, welcomed General Gordon to Khartoum and then filed regular dispatches to *The Times* during the Seige of Khartoum before he was killed trying to escape down the Nile; William Robinson (1838-1935), who began his career as a garden boy at Ballykilcavan and went on to become one of the most influential gardeners and horticultural writers of his time, leading the revolt against Victorian ideas in favor of simpler garden design; William Shoney O'Brien (1825?-1878), one of the so-called Irish-American Big Four or Bonanza Princes who became multimillionaires after paying $10,000 in 1859 for rights to the Comstock Lode, the now-famous silver strike in Nevada that ultimately produced over $500 million in silver.

Places of interest: Portarlington Power Station, Ireland's first turf-fired electrical generating plant; the Slieve Bloom mountains, a scenic range punctuated with green glens, helping enliven the county's generally plain topography; Abbeyleix, a planned village built in the 18th century, with modest but charming Georgian houses and impressive Abbeyleix Gardens; the Irish Steam Museum, Stradbally, with a diverse collection of steam-powered vehicles and machines; the Round Tower, Timahoe, a 12th-century specimen with an unusual and ornate double doorway.

Events: Stradbally Steam Rally (August); Vintage Car Rally, Portlaoise (July); Portarlington French Festival (July).

Newspapers: *Leinster Express* (weekly)

Miscellaneous: The name is usually pronounced LEASH or, less often, LEEKS. Until independence, it was called Queens County, originally in honor of the English queen, Mary Tudor, who tried to restore Catholicism in England after her father, Henry VIII, died.

LONGFORD
County town: Longford
Area: 403 sq.mi.
Notable natives: Poet and playwright Padraic Colum (1881-1972), whose plays were among the first staged at Dublin's Abbey Theatre; Oliver Goldsmith (1728-1774), writer, poet and playwright, whose works include *The Vicar of Wakefield* and *She Stoops to Conquer*; General Sean McEoin (1893-1973), the "blacksmith of Ballinalee:" IRA commander, veteran politician and twice a candidate for president; James A. Farrell (1863-1943), Irish-American "Steel King," who headed United States Steel, the nation's largest steelmaking firm; John Keegan Casey (1846-1870), Fenian and patriotic poet who died in prison at age 24 and is best remembered for his rousing ballad, "The Rising of the Moon;" Frank McCoppin (1834-1897), mayor of San Francisco after the Civil War, the first Irish-born mayor of a major U.S. city.

Places of interest: Inchmore Island, in Lough Gowna, where remains of a sixth-century church stand on a monastic site founded by St. Columcille; Edgeworthstown, ancestral home of the Edgeworth family, whose talented members included Maria, author of *Castle Rackrent*, a satire on the evils of the 19th-century Irish landowning system, and her father, Richard, an inventor of note; Inchlauran, an island-bound monastery site in Lough Ree, with several old churches and many early Christian grave slabs.

Events: Granard Harp Festival and Summer Harp School (August); Irish Hot-Air Balloon Championships, Ballymahon (September).

Newspapers: *Longford Leader* (weekly); *Longford News* (weekly)

LOUTH
County town: Dundalk
Area: 317 sq.mi. (Ireland's smallest county)
Notable natives: St. Brigid of Kildare (453-523), one of Ireland's three patron saints, who was born at Faughart, according to tradition; internationally famed architect Michael Scott (1905-), whose designs include the Irish Pavilion for the New York World's Fair (1939) and the Abbey Theatre, Dublin (1965); Paul Callan (1799-1864), priest, inventor and scientist, known for his pioneering work in electrical science, including invention of the induction coil – which made the modern transformer possible – and his discoveries involving high-tension electricity; John E. Cairnes (1823-1875), economist whose book, *The Slave Power*, did much to sway British opinion toward sympathy for the North during the Civil War; Paul Vincent Carroll (1900-1968), award-winning playwright (*Shadow and Substance, The White Steed*, etc.), known for his unsurpassed depictions of clergymen and clerical life; John O'Boyle Reilly (1844-1890), Irish-American poet, journalist and patriot; William D'Arcy McGee (1825-1868), writer and nationalist who emigrated to Boston, became editor of *The Pilot*, then worked as London correspondent for *The Nation* before breaking with the Young Irelanders over their revolutionary methods and emigrating to Canada. There he entered Parliament, served in the government and played a leading role in promoting Canadian federation before he was assassinated for denouncing a threatened Fenian invasion of Canada from the U.S.

Places of interest: The Cooley Peninsula – "Cuchullain Country" – setting for many ancient Irish sagas; Monasterboice, site of a once-great monastic settlement, of which remains a round tower and 17-foot Muiredach's Cross, finest of Ireland's high crosses; ruins of Mellifont Abbey, first and greatest monastic foundation of the Cistercians, who became the most influential Continental order in Ireland; Transport Museum, Dunleer; Shrine of St. Brigid (built 1933), Faughart, housing a relic of Ireland's patroness-saint.

Events: Dundalk Maytime Festival and Amateur Theatre International (May); Omeath Gala Week (August).

Newspapers: *Drogheda Independent* (weekly); *The Argus* (weekly); *Dundalk Democrat* (weekly)

MEATH
County town: Navan
Area: 903 sq.mi.
Notable natives: Turlogh O'Carolan (1670-1738), blind composer and
   harpist, one of the last and perhaps the greatest of Irish bards; Arthur
   Wellesley (1769-1852), first Duke of Wellington, victor of Waterloo
   and British prime minister; St. Oliver Plunkett (1629-1684), Catholic
   Archbishop of Armagh, martyred on perjured charges for alleged
   complicity in the so-called Popish Plot; Sir William Johnson (born
   MacShane; 1715-1774), Superintendent of Indian Affairs on the New
   York frontier and British-American hero of the French and Indian
   War; Rear-Admiral Sir Francis Beaufort (1774-1857), Royal Navy
   officer and hydrography pioneer, who originated the Beaufort scale
   of wind velocities and a tabulated system for recording weather, both
   still used; James Connell (1850?-1929), writer, nationalist and self-
   taught lawyer, best known as author of "The Red Flag," the socialist
   anthem; Sir Edward Lovett Pearce (1699-1733), architect of the Irish
   Houses of Parliament (now Bank of Ireland), which are considered
   among Europe's finest public buildings; Ambrose O'Higgins (1720?-
   1801), viceroy of Peru under Spanish rule and father of Bernardo
   O'Higgins, the "Liberator of Chile;" Thomas Hussey (1741-1803),
   first president of Maynooth College, Ireland's premier seminary;
   Trevor G. McVeagh (1908-1968), lawyer and sportsman
   extraordinary, who represented Ireland over 70 times in four different
   sports, gained international caps for tennis, hockey, squash rackets
   and cricket in 1938 and captained Ireland's hockey team to three
   straight Triple Crown wins.

Places of interest: Trim Castle, largest Anglo-Norman castle in Ireland;
   the Hill of Tara, containing ruins of the former religious and cultural
   capital of pre-Norman Ireland and seat of Ireland's High Kings;
   Newgrange, an important pre-Celtic burial site; the Hill of Slane,
   where St. Patrick is said to have first lit the Paschal Fire in 433 A.D.,
   in defiance of the pagan Druids.

Events: Moynalty Steam Threshing Festival, Moynalty (August)

Newspapers: *Meath Chronicle* (weekly)

Miscellaneous: The county is sometimes called "Royal Meath" because
   of the heritage of Tara and Ireland's High Kings.

OFFALY
County town: Tullamore
Area: 771 sq.mi.
Notable natives: Edward Hand (1744-1802), American military hero and major-general during the Revolution; Charles Jervas (1675?-1739), court painter to George I and George II, also known for his portraits of leading Irish figures of his day; Joseph Coyne (1803-1868), playwright, theatrical producer and writer, who excelled at writing farcical plays (*How to Settle Accounts with Your Laundress, The Widow Hunt,* etc.) and was one of the founders of *Punch,* the leading English magazine of satirical humor; Jasper Joly (1819-1892), book collector and philanthropist, whose collection of 23,000 books, prints and other items became the nucleus of the National Library, Dublin.

Places of interest: Birr Castle, with its museum, its impressive gardens and ruins of the Great Telescope, constructed for the third Earl of Rosse in 1845, which remained the world's largest for 75 years; Clonmacnoise, Shannonside remains of what was perhaps Ireland's most famous monastery; Clogan Castle, Banagher, built in 1120 and one of Ireland's oldest inhabited buildings.

Events: Birr Vintage Week (August); Irish Carriage Driving Championship, Birr Castle, Birr (September); Offaly Grand Canal Boat Rally (May/June); Edenderry Festival, Edenderry (July).

Newspapers: *Midland Tribune* (weekly); *Tullamore Tribune* (weekly); *Offaly Topic* (weekly).

Miscellaneous: Until independence, Offaly was called "Kings County," originally in honor of King Philip of Spain, husband of the English queen, Mary Tudor.

WESTMEATH
County town: Mullingar
Area: 681 sq.mi.
Notable natives: Michael J. Meany, father of George Meany (1894-1979), U.S. labor leader who was the first head of the combined AFL-CIO and American labor's leading spokesman; John McCormack (1884-1945), legendary Irish tenor, known for his renditions of popular Irish songs as well as his operatic performances; T.P. O'Connor (1848-1929), journalist, litterateur and nationalist member of parliament.

Places of interest: Tullynally Castle, Castlepollard, home of the Earls of Longford; Military Museum, St. Columb's Barracks, Mullingar; Athlone Castle Museum, The Castle, Athlone.

Newspapers: *Westmeath/Offaly Independent* (weekly); *Westmeath Examiner* (weekly); *Midland Topic* (weekly).

WEXFORD
County town: Wexford
Area: 908 sq.mi.
Notable natives: John Barry (1745-1803), U.S. naval officer and "Father of the U.S. Navy;" Patrick Kennedy, immigrant great-grandfather of President John F. Kennedy; Sir Robert McClure (1807-1873), who discovered the Northwest Passage linking the Atlantic and Pacific oceans; Admiral Sir David Beatty (1871-1936), British naval officer, who took command of the Grand Fleet in 1916 and successfully countered the U-boat threat, later serving as Admiral of the Fleet and First Sea Lord; Beauchamp Bagenal Harvey (1762-1798), Wexford landowner whose support for Catholic emancipation and parliamentary reform led him to join the United Irishmen, who subsequently elected him commander-in-chief of the rebel forces during the 1798 rising, after whose failure he was executed; Leo Rowsome (1900-1970), "King of Irish Pipers;" John Edward Redmond (1856-1918), nationalist leader who remained loyal to Parnell after the O'Shea affair, later becoming leader of the reunited Irish Parliamentary party, where he pushed through the Land Act of 1903, helped found the National University, and secured introduction of the third Home Rule Bill in 1912, before the polarization of opinion between the Ulster Unionist movement and the revolutionary nationalists undermined his moderate, parliamentary approach to independence.

Places of interest: Hook Lighthouse, near Fethard – one of the world's four oldest lighthouses, a 13th-century tower on a site where a light is said to have been kept continuously burning since the 3rd century; the Saltee Islands, Ireland's foremost birding spot, where over 3 million birds flock during warmer months; Wexford Wildfowl Reserve, a wintering spot for Greenland geese; Dunganstown, site of the Kennedy family homestead, from which JFK's great-grandfather emigrated; Johnstown Castle Gardens and Agricultural Museum, Wexford, where you can enjoy an impressive collection of trees set amid lakes and landscaped gardens, and then tour an exhibition illustrating the evolution of Irish agriculture and rural life; Wexford Maritime Museum, The Quay, Wexford; John F. Kennedy Park, New Ross, a 500-acre arboretum containing a wide range of flowers, shrubs and other plants as well as forested areas.

Events: Wexford Opera Festival, featuring little-performed opera classics (October); Enniscorthy Strawberry Festival (late June/early July); Wexford Mussel and Seafood Festival (August); Tagoat Steam Rally and Agricultural/Horticultural Show, Tagoat (August).

Newspapers: *Echo & South Leinster Advertiser* (weekly); *Enniscorthy-Gorey Guardian* (weekly); *New Ross Standard* (weekly); *Wexford People* (weekly).

WICKLOW
County town: Wicklow
Area: 782 sq.mi.
Notable natives: Charles Stewart Parnell (1846-1891), champion of Home Rule during the late 1800s, who was forced to retire from politics after a scandalous affair with a married woman; Michael O'Dwyer (1771-1826), patriot leader who took part in the abortive risings of 1798 and 1803 and then, after surrendering voluntarily, was transported to Australia, where he became high constable of Sydney in 1815; Robert Childers Barton (1881-1975), last surviving signer of the 1921 Anglo-Irish Treaty, who had resigned his commission in the Dublin Fusiliers and joined the Republicans when the 1916 Easter Rising erupted, later winning election as a Sinn Fein MP; Edwin L. Godkin (1831-1902) who, after covering the Crimean War for the *Daily News,* emigrated to America, founding *The Nation,* in which he opposed Tammany Hall, the Boer War, American annexation of Hawaii and the Philippines, and supported Home Rule.

Places of interest: Powerscourt, a 12,500-acre estate whose grand house was destroyed by fire in 1974, but whose gardens remain among Europe's finest, with magnificent Japanese and Italian-style gardens, a 400-foot waterfall, fountains, statuary and a deer park; Avondale House, near Rathdrum: birthplace of Charles Stewart Parnell, which houses the Parnell Museum; the Vale of Avoca, which inspired Thomas Moore's famous verses, "The Meeting of the Waters;" Glendalough, where St. Kevin founded a monastic community in the sixth century that became known as the "Rome of the Western World," and whose remains include the ruins of seven churches and a 100-foot round tower; Glenealy Agricultural Museum; Mount Usher, Ashford, magnificent gardens along the Vartry River where exotic plants from Africa, Sri Lanka and New Zealand flourish in summer; Woodenbridge Trout Farm, near Arklow, where you pay for what you catch using tackle provided free; The Maritime Museum, Arklow; Avoca, a center for distinctive handweaving; Hunter's Hotel, Rathnew, one of Ireland's oldest coaching inns; The Wicklow Way, Ireland's first government-sponsored hiking trail; the Beit Art Collection, Russborough, Blessington, which includes important Spanish, Dutch and Flemish Old Masters.

Events: Arklow Music Festival (March); Melody Fair, the Vale of Avoca, celebrating the popular Irish melodies of Thomas Moore (July); Blessington Horse Show, Blessington (July); Tinahely Agricultural Show, Tinahely (August).

Newspapers: *Wicklow People* (weekly)

Miscellaneous: Wicklow is known as the "Garden of Ireland." Relatively few Wicklow people emigrated to the United States, though a good number settled the Australian island of Tasmania.

PROVINCE OF MUNSTER

CLARE
County town: Ennis
Area: 1,231 sq.mi.
Notable natives: John P. Holland (1841-1914), Irish-American inventor of the submarine; Brian Boru (926-1014), high king and unifier of Ireland; Brian Merriman (ca. 1750-1803), Gaelic poet, schoolmaster, musician and mathematician, best known as the author of "Cuirt an Mhean Oiche" ("The Midnight Court"), one of the greatest poems ever written in Gaelic, and sometimes suppressed because of its ribald content; Willie Clancy (1921-1973), Uillean pipes virtuoso and "godfather" of the Irish traditional music revival, who thrilled audiences throughout Europe and the U.S. as well as Ireland; Michael Cusack (1847-1906), co-founder of the Gaelic Athletic Association (GAA); the Kirby family, a multigeneration dynasty of international handball champions; Harriet Smithson (1800-1854), actress who won the love of French composer Hector Berlioz, whose *Symphonie Fantastique* was dedicated to her, and to whom she was for a time married; Peadar Clancy (18??-1920), vice-commandant of the Dublin Brigade during the War of Independence, who acquired a reputation for springing prisoners from British jails; Austin Hogan (1907-1974), co-founder with Kerryman Mike Quill of the Transport Workers Union of America (TWU); Dr. Patrick Hillery (1923-), President of Ireland, 1976-date; St. Senan (?-560), who founded 20 monasteries.

Places of interest: Bunratty Castle and Folk Park, which includes Ireland's finest remaining medieval castle as well as reconstructions of turn-of-the-century rural homes and a 19th-century village street; Knappogue Castle, one of 42 built by the McNamaras; Ballycasey Craft Workshop; Clare Heritage Centre, Corofin; the Cliffs of Moher, nearly five miles of sheer cliffs towering as high as 700 feet above the sea; Craggaunowen Castle, Quin, whose grounds house a rebuilt crannog, or Bronze Age lake dwelling; the Burren, an enormous limestone area unique in Europe and featuring spectacular caves, underwater streams and plants native to the Arctic thriving next to others native to subtropical regions; Lisdoonvarna, a Burren town renowned as a spa and also as a mecca for Irish bachelors and spinsters in search of mates; Lahinch, site of Ireland's oldest golf course, also one of the country's three finest; Shannon International Airport, a major engineering feat when constructed during the 1930s – the first airport built to serve commercial transatlantic air traffic – and the focus of much of Ireland's industrial development effort; Quin Abbey, an excellent example of a medieval Franciscan friary, with well-preserved cloisters.

Events: Lisdoonvarna Folk Festival (July); Matchmaking Festival of Ireland, Lisdoonvarna (September); Willie Clancy School of Irish Music, Miltown Malbay (July); Merriman Summer School, Lisdoonvarna (August); Fleadh Nua, Ennis, celebrating traditional music (May); Ennis Harvest Festival (August); Queen of the Burren Autumn Festival, Lisdoonvarna (October); Burren Landscape Painting School, Lisdoonvarna (May).

Newspapers: *Clare Champion* (weekly)

CORK
County borough: Cork
Area: 2,881 sq.mi. (Ireland's largest county)
Notable natives: Thomas Davis (1814-1845), poet, leader of the Young Ireland movement and a founder of *The Nation;* William R. Grace (1832-1904), U.S. steamship magnate and first Catholic mayor of New York; Sean O'Faolain (1900-), versatile writer who produced stories, novels, a play, a travel book, literary criticism, translations and autobiography as well as numerous biographies of famous Irishmen; William Penn (1644-1718), Quaker leader who founded Pennsylvania; Michael Collins (1890-1922), veteran of the Easter Rising who later served as commander-in-chief of the Free State Army; Patrick Cleburne (1828-1864), Confederate general known for his bravery and leadership in battle; Jeremiah O'Brien (1740-1818), who captured the British schooner *Margaretta* in the "first naval action of the American Revolution;" Sir Richard Church (1784-1873), the "Liberator of Greece"— a Quaker merchant's son who ran away to join the British army, where he became sympathetic to the cause of Greek independence and, after briefly commanding the forces of the King of Naples, accepted an invitation to become commander-in-chief in the struggle that secured Greece's freedom from Turkish rule;

James Barry (1741-1806), painter who drew subject matter from ancient Irish history (e.g., *The Conversion by St. Patrick of the King of Cashel*) and later, classical antiquity; writer Frank O'Connor (born Michael O'Donovan; 1903-1966), known for his short stories; Elizabeth Bowen (1899-1973), novelist and short-story writer, whose works include the best-selling *Heat of the Day*, as well as *A Summer's Night* — a short story set in Cork and said only to be surpassed by Joyce's *The Dead* — and *The Last September* (1929), a novel describing life in a great house in Cork during "The Troubles;" Timothy M. Healy (1855-1931), nationalist politician and first Governor-General of the Irish Free State; Richard Hennessy (1720-1800), French-Irish soldier and distiller whose name is immortalized in world-famous Hennessy's brandy; Archbishop Thomas W. Croke (1824-1902), who worked actively for temperance, the Land League and the Gaelic Athletic Association, and is commemorated for the last in Croke Park, Dublin; Jack Lynch (1917-), Prime Minister of Ireland, 1966-1973 and 1977-1979.

Places of interest: Blarney Castle (and its Stone); the port of Kinsale, a center for first-rate deep-sea fishing; Cobh (formerly Queenstown), in Cork Harbor, where transatlantic liners once called; Bantry Bay, widely considered Ireland's most beautiful bay; Castletownbere, with its nightly fish auction; Crawford Municipal School of Art & Gallery, Cork, a showcase for 20th-century Irish painting; the Opera House, Cork, featuring opera and ballet performances by the Irish Ballet Company; West Cork Regional Museum, Clonakilty; Garinish Island, whose Italian-style garden features plants and shrubs from around the world set among shelter trees, with coastal and mountain vistas as a backdrop; Fota House, Carrigtwohill, a restored Regency great house (early 1800s), containing the nation's finest collection (after the National Gallery's) of Irish landscapes painted between 1750 and 1870; Fota Arboretum, a magnificent collection of trees and shrubs from around the world.

Events: Cork Film Festival (June); Cork International Choral & Folk Dance Festival (May); Guinness Jazz Festival, Cork (October); Cobh International Folk Dance Festival (July); West Cork Drama Festival (March); Midleton Art Fest (April); Cork Western Music Jamboree (March); Macroom Mountain Dew Festival, featuring outdoor concerts (June); Kinsale Gourmet Food Festival (October); Dungannon Horse Fair (August); Cork International Film Festival, Cork (October); Baltimore Sailing Regatta, Baltimore (August).

Newspapers: *Cork Evening Echo* (daily); *Cork Examiner* (daily); *Cork Weekly Examiner* (weekly); *Southern Star* (weekly).

KERRY

County town: Tralee

Area: 1,815 sq.mi.

Notable natives: Daniel O'Connell (1775-1847), "The Liberator," who won election to the British Parliament, where he was instrumental in the 1829 passage of the Catholic Emancipation Bill; St. Brendan the Navigator (484?-577), who is believed by some to have sailed to America nearly one thousand years before Columbus; Horatio Herbert, Lord Kitchener (1850-1916), British soldier, commander-in-chief against the Boers and Secretary for War, 1914; Peig Sayers (1873-1958), traditional Irish storyteller, who preserved hundreds of old Gaelic tales and folksongs that would otherwise have been lost, and whose autobiography is a classic of its kind, recounting a life filled with more than its share of tragedy and sadness, much of it on the bleak Great Blasket Island; Maurice Walsh (1879-1964), novelist and short-story writer, whose best-known work, *The Quiet Man*, was made into the popular film.

Places of interest: The Dingle Peninsula, one of Ireland's most picturesque areas; Muckross House, Killarney, with exhibits of Kerry folk life and demonstrations of traditional crafts as well as a variety of gardens worth seeing; Carrantuohill, Ireland's highest mountain (3,414 feet), part of the famed McGillicuddy's Reeks; Derrynane Abbey, Caherdaniel; Waterville, a favorite spot for game fishermen; Gallarus Oratory, Kerry, one of Ireland's earliest churches, a well-preserved structure that is simple in form and built entirely of unmortared stone; the famous Ring of Kerry, a 112-mile route snaking through some of the most scenic country anywhere, offering mountain, lake and seaside vistas.

Events: Puck Fair, Killorglin (August); Fleadh Cheoil na hEireann, traditional music competition (July); Rose of Tralee International Festival (September); Killarney Bach Festival (July); Pan-Celtic Festival, Killarney (May); Kenmare Seafood Festival (September); Siamsa Tire Theatre, home of the National Folk Theatre of Ireland, which performs from mid-June to mid-September; Lamb Festival, Sneem (June); Dingle Races, Dingle, featuring horse and curragh racing (August); Kerry Summer Painting School, Cahirciveen (July); Ballybunion International Batchelor Festival, Ballybunion (June); Rally of the Lakes, Killarney, a motor-sports event (December).

Newspapers: *The Kerryman* (weekly); *Kerry's Eye* (weekly)

Miscellaneous: Kerry lays claim to the mildest climate in Ireland, since its position as the island's most westerly county gives it the benefit of the Gulf Stream's warming effects. Some of its sheltered bays are lined with subtropical plants.

LIMERICK
County borough: Limerick
Area: 1,037 sq.mi.
Notable natives: James O'Neill (1847-1920), Irish-American stage
    actor and father of playwright Eugene O'Neill; Lola Montez (1818-
    1861), born Maria Dolores Eliza Rosanna Gilbert, the famous adven-
    turess and dancer who, as the favorite of Ludwig I, the "Mad King"
    of Bavaria, became virtual ruler of that German principality; poet and
    activist-nationalist Aubrey Thomas de Vere (1814-1902); Philip
    Embury (1728-1773), the "Father of American Methodism," who
    estab-lished America's first Methodist Episcopal church in New York
    City; Ada Rehan (born Ada Crehan; 1860-1916), Irish-American
    comic actress well-loved on the stages of New York and London;
    Francis Bindon (1690?-1765), painter and architect, who executed
    many fine portraits as well as designs for such great Irish houses as
    Dunsandle (County Galway), New Hall (County Clare) and
    Bessborough, Woodstock and Castle Morres in County Wicklow;
    Richard Harris (1933-), film and television actor whose film credits
    include *Camelot, A Man Called Horse, This Sporting Life* and *The
    Molly Maguires*.

Places of interest: St. Mary's Cathedral, Limerick, built in 1172 by
    Donal Mor O'Brien, last king of Munster; Lough Gur Stone Age
    Centre; King John's Castle, Limerick, a massive, reasonably intact
    Anglo-Norman fortress dating from 1210; The Hunt Collection,
    National Instutite of Higher Education, Plassey, Castleroy; Good
    Shepherd Convent, Limerick, where the nuns make Limerick lace in
    the age-old manner.

Events: Limerick Game and Country Fair, Adare (May); Limerick Civic
    Week (March); Limerick Theatre Festival (March); Church Music
    International Choral Festival, Limerick (March); Charleville Cheese
    Festival (June).

Newspapers: *Limerick Chronicle* (three times weekly); *Limerick Leader*
    (three times weekly); *Limerick Weekly Echo & Shannon News*
    (weekly).

TIPPERARY
County town: Clonmel
Area: 1,643 sq.mi.
Notable natives: Laurence Sterne (1713-1768), author of *Tristam
    Shandy* and other novels; Father Theobald Mathew (1790-1856), the
    "Apostle of Temperance," who successfully encouraged sobriety
    among many of Irish heritage in Britain and America as well as

Ireland; Brendan R. Bracken, Viscount Bracken (1901-1958), son of a founder of the Gaelic Athletic Association, who entered British publishing, acquiring a stable of financial publications and subsequently serving as a member of Parliament, Parliamentary Private Secretary and confidante to Winston Churchill, and wartime Minister of Information; Dan Breen (1894-1969), IRA leader during the War of Independence, when he gained a reputation for escaping from tight spots, and for three decades a representative in the Dail for Tipperary; John Burke (1787-1848), genealogist and creator of the two famous handbooks that bear his name: *Burke's Peerage* (once described as "a stud book of humanity") and *Burke's Landed Gentry,* both still published today; Geoffrey Keating (1570?-1650) historian, poet and priest, whose narrative *History of Ireland,* written in early Modern Irish between 1620 and 1634, defended Ireland against the criticisms of some English writers.

Places of interest: Holy Cross Abbey; Hayes's Hotel, Thurles, where the Gaelic Athletic Association (GAA) was founded in 1884; Ballyporeen, the birthplace of Ronald Reagan's paternal great-grandfather; the Falconry of Ireland, with one of the world's largest collections of birds of prey, which presents demonstrations of falconry for visitors; the Irish Coursing Club, Clonmel, headquarters of Irish greyhound racing; the Rock of Cashel, one of Ireland's most historic sites, a massive stone outcrop on which stand a ruined 12th-century cathedral, a 92-foot round tower and other religious structures: Cashel was the ancient capital of the kings of Munster and, in medieval times, Munster's religious center.

Events: Bianconi Days Festival (May); National Coursing Meeting, Clonmel, Ireland's premier greyhound racing event (early February).

Newspapers: *The Nationalist & Munster Advertiser* (weekly); *Clonmel Express* (weekly); *The Nenagh Guardian* (weekly); *Tipperary Star* (weekly).

WATERFORD
County borough: Waterford
Area: 710 sq.mi.
Notable natives: Sir Robert Boyle (1627-1691), Anglo-Irish physicist and first president of The Royal Society; Thomas F. Meagher (1823-1867), Young Ireland leader who escaped prison to distinguish himself as a Union general in the Civil War; actor and comedian William Grattan Tyrone Power (1797-1841), whose great-grandsons included the American film star, Tyrone Power (1913-1958) and the director,

Sir Tyrone Guthrie (1900-1971); Charles Kean (1813-1868), a leading actor on the 19th-century London stage; William Vincent Wallace (1812-1865), composer of operas and piano music and best known for *Maritana* and *Lurline*, two operas that were quite popular in their time but rarely heard today; General Richard Mulcahy (1886-1971), soldier and politician, who fought with the Irish Volunteers in 1916, became commander-in-chief of the Republican Army, General Officer Commanding the Provisional government forces during the civil war, and later a Dail member, cabinet minister and leader of the Fine Gael party; Thomas Roberts (1748-1778), artist whose paintings for well-heeled patrons include some of the most inspiring scenery of Ireland ever put on canvas.

Places of interest: Waterford Glass Works; The Theatre Royal (1788), where internationally famed performers have appeared — and professional Irish touring companies still perform; Waterford Maritime Museum, The Quay, Waterford; Municipal Art Gallery, Waterford.

Events: International Festival of Light Opera (late September/early October); Waterford Glass Angling Competition, Dungarvan (June).

Newspapers: *Dungarvan Observer & Munster Industrial Advocate* (weekly); *Munster Express* (weekly); *Waterford News & Star* (weekly); *East Cork News* (weekly).

PROVINCE OF ULSTER (Republic of Ireland)

CAVAN
County town: Cavan
Area: 730 sq.mi.
Notable natives: Thomas Brady (1752-1827), born a farmer's son, who emigrated to Austria and rose to become a field marshal in the imperial army; Patrick Donahue (1811-1901), founder of *The Boston Pilot,* the leading Irish-American journal of its day; Mary Anne Sadlier (born Mary Madden; 1820-1903), Irish-Canadian author of some 60 popular novels, including *The Red Hand of Ulster* and *The Old House by the Boyne;* Philip H. Sheridan (1831-1888), U.S. soldier renowned for his exploits as a major-general of cavalry during the Civil War, winning the last major battle of the conflict, Five Forks, and later, after serving as military governor of Texas and

Louisiana and fighting Indians on the frontier, rising to become U.S. army commander-in-chief.

Places of interest: Cavan Crystal Ireland Ltd., Cavan; Derragara Folk Museum, Butlersbridge; Derragara Inn, Butlersbridge, one of Ireland's oldest inns — and with pub food that has won seven national awards; Bellamont Forest, near Cootehill, one of Ireland's finest Palladian-style great houses.

Events: Water Sports Regatta, Lough Sillan (August); Cavan International Song Contest (February); Summer Craft School, Mountnugent (July/August); Belturbet Festival of the Erne, a coarse fishing event (July).

Newspapers: *The Anglo-Celt* (weekly)

DONEGAL

County town: Lifford

Area: 1,865 sq.mi.

Notable natives: St. Columcille, also called Columba (521-597), one of Ireland's three patron saints, who founded the famous monastery of Iona and others in his efforts to convert the tribes of Scotland; Francis Makemie (1658-1708), "Father of American Presbyterianism;" Isaac Butt (1813-1879), "Father of Home Rule," who lost leadership of the movement to Parnell; William Allingham (1824-1889), poet (*Day and Night Songs,*) member of the pre-Raphaelite circle and author of *Laurence Bloomfield in Ireland,* which has been called "an epic of Irish philanthropic landlordism;" Michael O'Clery (1575-1643), chronicler of Irish history, who compiled a *Martyrologium* of Irish saints, lists of Irish kings and their pedigrees, and was the chief author of the so-called *Annals of the Four Masters,* an indispensable record of Irish history up to 1616.

Places of interest: Lough Derg, site of an annual pilgrimage; Killybegs, a major Irish fishing port; Glencolumbkille, which has a Folk Museum with a recreation of a traditional country village; Donegal Abbey, where the "Four Masters" are said to have written their famous *Annals* during the early 1600s; Slieve League, Europe's highest cliffs (1,972 feet); Ardara, a center for the weaving and sale of famous handwoven Donegal tweed; the Donegal Gaeltacht, a traditional Gaelic-speaking district; the Grianan of Aileach, a splendidly preserved circular stone fort, built atop Greenan Mountain around 1,700 B.C.; Glenveagh National Park, in the Donegal Highlands, with 25,000 acres of memorable views; the Bloody Foreland, a headland between Falcarragh and Gweedore whose rocks turn the color of blood as the sun goes down; Mountcharles, a town that ascends a steep hill whose top offers stunning views of Donegal Bay; Malin Head, Ireland's most northerly point; Falcarragh, a seaside village in the Donegal Gaeltacht, and a good starting point for climbing 2,200-foot Muckish Mountain and 2,460-foot Errigal, which offer rewarding views.

Events: Letterkenny International Folk Dance Festival (August); Donegal International Car Rally, Letterkenny (June); Glengad/ Malin Sea Angling Competition, Malin (September); Killybegs Festival, Killybegs (August).

Newspapers: *Donegal Democrat* (weekly); *Donegal People's Press* (weekly); *Derry People and Donegal News* (weekly).

MONAGHAN
County town: Monaghan
Area: 498 sq.mi.
Notable natives: James Connolly (1870-1916), first active socialist in Irish history and a leader of the Easter Rising of 1916, for which he was executed; Ann Jane Carlile (1775-1864), pioneering Irish temperance leader; John O'Neill (1834-1878), who led the Fenians' raids into Canada from the U.S. after the Civil War; John Bagenal Bury (1861-1927), classical scholar and historian, whose monumental *History of the Later Roman Empire* — completed at age 28 — placed him among the world's foremost historians; Patrick Kavanagh (1907-1967), poet and writer whose works celebrated rural Irish life; John Robert Gregg (1867-1948), Irish-American inventor of Gregg shorthand, which is still used in this age of dictating machines and word processors; Richard Pockrich (1690-1759), inventor of the musical glasses, sometimes called the "glass harmonica;" Sir Charles Gavan Duffy (1816-1903), nationalist co-founder of *The Nation* who, after imprisonment for his role in the abortive 1848 rising, entered Parliament and then, discouraged about reform prospects, emigrated to Australia, where he became prime minister of the state of Victoria;

Thomas Taggart (1856-1929), mayor of Indianapolis, chairman of the Democratic National Committee and U.S. Senator from Indiana.

Places of interest: Carrickmacross, a scenic town where the handmaking of lace flourishes; Folk Museum, Iniskeen.

Events: Farney Coarse Fishing Festival, Carrickmacross (April or May); Clones Agricultural Show, Clones (August).

Newspapers: *Northern Standard* (weekly); *Monaghan Democrat* (weekly).

PROVINCE OF ULSTER (Northern Ireland)

ANTRIM
County town: Ballymena
Area: 1,122 sq.mi.
Notable natives: James Galway (1939-), world-famous concert flutist; Siobhan McKenna (1923-), stage and screen actress; Alexander T. Stewart (1803-1876), U.S. department store pioneer; Samuel S. McClure (1857-1949), founder of the first U.S. newspaper syndicate; Sir Hamilton Harty (1879-1941), composer and former conductor of the Halle Orchestra; James McHenry (1753-1816), private secretary to George Washington, delegate to the Constitutional Convention and Secretary of War, 1796-1800 (Fort McHenry, Baltimore, whose successful stand against a British naval bombardment inspired *The Star-Spangled Banner,* is named for him); Thomas Hunter (1831-1915), Anglican Young Irelander who emigrated to New York, becoming a noted educational reformer — the city's Hunter College commemorates him; C.S. Lewis (1898-1963), noted writer and theologian; Sir Roger Casement (1864-1916), British diplomat and Irish patriot, executed on charges of treason for arranging German arms shipments to aid the 1916 Easter Rising; Sir Samuel Ferguson (1810-1886), poet and antiquary known for his translations of old Irish poems and sagas; James Bryce, Viscount Bryce (1838-1922), historian and diplomat, whose masterly *The American Commonwealth* (1888) is considered one of the most perceptive books ever written about the U.S., where he later served as British ambassador; James B. Armour (1841-1928), liberal Presbyterian leader who

supported Home Rule and opposed Sir Edward Carson and others favoring partition, contending it would tend to exaggerate "racial and religious hatreds;" Field Marshall Sir George White (1835-1925), hero of the Siege of Ladysmith (Boer War), which earned him the Victoria Cross; Sean Lester (1888-1959), last Secretary-General of the League of Nations; Timothy Eaton (1834-1907), founder of Eaton's, the Toronto-based department-store chain that ranks among North America's largest; William Thomson Kelvin, first Baron Kelvin (1824-1907), scientist and inventor who, after entering Glasgow University at age 11, went on to discover the Second Law of Thermodynamics, conducted research on electrical currents that assured the success of the Atlantic Cable, invented a variety of nautical and electrical instruments, and is immortalized in the Kelvin Scale for measuring absolute temperature; St. Clair Mulholland (1839-1910), U.S. soldier, a major-general in the Civil War, who won the Medal of Honor and later served as chief of police in Philadelphia.

Places of interest: The Giant's Causeway, a geological wonder of volcanic origin; Old Bushmill's Distillery, world's oldest, dating from the early 1600s; Carrickfergus Castle, largest and best-preserved medieval castle in the North; Dunluce Castle; Carrick-a-Rede Rope Bridge, an adventure for the stouthearted, near Ballycastle; Belfast Pottery; Slemish Mountain, where St. Patrick is said to have herded pigs as a boy-slave; Ulster Museum, the Botanic Garden, Belfast, which contains Irish antiquities, treasures from a Spanish Armada wreck, costume and fine arts collections, and exhibits portraying the early industrialization of the province; Belfast Zoo, set in a mountain park above the city; the Glens of Antrim, nine of which open onto the sea, providing panoramas of rocky cliffs, green swatches and cascading waterfalls; the Round Tower, Antrim, one of Ireland's best-preserved; Crown Liquor Saloon, Belfast, a high Victorian pub with elaborate decoration and fine woodwork, glass and tiles; Sixmilewater, where you can board an excursion boat for a cruise on Lough Neagh, largest lake in the British Isles.

Events: Royal Ulster Agricultural Show, Belfast (May); Belfast Festival, featuring music, drama, opera and film (November); The Lord Mayor's Show, Belfast, a parade featuring scores of bands and floats (May); Slemish Pilgrimage (St. Patrick's Day); Glens of Antrim Feis, Glenariff (July); Oul' Lammas Fair, Ballycastle, the North's oldest and largest (August); Lady Day: Ancient Order of Hibernians Celebrations (August 15); Orangemen's Day (July 12).

Newspapers: *Belfast Telegraph* (daily); *Irish News & Belfast Morning News* (daily); *News Letter* (daily); *Sunday News* (weekly); *Ballymena Observer* (weekly); *Ballymena Chronicle & Antrim Observer* (weekly); *Ballymena Guardian* (weekly).

ARMAGH
County town: Armagh
Area: 489 sq.mi.
Notable natives: George William Russell (1867-1935), poet, essayist and painter, who wrote under the pseudonym "AE" and is known for his contributions to the Irish Literary Revival; James Logan (1674-1751), secretary to William Penn, who emigrated with him to Pennsylvania, rising to become chief justice of the colony's Supreme Court as well as a scholar of some note; Thomas Cardinal O'Fiaich (1923-), Primate of All Ireland; Edward Bunting (1773-1843) who, while not as famous as Thomas Moore, collected and published hundreds of old Irish airs and tunes, many of them set to words by Moore in *Irish Melodies;* Tommy Makem (1932-), musician and entertainer, known for his lively performances of Irish music.

Places of interest: Armagh Town is the seat of ecclesiastical authority for both the Roman Catholic Church and the (Protestant) Church of Ireland: their respective cathedrals face each other from opposite hills, the latter containing a tablet said to mark the grave of Brian Boru; Navan Fort, hilltop-capital of the Conor and other kings of Ulster from about 600 B.C. (and also linked with the hero Cuchullain and the Red Branch Knights); Planetarium & Astronomy Centre, Armagh.

Events: Ulster Road Bowls Finals, Armagh (July or August); Lady Day: Ancient Order of Hibernians Celebrations (August 15); Orangemen's Day (July 12); Armagh Apple Blossom Festival (late May/early June).

Newspapers: *Armagh Observer* (weekly); *Ulster Gazette & Armagh Standard* (weekly).

DERRY/LONDONDERRY*
County borough: Derry/Londonderry*
Area: 804 sq.mi.
Notable natives: The parents of John Cardinal McCloskey (1810-1885), America's first native-born Catholic cardinal; John Mitchel (1815-1875), Presbyterian leader of the Young Ireland movement, who wrote *Jail Journal*; George Farquhar (1678-1707), playwright known for two Restoration comedies, *The Recruiting Officer* and *The Beaux' Strategem;* Charles Thomson (1729-1824), first secretary of the U.S. Continental Congress, a drafter of the Declaration of Independence, and designer of the Great Seal of the United States; Rev. Charles H. McKenna (1835-1917), "Apostle of the Holy Name Society," who emigrated to America, where he founded this popular organization for Catholic laymen as well as other devotional activities; Oliver Pollock (1737-1823), wealthy American patriot who helped finance George Washington's army; William Ferguson Massey (1856-1925), Prime Minister of New Zealand, 1913-1925, the only premier in the world to continue in office from the pre-World War I period through the end of the war; Matthew Thornton (1714-1803), Signer of the Declaration of Independence; Charles Donagh Maginnis (1867-1955), world-renowned architect whose commissions included the National Shrine of the Immaculate Conception, Washington, DC.

Places of interest: Mussenden Temple, Downhill, an oddity of 18th-century classical architecture built by Frederick Hervey, Earl of Bristol and Anglican Bishop of Derry; the Sperrin Mountains, a less-visited area featuring whitewashed cottages and sparsely settled moors crossed by narrow, winding roads; the Guild House, Derry, whose beautiful stained-glass windows depict highlights of the city's history; the City Wall, Derry, a 20-foot-thick, mile-long enclosure that helped the city's Protestant inhabitants withstand the famous 105-day siege by James II's Catholic forces in 1689; Cathedral of St. Columb, Derry, in Gothic style (built 1633) with a chapter house that displays relics of the 1689 siege; Movanagher Fish Farm, Kilrea, where you can see several million trout at various stages of growth.

Events: Portstewart Music Festival (late May/early June); Portstewart Regatta (summer); Relief of Derry Celebration/ Apprentice Boys' March (August 12); Lady Day: Ancient Order of Hibernians Celebrations (August 15); Orangemen's Day (July 12).

Newspapers: *Derry Journal* (twice weekly); *Sentinel* (weekly).

* Note: Irishmen south of the border and nationalists in the North have traditionally called the town and county "Derry," its original name. After Scottish and English Protestants settled the area under a charter from James I early in the 17th century, they changed the name to "Londonderry," in honor of the London company that had organized the so-called Plantation. The newer name is the official one in Northern Ireland and Britain as well as the name recognized by Unionists. In 1984, however, the City Council of Londonderry voted to formally remove "London" from its name. Partly, perhaps, as a result of this, the name "Derry" seems to be growing in popularity throughout the community.

DOWN
County town: Downpatrick
Area: 952 sq.mi.
Notable natives: Rev. Patrick Bronte (born Prunty; 1777-1861), clergyman and writer, better known as the father of the three Bronte sisters — novelists who among them wrote such classics as *Jane Eyre, Wuthering Heights* and *Agnes Grey;* Harry Brogan (1905-1977), who made his stage debut at age 13 with Countess Markievicz, then, after a stint with touring actors, became active in the Abbey Theatre company and appeared in nearly every feature film made in Ireland during his career; Harry B. Ferguson (1884-1960), engineer and inventor, who in 1909 became the first person in Ireland to fly (in a monoplane he designed and built) and later designed a revolutionary tractor manufactured by Ford Motor Company in the only partnership Henry Ford ever entered.

Places of interest: Down Cathedral, Downpatrick, built on the supposed site of St. Patrick's first stone church (tradition holds that the remains of Sts. Patrick, Brigid and Columba lie within the churchyard); St. Patrick Heritage Centre, Downpatrick; Mountstewart Gardens, where a mild climate supports eucalyptus, bamboo and other subtropical plants; Saul, site of Ireland's first Christian church, built by St. Patrick about 432 A.D.; the Mountains of Mourne, "...that sweep down to the sea," best explored by foot or pony; Ulster Folk Village and Transport Museum, Cultra Park, Holywood, where traditional life in rural Ulster has been recreated through cottages, churches, mills and other buildings moved here from throughout the province and restored to their original state (some are centuries old); Ballycopeland Windmill, thought to be Ireland's only working example; the Ards Peninsula, an unspoiled finger of land between Strangford Lough and the sea, dotted with charming shoreside villages, windmill towers and the ruins of ancient hilltop strongholds; Newry Canal, Newry, the first canal in the British Isles, which proved their practicability.

Events: Ulster Harp National Steeplechase, Downpatrick (late February/ early March); Lady Day: Ancient Order of Hibernians Celebrations (August 15); Orangemen's Day (July 12).

Newspapers: *County Down Spectator* (weekly)

FERMANAGH
County town: Enniskillen
Area: 653 sq.mi.
Notable natives: Rev. James MacDonald (late 1700s), great-grandfather of both Rudyard Kipling (1865-1936), the British novelist and "Poet of Empire," and Stanley Baldwin (1867-1947), British prime minister intermittently from 1923 to 1937; Field Marshall Sir Alan Brooke, the Viscount Alanbrooke (1883-1963), leading British commander during WWII; T.P. Flanagan (1929-), artist known for his watercolors of literary and historical landscapes; Shan Bullock (1865-1935), writer whose works include several novels of Fermanagh life (*By Thrasna River, The Squireen, Dan the Dollar* and *The Loughsiders*) as well as poetry and autobiography; Hugh O'Brien (1827-1895), first Irish-American mayor of Boston, who was inaugurated for the first of his three terms in 1885.

Places of interest: The Belleek Pottery, Ltd., home of world-famous china ware; Upper and Lower Lough Erne, a mecca for fishing and cruising enthusiasts; the Royal School (1777), Portara, where both Oscar Wilde and Samuel Beckett studied; Castlecoole, a magnificant late Georgian house and estate, near Enniskillen; Devenish Island, a medieval monastic site, with Ireland's best-preserved round tower as well as church and abbey ruins.

Events: Lady Day: Ancient Order of Hibernians Celebrations (August 15); Orangemen's Day (July 12); Enniskillen Agricultural and Industrial Show (August).

Newspapers: *Fermanagh Herald* (weekly)

Miscellaneous: Bountifully blessed with lakes and waterways, Fermanagh is sometimes called the "Lake District of Northern Ireland." The correct pronunciation is fer-MA-na.

TYRONE
County town: Omagh
Area: 1,218 sq.mi.
Notable natives: James Shields (1810-1879), U.S. military officer and statesman, the only person ever elected a U.S. senator by three states; Bernadette Devlin (1947-), the fiery nationalist-socialist who became the youngest member of the House of Commons in 1968; John Joseph Hughes (1797-1864), first Catholic Archbishop of New York and builder of St. Patrick's Cathedral; John Dunlap (1747-1812), Irish-American printer and publisher, who issued America's first daily newspaper, *The Pennsylvania Packet,* and printed the first copies of the Declaration of Independence; Flann O'Brien (1912-1966), popular writer of comic plays, novels and broadcast humor in both English and Gaelic; Field Marshall Sir Harold Alexander, first Viscount Alexander of Tunis and Errigal (1891-1961), British World War II commander who won fame in the North African campaign and Italy; Brian Friel (1930-), dramatist, author of *Philadelphia, Here I Come* and other plays; Jimmy Kennedy (20th cent.), prolific song-writer who produced over 2,000 songs, including "Red Sails in the Sunset," "The Isle of Capri," "South of the Border" and "Did Your Mother Come from Ireland?".

Places of interest: Woodrow Wilson Ancestral Home, near Strabane; Ulster-American Folk Park, outside Omagh, which recreates the rural lifestyle of Ulster emigrants both in Ireland and America; the 18-foot Arboe Cross, Ireland's finest high cross, with sculpted panels depicting biblical scenes; Tullaghoge Fort, near Cookstown, a fine hilltop enclosure that served as headquarters and coronation site for the O'Neills, chiefs of Ulster (12th-17th centuries); Gray's Printing Press, Strabane, an 18th-century printing shop where both James Dunlap, printer of the American Declaration of Independence, and President Woodrow Wilson's grandfather, James Wilson, are thought to have learned the trade.

Events: Lady Day: Ancient Order of Hibernians Celebrations (August 15); Orangemen's Day (July 12); Traditional Irish Music Summer

School, Benburb (July).

Newspapers: *Derry People & Donegal News* (Saturday); *Strabane Weekly News* (weekly); *Tyrone Constitution* (weekly).

The Green Pages

TABLE OF LISTINGS

Begins on Page

Begins on Page

Listings by Category

AIRLINES – SCHEDULED SERVICE BETWEEN THE U.S. & IRELAND

AER LINGUS: IRISH INTERNATIONAL AIRLINES
(800) 223-6537; in New York State, (800) 631-7917

Regularly scheduled 747 service connecting New York/Shannon/ Dublin and Boston/Shannon/ Dublin. Service to and from New York is offered daily year-round. The Boston flights operate three days weekly, April - September; and once a week, October - March. Phone toll-free for fares, flight schedules, terms/conditions and other information.

DELTA AIR LINES
(800) 221-1212

Delta inaugurated direct flights between Atlanta International and Shannon in May 1986. Six flights are scheduled each week using wide-body aircraft — three direct to Shannon, and three with stop-overs but no change of planes at London/Gatwick. Phone toll-free for further information and reservations.

NORTHWEST ORIENT AIRLINES
(800) 447-4747

Regularly scheduled 747 flights from April through October connecting New York/Shannon/Dublin and Boston/ Shannon/Dublin. Phone toll-free for fares, schedules, conditions and other details.

PAN AMERICAN WORLD AIRWAYS
(800) 221-1111

After more than a decade, Pan Am resumed service between the U.S. and Ireland in April 1986. Daily wide-body flights connect New York's JFK International Airport and Shannon.

ALCOHOLIC BEVERAGES – U.S. DISTRIBUTORS OF IRISH PRODUCTS

Finding the Irish liquor brands listed below at a store in your community should be no problem. If you're unable to locate one, however, contact the appropriate distributor below for the location of your nearest retail dealer.

HEUBLEIN INCORPORATED
Munson Road
Farmington, CT 06032
(203) 677-4061

Irish Mist Liqueur.

GUINNESS IMPORT COMPANY
Six Landmark Square
Stamford, CT 06901
(203) 323-3311

Guinness Stout. Harp Irish Lager.

**THE JOSEPH GARNEAU
COMPANY**
P.O. Box 1080
Louisville, KY 40201
(502) 585-1100

Old Bushmills Irish Whiskey.

FLEISCHMANN DISTILLING
COMPANY
One Hollow Lane
Lake Success, NY 11042
(516) 222-8100

Dunphy's Irish Whiskey. Dunphy's
Cream Liqueur.

AUSTIN, NICHOLS & CO.
1290 Avenue of the Americas
New York, NY 10019
(212) 974-8080

Paddy Irish Whiskey. Murphy's Irish
Whiskey.

**THE PADDINGTON
CORPORATION**
1290 Avenue of the Americas
New York, NY 10014
(212) 957-7860

Bailey's Original Irish Cream Liqueur.

**ST. BRENDAN'S IRISH
IMPORTS LTD.**
1345 Avenue of the Americas
New York, NY 10019
(212) 333-3877

St. Brendan's Irish Cream Liqueur.

375 SPIRITS
375 Park Avenue
New York, NY 10152
(212) 572-7000

Jameson Irish Whiskey. Jameson
1780.

**IRISH WHISKEY
INFORMATION BUREAU**
c/o Irish Distillers International
Water Mill Center
800 South Street
Waltham, MA 02154
(617)891-9008

General information on Irish whiskey
and on the various IDI brands, which
are imported by other firms listed here.

**A & M IMPORTING
DISTRIBUTORS**
1943-49 Wakeling Street
Philadelphia, PA 19124
(215) 288-2012

Imports and distributes Dempsey's
Irish Beer.

**SCHENLEY AFFILIATED
BRANDS CORP.**
12770 Merit Drive
Dallas, TX 75251
(214) 450-6400

Power's Irish Whiskey.

ANTIQUITIES – CELTIC – REPRODUCTIONS

ALL THINGS IRISH, INC.
P.O. Box 94
Glenview, IL 60025
(312) 998-4510

As agent for the Wild Goose Studio, Kinsale, County Cork, this firm sells small sculptures, bas-reliefs, statues and pendants hand-cast from models of medieval Celtic art or interpretations by contemporary artists. Each piece consists of a thick shell cast in bronze, iron or nickel silver and backed by ceramic resin compound. Among the pieces are a seven-inch statue of St. Patrick modelled after a carving on a 12th-century cross at Kilfenora; a replica of a 16th-century lion from Lynch's Castle, Galway; and several Celtic crosses. Request free catalog.

ARTISTS – LANDSCAPES & OTHER IRISH SUBJECTS

MARION J. SULLIVAN
1511 Old Oak Road
Brentwood, CA 90049
(213) 459-9705

In addition to other subject matter, Ms. Sullivan paints Irish portraits and landscapes.

IRISH ARTS
7364 El Dorado Drive
Buena Park, CA 90620
(714) 739-4195

Peter Walsh, the owner, paints in oils, specializing in Irish landscapes. He also represents Edmund Sullivan, the New York-based landscape painter, and Jim Fitzpatrick, who has made his reputation painting Irish historical scenes. Write for descriptive literature, or phone during evening or weekend hours.

THE ART OF THE IRISH
1 Evans Road
Brookline, MA 02146
(617) 566-1147

Imports and sells works of Irish artists, including watercolors, oils, lithographs and prints.

KEVIN O'BRIEN
51 Church Street
Somerville, MA 02143
(617) 625-0835

Mr. O'Brien is known for his Irish landscapes, done in both pastels and watercolors.

VAL McGANN
Val McGann Studio & Gallery
Route 1 – Box 395
Ogunquit, ME 03907
(207) 646-3167

Request free brochure with representative Irish scenes by McGann.

ED HAVAS
Department of Art and Music
Seton Hall University
South Orange, NJ 07079
(201) 761-9000

An art professor at Seton Hall University, Ed Havas also practices what he teaches. His watercolors of Irish landscapes – his specialty – have earned well-deserved praise. Havas has presented one-man shows at the Kennedy Memorial Library, Boston, and the American Irish Historical Society, New York. Contact him for details on pieces currently available for sale.

EDMUND SULLIVAN
166 Brookdale Drive
Yonkers, NY 10710
(914) 337-1585

Artist Sullivan offers realistic paintings of Irish landscapes, equestrian scenes and other subjects by Irish and Irish-American artists. For a viewing, phone between 11 am and 6 pm. Sullivan also sells his own paintings –both as originals and as numbered prints in limited editions, suitable for framing. Request free color catalog.

BRAD BENNETT STUDIO
405 65th Street
Kenosha, WI 53140
(414) 652-9443

An award-winning artist, Bennett has created limited-edition lithographed prints of four original watercolors he painted of scenes in Ireland: *Adare Cottages; Dingle at Low Tide; Creamery;* and *O'Donoghue's Pub.* They are available at $85. each or $300. for the set. Request free brochure showing prints.

BAKERIES – (See also "Food Specialties")

STAR BAKERY
1701 Church Street
San Francisco, CA 94131
(415) 648-0785

Irish soda bread and other specialties. Open seven days.

O'BRIEN'S BAKERY
9 Beale Street
Wollaston, MA 02170
(617) 472-4025/4027

Features Irish breads, cakes, cookies and rolls.

THE IRISH BAKERY
367 East 204th Street
Bronx, NY 10467
(212) 652-6854

Sells soda bread, scones, barmbrack, Irish sausages, Irish bacon and black pudding.

GAELIC IMPORTS
4882 Pearl Road
Cleveland, OH 44109
(216) 398-1548

Sells fresh soda bread, potato bread and scones. Also makes black pudding, white pudding and Irish sausages as well as stocking a variety of biscuits, sauces and other imported grocery items.

BANKS – IRISH – U.S. OFFICES

ALLIED IRISH BANK, LTD.
U.S. branch offices at:

405 Park Avenue
New York, NY 10022
(212) 223-1230

3 First National Plaza
Suite 4412
Chicago, IL 60602
(312) 630-0044

A full-service bank serving both individuals and businesses. Consumer banking services include checking accounts; money market funds; traveler's checks; international money orders; and changing of money into Irish currency.

BANK OF IRELAND
Branch office at:

640 Fifth Avenue
New York, NY 10019
(212) 397-1700

Representative office at:

135 S. LaSalle – Suite 4004
Chicago, IL 60603
(312) 236-6195

A full-service bank catering to both individuals and corporate customers. Among its services are traveler's checks; savings and checking accounts; international money orders; and currency exchange.

BOOKS – GAELIC-LANGUAGE

ALICORN/IRISH BOOKS & THINGS
3428 Balboa Street
San Francisco, CA 94118
(415) 751-9129

Books in Gaelic, both current and out-of-print. Also, Gaelic dictionaries, grammars and other language-learning materials.

IRISH BOOKS AND MEDIA
2115 Summit Avenue
Box 5026
St. Paul, MN 55105
(612) 647-5678

A mail-order service. Stocks a wide selection of Irish-language titles, including children's books, literary classics, dictionaries and grammars, and contemporary fiction. Write for a free list, enclosing a self-addressed stamped envelope.

KESHCARRIGAN BOOK SHOP
90 West Broadway
New York, NY 10007
(212) 962-4237

In addition to its impressive selection of new and used English-language books, Keshcarrigan has stocked its smallish shop with what may be the largest selection of Gaelic-language books on this side of the Atlantic, including adult and children's titles. Request free Gaelic title list.

BOOKS – PUBLISHERS & DISTRIBUTORS
(See also "Genealogical Resources" & "Directories – Irish-American")

CELTIC BOOK COMPANY
P.O. Box 5935
Berkeley, CA 94705
(415) 548-9214

Publishes the "Library of Irish-American Literature and Culture." Request details on titles.

THE DEVIN-ADAIR COMPANY, PUBLISHERS
6 North Water Street
Greenwich, CT 06830
(203) 531-7755

Publishes "Books of Irish Interest," including reprints of out-of-print titles as well as newer works. Among subjects covered are poetry, history, politics, fiction, travel, culture, customs and folklore. Request free copy of their descriptive price list.

GREENWOOD PRESS
88 Post Road West
P.O. Box 5007
Westport, CT 06881
(203) 226-3571

Among the 600 books GP issues each year is a small but growing number of Irish-related reference works. These include *Irish-American Voluntary Organizations* (1983), edited by Michael Funchion; *Irish Research: A Guide to Collections in North America, Ireland and Great Britain,* edited by DeeGee Lester (publication scheduled for late 1986); *A Companion to Joyce Studies* (1983), edited by Zack R. Bowen and James F. Carens; *Dictionary of Irish Literature* (1979), Robert Hogan, Editor-in-Chief; and *Sean O'Casey's Autobiographies: An Annotated Index* (1983), by Robert G. Lowery. Request free catalog or descriptive literature.

PROSCENIUM PRESS
P.O. Box 361
Newark, DE 19715

In addition to *The Journal of Irish Literature,* Proscenium publishes books of Irish fiction, poetry collections and full-length plays by Irish and Irish-American writers. Request publication price list.

QUINLIN, CAMPBELL PUBLISHERS
P.O. Box 651
Boston, MA 02134
(617)787-0178

Publishes or distributes a small but growing list of titles on Irish history, politics and nationalism, women's studies – plus such topical works as *Guide to the Boston Irish* and *Irish Trivia*. Also sells Irish records and subscriptions to selected Irish journals. Request free descriptive brochures.

LINDISFARNE PRESS
RD #2
West Stockbridge, MA 01266
(413) 232-4377

Publishes a limited selection of works
on such topics as Celtic Christianity,
Irish fairy and folk tales, Celtic myths
and legends, and the 1916 Easter
Rising. Request free catalog.

**CATHOLIC UNIVERSITY OF
AMERICA PRESS**
P.O. Box 4852
Hampden Station
Baltimore, MD 21211
(301) 338-7817

Publishes "Reprints in Irish History" –
important works previously out of
print.

**LONGWOOD PUBLISHING
GROUP, INC.**
27 South Main Street
Wolfeboro, NH 03894-2069
(603) 569-4576/4577

Distributes a variety of books on Irish
subjects from Irish and British
publishers, including The University
Press of Ireland, Brandon Book
Publishers, Caliban Books, Blackstaff
Press and Manchester University
Press. Some titles are scholarly,
others aimed at general readers.
Request free *Irish Books* catalog.

SALEM HOUSE
426 Boston Street
Topsfield, MA 01983
(617) 887-8199

Publishes books on a wide range of
Irish and Irish-American subjects – as

well as co-editions with Irish and
American houses.

**HUMANITIES PRESS
INTERNATIONAL**
Atlantic Highlands, NJ 07716-1289
(201) 872-1441; (800) 221-3845

HPI's "Irish Studies" series includes
titles in history, poetry, drama,
literature, literary criticism and other
categories. Request free catalog(s)
covering history and/or literature.

**CAMBRIDGE UNIVERSITY
PRESS**
32 East 57th Street
New York, NY 10022
(212) 688-8885

Publishes a growing list of books on
Irish subjects, particularly history,
biography, literature and criticism.
Also issues an annual interdisciplinary
journal, *Irish Studies*, each edition
devoted to a special theme. (See
"Magazines and Journals")

**SYRACUSE UNIVERSITY
PRESS**
1600 Jamesville Avenue
Syracuse, NY 13210
(315) 423-2596

SUP's "Irish Studies" series includes
books on literary history and criticism;
politics; history; and biography.
Request brochure.

BOOKS – RETAIL STORES & MAIL – ORDER SERVICES

HELEN HARTE, BOOKSELLER
2249 Glendon Avenue
Los Angeles, CA 90064
(213) 474-0181

Fills mail orders; also open by
appointment. $2 catalog charge
credited on first offer. Also publishes
bi-monthly newsletter, *Irish Book
Collecting,* @ $20/yr.

ROWAN'S BOOKS
P.O. Box 1822
Orange, CA 92666

Irish books, records and tapes.
Request free catalog/price list.

ALICORN/IRISH BOOKS & THINGS
3428 Balboa Street
San Francisco, CA 94121
(415) 221-5522

Books of Irish interest: new, used and
out-of-print. Includes texts and tapes
for language instruction; cookbooks;
and genealogical material as well as
books on various cultural and
historical topics. Also: Irish records
and books about other Celtic nations.
Request free catalog.

DONEGAL IMPORTS
5358 West Devon Avenue
Chicago, IL 60646
(312) 792-2337

This import store stocks a good
selection of books.

GUILD BOOKS
2456 N. Lincoln Avenue
Chicago, IL 60614
(312) 525-3667

Perhaps the largest, most diverse
selection of Irish literature, history and
music in Chicago, including many
imported items.

POWELL'S BOOK STORE
1501 East 57th
Chicago, IL 60637
(312) 955-7780

Stocks several hundred Irish-related
titles, mostly history and literature.

IRISH BOOKS AND MEDIA
2115 Summit Avenue
Box 5026
St. Paul, MN 55105
(612) 647-5678

This mail-order book service, affiliated
with the Irish American Cultural
Institute, is "the largest supplier of
books on Ireland in the U.S., and a
distributor for all major Irish
publishing houses." Request
catalog(s).

FACSIMILE BOOK SHOP
16 West 55th Street
New York, NY 10019
(212) 58?-25?2

OUT OF BUSINESS

A wide selection of books from and about Ireland and the Irish. Also stocks periodicals, music recordings, books, records, greeting cards, maps and related items.

IRISH BOOK CENTER
245 West 104th Street
New York, NY 10025
(212) 866-0309

Imports, sells books of most major Irish publishers. Free catalog. Write or phone only.

KESHCARRIGAN BOOK SHOP
90 West Broadway
New York, NY 10007
(212) 962-4237

Stocks new and backlist works as well as out-of-print titles. In addition to English-language materials, Keshcarrigan carries a large number of Gaelic-language books for adults and children. Three separate catalogs – available on request – cover history and literature; Irish-language books; and Christmas gift recommendations (*Winter Book News*).

RIVENDELL BOOK SHOP
109 St. Marks Place
New York, NY 10009
(212) 533-2501

Books on the Irish and sister Celtic nations, covering such subjects as history, languages, art, folklore and music. Also: music recordings; language-learning tapes, records. Catalog: $1.

CELTIC HERITAGE BOOKS
59-10 Queens Boulevard - # 9B
Woodside, NY 11377
(718) 478-8162

Books from Irish, British and U.S. publishers on various Celtic nations and their cultures: Scottish, Irish, Welsh, Manx and Breton. Categories covered include archaeology, art, history, literature, music and children's literature. Also: maps and cut-out models. Request free catalog.

BOOKS – SPECIALISTS IN OUT-OF-PRINT, USED, RARE & ANTIQUARIAN TITLES

HOUSE OF BOOKS
1758 Gardenaire Lane
Anaheim, CA 92804

HELEN HARTE, BOOKSELLER
2249 Glendon Avenue
Los Angeles, CA 90064
(213) 474-0181

Visitors welcome by appointment. Bi-monthly newsletter (*Irish Book Collecting*) and periodic catalog (*Books about Ireland and the Irish*) available by subscription @ $20/yr.

ALICORN/IRISH BOOKS & THINGS
3428 Balboa Street
San Francisco, CA 94121
(415) 221-5522

Books of Irish interest: new, used and out of print.

THOMAS J. JOYCE & CO.
431 South Dearborn Street
Chicago, IL 60603

History and literature.

MURPHY BROOKFIELD BOOKS
219 North Gilbert
Iowa City, IA 52240

History and literature.

STEPHEN GRIFFIN
9 Irvington Road
Medford, MA 02155
(617) 396-8440

Irish books bought and sold: used and out-of-print; English- and Gaelic-language items.

LITTLE FARM BOOKSHOP
169 Wheeler Street
Rehoboth, MA 02769

Covers books on the Irish in America.

J.& J. O'DONOGHUE BOOKS
1926 2nd Avenue South
Anoka, MN 55303
(612) 427-4320

KESHCARRIGAN BOOKSHOP
90 West Broadway
New York, NY 10007
(212) 962-4237

CALENDARS & APPOINTMENT BOOKS

Most of the bookshops and mail-order sources listed above also offer a selection of calendars and appointment books produced in Ireland or by Irish-American organizations. Also check:

IRISH CASTLE GIFT SHOP
537 Geary Boulevard
San Francisco, CA 94102
(415) IRISH 32

GATEWAY
Box 403
Greenwich, CT 06830-0403
(203) 531-7400

Offers a variety of Irish calendars, including *Beautiful Ireland*. Request free color catalog, *Best of Ireland*.

IRISH BOOKS AND MEDIA
2115 Summit Avenue
Box 5026
St. Paul, MN 55105
(612) 647-5678

Write for information in the fall, when Irish Books and Media begins stocking several Irish- and American-produced calendars for the coming year.

GALLOWGLASS CELTICA
4 Greenlay
Nashua, NH 03063
(603) 880-3706

Distributes the annual calendar of The Institute of Celtic Studies East, which is illustrated with drawings and notes all major Celtic holidays.

CELTIC LEAGUE AMERICAN BRANCH
2973 Valentine Avenue
Bronx, NY 10458

A calendar that celebrates not only the holidays and heritage of the Irish, but also those of their sister Celtic nations, the Scots, Manx, Cornish, Welsh and Bretons. Illustrated with drawings in the traditional Celtic style. Send $6 per calendar.

KESHCARRIGAN BOOKSHOP
90 West Broadway
New York, NY 10007
(212)962-4237

As the old year wanes and the new one begins, you'll find several calendars of Irish and Celtic interest in this singular bookstore. Request a copy of Keshcarrigan's *Book News*.

BUDWEISER IRISH CALENDAR
P.O. Box 61
Maryland Heights, MO 63043

Budweiser has produced a 1986 calendar – *Images of Ireland* – featuring 12 full-color photos of charming, peaceful Irish scenes. Send check or money order for $5.95, payable to

"Budweiser Irish Calendar Offer," to the address above. This price includes postage and handling.

CALLIGRAPHY & GRAPHIC DESIGN – CELTIC-STYLE
(See also "Typesetting – Gaelic")

Celtic-style hand-lettering and decoration by a professional can add special touches to invitations, announcements, posters and other printed material. Following is a selection of sources who can provide one or both services. We suggest you request samples of their work:

CALLIGRAPHIC DESIGN STUDIO
10141 S. Kedvale
Oak Lawn, IL 60453
(312) 425-9348

Celtic-style hand-lettering for your posters, invitations, announcements and other graphic decoration needs.

CELTIC IMAGE
14A Marine Road
South Boston, MA 02127
(617) 268-6702

Celtic-style calligraphy and graphic design in traditional Celtic/Irish motifs.

CELTIC FOLKWORKS
RD #4, Box 210
Willow Grove Road
Newfield, NJ 08344
(609) 691-5968

Custom design of various items using
Celtic motifs: banners; wall hangings;
logos for business cards and
letterheads; also stocks a variety of
ready-made items. Request free
catalog.

ARIES GRAPHICS
40 Massabesic Street
Manchester, NH 03053
(603) 668-0811

Design of books, booklets, brochures,
mastheads, logos, album covers and
other graphic materials with Celtic
motifs.

CEMETERY MONUMENTS –
IMPORTED– TRADITIONAL

IRISH ART INDUSTRIES OF
AMERICA
1921 Bellaire Avenue
Royal Oak, MI 48067
(313) 399-8804

Irish stonemasons began carving the
famous high crosses of Ireland over
1,000 years ago. Today IAI carries on
this tradition, employing master
stonecarvers at Durrow, County Laois,
to produce cemetery monuments
reminiscent of the great Celtic high
crosses. Three standard crosses are
available – each in three sizes,
mounted on a pedestal that can be
suitably inscribed. The face of the
cross may be ordered with ivy leaf,

shamrock or interlace pattern. IAI also
offers a contemporary memorial that
combines a rectangular stone with a
Celtic cross carved adjacent; and a flat
marker stone inspired by the Celtic
grave slabs at the monastery of
Clonmacnois. Monuments may also
be custom-carved to your order.
Request free color brochure.

CEMETERY PLOTS –
IRELAND – MAINTENANCE &
RESTORATION SERVICES

CELTIC GRAVE DECOR
Box 586
125 Glen Ridge Avenue
Montclair, NJ 07042

If you have loved ones buried in
Ireland, this firm's services may
interest you. For gravesites anywhere
within the Republic, Celtic Grave
Decor can arrange (1) year-round clean-
up and maintenance; (2) special
holiday wreaths and floral coverings;
and (3) cleaning and restoration of
monumental stones. If you wish, they
can also provide photographs showing
the site before and after any of these
procedures. Write for further
information.

CHARITABLE ORGANIZA-TIONS – GRANT-MAKING FOUNDATIONS (See also "Sports – Organizations")

AMERICAN IRISH FOUNDATION
Executive Offices
81 Shore View Drive
San Francisco, CA 94121
(415) 775-6662

Formed in 1963 by John F. Kennedy and Eamon de Valera, AIF works actively to foster America's Irish heritage and to strengthen the bonds between the U.S. and Ireland. The group aids deserving projects in Ireland – and in the U.S. – through a program of grants. AIF's membership consists largely of business and professional people in both countries, and its directors include all those who have served as Irish ambassador to the U.S. – or U.S. ambassador to Ireland – since the organization's founding. Members provide over one-half million dollars each year and this, together with interest from AIF's half-million-dollar perpetual endowment, has in recent years benefited such causes as (1) restoration of historic Marsh's Library, Dublin; (2) establishment of the Fota Island Wildlife Park, County Cork; and (3) endowment of Ireland's first university chair in American Studies. The Foundation also makes an Annual Literary Award of $10,000 to an Irish creative writer. AIF is a non-sectarian, non-political organization and welcomes those who share its objectives as members. Membership contributions are tax-deductible. For information, write the Membership Secretary at the address above. (See advertisement on pages 182-183.)

FUND FOR RECONCILIATION IN NORTHERN IRELAND
Nat'l Conference of Catholic Bishops
1312 Massachusetts Avenue, N.W.
Washington, DC 20005

This fund, established by NCCB in cooperation with the Irish Episcopal Conference, provides money to existing organizations working to help improve the human climate in Northern Ireland. The emphasis is on programs that promote inter-religious human relations and reconciliation of traditionally hostile groups. Contributions are tax-deductible, and checks or money orders should be made payable to "NCCB Fund for Reconciliation."

THE IRELAND FUND
Attn.: William J. McNally,
Executive Director
100 Federal Street – 34th Floor
Boston, MA 02110
(617) 423-9866

Founded in 1976, IF provides funds to help those affected by Ireland's political turmoil: – Catholic or Protestant – in any of the 32 counties. It has made some $4 million in grants to date. These have helped further the work of the Corrymeela Community, the Glencree Center for Reconciliation and over 350 other charities serving children, elderly, injured and unemployed in Ireland. To raise the money it disburses, the Fund runs fund raising events across the U.S. It also welcomes donations in any amount as well as deferred gifts and bequests. All are tax-deductible. You may restrict your

the american irish foundation

WE THINK OUR LIST SPEAKS FOR ITSELF.
BUT WE'D LIKE IT TO SPEAK FOR YOU, TOO...

Since 1963, Americans have had a special way to demonstrate their concern for Ireland.

The American Irish Foundation, established that year by Presidents John F. Kennedy and Eamon de Valera, has worked actively to strengthen the historic friendship between the United States and Ireland, and to sustain Ireland's cultural heritage. These efforts have been possible only through the interest and generosity of AIF members, who include business and professional leaders and the Ambassadors of both Ireland and the United States.

The list on the opposite page reflects just a fraction of the great good that has been accomplished through the support of AIF members.

So think a bit about Ireland—and the many projects that deserve and await Foundation support. Your tax-deductible contribution or $200 membership will help continue and broaden AIF grants—all made on a non-political, non-sectarian basis.

I WANT TO SUPPORT THE GRANT PROGRAMS OF
the american irish foundation

☐ Contributor, $_____   ☐ Member, $200   ☐ National Committee, $1,000
☐ Ambassadors Circle, $5,000

Name_____Street_____

City/State_____Zip_____

Please send this form and your contribution to:
the american irish foundation
81 Shore View Avenue   San Francisco, CA 94121

GRANT RECIPIENTS

Willie Clancy School of Irish Music, *Co. Clare*
Irish Children Summer Holidays, *North Carolina*
Siamsa Tire—National Folk Theatre, *Co. Clare*
Duiske Abbey Restoration, *Co. Kilkenny*
Flax Trust Theatre, *Belfast*
O'Conor Family Archives,*Co. Roscommon*
Central Remedial Clinic for Handicapped, *Dublin*
University College, Dublin—*Chair of American Studies*
Listowel Writers Week, *Co. Kerry*
Derry Unemployed Workers Program, *Co. Derry*
Druid Theatre, *Co. Galway*
Marsh's Library Restoration, *Dublin*
National Irish Ballet Company, *Co. Cork*
National Gallery of Ireland, *Dublin*
Fota Island Zoological Park, *Co. Cork*
Irish Cultural Directory of So. California, *California*
Trinity College Genetics Program, *Dublin*
Glencree Centre for Reconciliation, *Co. Wicklow*
St. Patrick's College Library, Maynooth, *Co. Kildare*
Oidhreacht Chorca Dhuibhne, *Co. Kerry*
The Jewish Home of Ireland, *Dublin*
King's Inns Library, Constitutional Law Collection, *Dublin*
University College, *Co. Cork*
Field Day Theatre, *Co. Donegal*
National Feis, *Washington, D.C.*
Wexford Opera Festival, *Co. Wexford*
The Robert Emmet Memorial, *Dublin*
Guide to Irish Research in the U.S., *Tennessee*
Ballinafad Educational Trust, *Co. Mayo*
Voluntary Services Playschemes, *Belfast*
St. Canice's Cathedral Restoration, *Co. Kilkenny*
Northeastern University Press, *Massachusetts*
St. Vincent Employment Program, *Co. Tyrone*
Holy Trinity Church Restoration, *Co. Mayo*
Galway Theatre Workshop, *Co. Galway*
Cahir Swiss Cottage Restoration, *Co. Tipperary*

gift to benefit your favorite Irish charity, as long as it is non-sectarian and non-denominational. Request free brochure describing the Ireland Fund in more detail.

CHARITABLE ORGANIZA-TIONS – MISCELLANEOUS

Among the charities listed below, those involved in aiding victims of "The Troubles" in Northern Ireland do so without taking sides in the conflict. Contributions are tax-deductible under U.S. law:

IRISH CHILDREN'S FUND
c/o Robert N. O'Connor
5602 Hillcrest Road
Downers Grove, IL 60510

Since the early 1980s, ICF has been bringing 11- and 12-year-old boys and girls – Catholic and Protestant – from Northern Ireland to the Chicago area for six-week summer stays with local families. After the children return home, the program works to follow up with them in an effort to reinforce healthy values and attitudes that will work against the prevailing cycle of bitterness and hatred. Please make checks, which are tax-deductible, payable to "Irish Children's Fund."

THE IRISH WAY
Irish American Cultural Institute
2115 Summit Avenue
Box 5026
St. Paul, MN 55105
(612) 647-5678

IACI welcomes contributions to help it finance the Irish Way program, which sends American high-school students to Ireland each summer to experience Irish life and culture first-hand. Information on the program will be sent to you on request. Or see description under "Travel to Ireland – Student Travel and Travel/Study Programs"

TREES FOR IRELAND
Irish American Cultural Institute
2115 Summit Avenue
Box 5026
St. Paul, MN 55105
(612) 647-5678

For a $10 donation – tax-deductible – you can aid the Irish government's reforestation program and have a tree planted in any county of the Republic. The name in which each donation is made – whether your own, a friend's or a relative's –will be recorded in the local register of the Forestry and Wildlife Service, and a certificate will be issued and sent to you by the IACI's "Trees for Ireland" program. Contact IACI for details.

PROJECT CHILDREN
c/o Gaelic Cultural Society
P.O. Box 933-L
Greenwood Lake, NY 10925

This organization brings Protestant and Catholic children from Northern Ireland to the U.S. each summer for six-week vacations, which are spent with families on the Eastern seaboard of the United States. From 1975 through 1986, over 2,500 Irish children have been guests of American families under this program. Donations are tax-deductible; checks should be payable to "Project Children."

THE UNITED IRISH FOUNDATION, INC.
319 West 48th Street
New York, NY 10036
(212) 581-1619

A non-member agency under The United Way. Aids elderly and needy residents of New York City – of Irish and other heritages – through counseling services and referrals to appropriate government agencies and non-profit organizations.

CHINA – IMPORTED

Most Irish import shops stock some Irish china ware. The following sources specialize in these products or represent the Irish manufacturers:

ROYAL TARA CHINA
P.O. Box 341
Kearny, NJ 07032

Royal Tara fine bone china, handmade in County Galway, is available from Irish import stores and selected gift shops in the U.S. Write for a free catalog sheet and addresses of local dealers.

IRISH CRYSTAL & CHINA
120 Midland Avenue
Kearny, NJ 07032
(201) 997-1059

Stocks Royal Tara's china line but no longer carries crystal, despite its name. Free catalog.

THE BELLEEK COLLECTORS' SOCIETY
P.O. Box 675
Pine Brook, NJ 07058
(201) 882-0894

For generations, Belleek china has been not only a popular, prestigious giftware, but has attracted avid collectors. The Collectors' Society serves a growing number of enthusiasts – now 5,000 in the U.S. – by informing them of newly issued Belleek items, product revivals, and retirements in the current product line. Other benefits include (1) a special new-member presentation package; (2) a four-color quarterly publication; (3) chances to acquire special limited editions; (4) local chapter events; and (5) Belleek's annual Collectors' Tour of Ireland and the Belleek Pottery. Request further information.

BELLEEK IRELAND, INC.
1 Chapin Road
P.O. Box 675
Pine Brook, NJ 07058
(201) 882-0507

Belleek, the classic Irish porcelain chinaware, has 2,000 dealers throughout the U.S. Its U.S. headquarters will be pleased to refer you to dealers in your area, and will also send you literature about Belleek products. (See advertisement inside front cover.)

EBELING & REUSS COMPANY
1041 West Valley Road
Devon, PA 19333
(215) 687-8930

This is the U.S. distributor for Irish Dresden, Ltd., makers of porcelain figurines. They don't sell directly to individuals, but will refer you to local dealers.

DENNA IRISH IMPORTS
I-95 Market Place
Routes 1 & 413
Levittown, PA 19056
(215) 632-5792 or 752-3662

Stocks Belleek and Royal Tara china.

CORPORATIONS (U.S.) OPERATING IN IRELAND

UNIWORLD BUSINESS PUBLICATIONS, INC.
50 East 42nd Street
New York, NY 10017
(212) 697-4999

Publishes *The Directory of American Firms Operating in Foreign Countries,* which includes a listing of U.S. businesses with offices, factories or other operations in Ireland. Updated regularly, the directory may be ordered from Uniworld or used without charge at many public, corporate and college libraries.

CRAFTS & CRAFTSPEOPLE – TRADITIONAL (See also "Needlecrafts – Traditional" and "Musical Instruments – Traditional – Sources")

LUCILLE DZUGAJ
1021 East Fifth Street
Long Beach, CA 90802
(213) 436-6664

Ms. Dzugaj, who attended school in Ireland, handcrafts St. Brigid's crosses.

LONG SHOTS
809 North Lafayette Park Place
Los Angeles, CA 90026
(213) 413-1374

Traditional Irish fabrics, designed and woven by Eileen O'Dwyer using centuries-old techniques. To assure authenticity, Ms. O'Dwyer – a UCLA graduate in Ethnic Arts specializing in folklife studies – researches each new project. In addition to looming tweeds and other fabrics, she makes crios (belts) and spins some of her own thread and yarn, dyeing them with either vegetable or synthetic dyes. Ms. O'Dwyer also fills orders for customized items; exhibits her work; and gives public demonstrations of her crafts.

LAURIE RILEY
Box 927
Estes Park, CO 80517
(707) 964-5569

Handforged jewelry in gold, silver or bronze: pendants, torcs, earrings, buttons, plaid pins and penannular brooches. Most of Ms. Riley's items incorporate a "Celtic knotwork" interlace pattern. Many are modelled after originals made many centuries ago and now in museums or private collections. Custom-made items available by arrangement. Free catalog on request. (Note: The phone number above is in California, where Ms. Riley may be reached. Mail, however, should be sent to the Colorado address for forwarding.)

JAMES McLOUGHLIN
18 Madison Avenue
Danbury, CT 06810
(203) 792-3740

Mayo-born McLoughlin, a carpenter and cabinetmaker by trade, handcrafts traditional Irish spinning wheels. These are authentic, full-size working wheels made of oak or other woods. And, in skilled hands, they are fully capable of turning wool into yarn for knitting – as they have done for centuries in Irish homes.
McLoughlin's creations, which have won prizes in Irish competitions, are usually bought for decorative use these days, he reports. The pedal-powered wheels are individually made to order, and cost about $350 each. Call for details.

LENORE KEANE
8420 South Kenneth Avenue
Chicago, IL 60652
(312) 582-3097

Trained in Ireland, Ms. Keane is a skilled maker of Carrickmacross lace, Limerick lace, traditional Irish crochet items and Mount Mellick embroidery. Though she does not make items for sale, she does teach, demonstrate and exhibit throughout the U.S.

KILTARTON STUDIOS
P.O. Box 403
Oradell, NJ 07649
(201) 261-4759

Sells Irish-made St. Brigid's crosses, a traditional house blessing. Handcrafted from rush in 9"x9" size. $5 each, postpaid. Write for details.

CELTIC FOLKWORKS
RD #4, Box 210
Willow Grove Road
Newfield, NJ 08344
(609) 691-5968

Hand-etched brass earrings, brooches and bracelets incorporating serpentine, interlace, zoomorphic and other traditional Celtic motifs. Also, sterling silver pendant necklaces and brooches made in Dublin, in interlace patterns and other designs taken from the *Book of Kells*. Request free catalog.

SIMON PEARCE GLASS
Quechee, VT 05059
(802) 295-2711

County Cork-born Simon Pearce was surprised to find several years ago that no one was still making Irish glassware using traditional styles, materials and techniques. So he came to the U.S., and set up an authentic traditional glass mill in Vermont. Here you can watch lead-glass items being hand-blown and -worked: everything from pitchers, wine glasses and tumblers to bowls, vases and candlesticks. The designs are simple yet elegant, and authentic. You can also enjoy a traditional Irish meal in the mill's own restaurant. Send $2 for catalog, which also includes traditional clay dinnerware handmade in Ireland by the potteries of Simon's father and brother.

CELTIC SWAN FORGE
P.O. Box 123
Freeland, WA 98249
(206) 221-8734

The ancient Celts were known for their jewelry and metalwork. Splendidly worked items of precious metal or bronze sometimes served practical purposes as well, such as fastening clothing. Celtic Swan Forge recreates these items today, handforging and working each so that no two are exactly alike. Among the items they make are Celtic-inspired torcs, or neck rings; lyre-shaped penannular brooches, which are attractive fasteners for scarves, shawls and sweaters; straight shawl pins; bracelets; sleying hooks for weavers; crochet hooks; and threading hooks for spinners. Some items can be ordered in bronze, some in .999 pure silver, and some in either metal. Write or call for free descriptive literature and price list.

CRYSTAL & GLASS – IMPORTED (See also "Crafts & Craftspeople – Traditional")

Most Irish import shops carry at least some of the famous crystal ware of Ireland. The following specialize in these products:

IRISH CRYSTAL COMPANY
1815 East Thousand Oaks Boulevard
Thousand Oaks, CA 91360
(805) 496-8363

Sells Tyrone crystal exclusively, at discounted prices.

IRISH TREASURE TROVE LTD.
17W424 22nd Street
Oakbrook Terrace, IL 60181
(312) 530-2522

Stocks Waterford's entire line of crystal items. Request free catalog.

IRISH CRYSTAL OF CHICAGO
815 East Nerge Road
Roselle, IL 60172
(312) 351-3722

Claims to be "the only factory-direct warehouse in the U.S.A.," offering "50% savings and more." Stocks over 300 items. Specializes in custom pieces and hand engraving for trophies, business gifts and presentation awards.

IRISH IMPORTS
249 Newbury Street
Boston, MA 02116
(617) 267-9024

Sells a variety of glass items handblown at Jerpoint Glass Studio, County Kilkenny, including wine goblets, carafes, vases, bowls and whiskey glasses.

WARD'S
24-26 High Street
Medford, MA 02155
(617) 395-4099 or 395-2420

Stocks Waterford and Galway crystal.

MARKET IRELAND
1224 Washington Street
Hoboken, NJ 07030
(201) 963-4127

Sells handblown glass items from Jerpoint Glass Studios, County Kilkenny.

WATERFORD CRYSTAL
P. O. Box 2298
Ocean, NJ 07712
(201) 493-2900

Waterford's U.S. headquarters will
send you information on their famous
crystal products and provide the names
of dealers in your area.

IRISH IMPORTS
Bowen's Wharf
Newport, RI 02840
(401) 847-3331

See listing for Irish Imports, Boston,
MA.

IRISH CRYSTAL COMPANY
4046 Westheimer
Highland Village
Houston, TX 77027
(713) 963-0550

Offers Tyrone Crystal's full line.
Request free catalog.

DANCE – INSTRUCTION

Irish dancing schools aren't usually
located in a fixed place. Instead,
instructors – often national or world
champions in one or more events –
typically rent rooms at schools or
commercial dance studios. Many teach
in different locations, even different
states, on different days or evenings,
permitting them to "bring the school to
their students." You can reach the
individuals who operate the following
schools at the numbers given. In most
cases, they'll be able to send you a
current class schedule:

**McTEGGART SCHOOL OF
IRISH DANCE**
Phoenix & Tucson, AZ
(602) 942-1774

**KELLY SCHOOL OF
TRADITIONAL IRISH
DANCING**
1217 East Oak Avenue
El Segundo, CA 90245
(213) 322-2802

Classes in El Segundo, Manhattan
Beach, San Pedro and Palos Verdes.

**McTEGGART SCHOOL OF
IRISH DANCE**
Fresno, CA
(209) 439-2815

Also offers classes in Denver, CO.

PLUMMER STUDIOS
Southern California
(619) 747-0071 or (818) 781-3325;
ask for Mrs. Thomas

Classes in Escondido, Los Angeles
and San Diego.

**PRIDE OF ERIN CEILI
DANCERS**
13827 Olive Park Place
Poway, CA 92064
(619) 748-6807

Classes held in San Diego.

**TARA SCHOOL OF TRADI-
TIONAL IRISH DANCING**
West Los Angeles, CA
(213) 559-5050

Daily classes.

MYRA BRENNAN SCHOOL OF
IRISH DANCE
10125 Grayling
Whittier, CA 90603
(213) 947-6724

GREATER WASHINGTON
CEILI CLUB
Washington, DC; suburban MD & VA
(301) 279-1496

DENNEHY SCHOOL
Chicago, IL area
(312) 636-8241

FLATLEY SCHOOL
Chicago, IL area
(312) 448-4448

JIM McGING SCHOOL OF
IRISH DANCING
Chicago, IL area
(312) 775-6714

TRINITY ACADEMY OF IRISH
DANCING
Chicago, IL area
(312) 631-6243

Also offers classes in Milwaukee, WI,
and St. Louis, MO.

COMHALTAS CEOLTOIRI
EIREANN
New Orleans, LA
(504) 488-3338

Ceili and stepdancing classes for adults
and children.

ROISIN DUBH DANCERS
Baltimore, MD
(301) 665-8402 or 433-3385

Ceili dancing instruction for adults.

FITZMAURICE-MORAN
ACADEMY
Boston, MA suburbs
(617) 862-8655

Daytime and Saturday morning
stepdancing classes in Arlington,
Lexington and Malden.

MAUREEN GREEN SCHOOL
OF DANCING
Boston, MA suburbs
(617) 323-0872

Adult ceili and stepdancing classes:
Needham and West Roxbury.

MAUREEN HEALY SCHOOL
OF DANCING
Boston, MA suburbs
(617) 447-3081

Classes in adult ceili and stepdancing.
Held in Brockton, Duxbury, Kingston
and Whitman.

MAURA C. NEVINS SCHOOL
OF IRISH DANCING
Boston, MA suburbs
(617) 749-7663

Ceili and stepdancing instruction in
Hingham, Scituate and Weymouth.

RITA O'SHEA ACADEMY
Boston, MA suburbs
(617) 665-3110

Stepdancing classes in Lawrence, Lowell, Malden, Framingham, Quincy, Winchester, Norwood and Needham.

SMITH ACADEMY OF IRISH STEPDANCING
Boston, MA area.
(617) 265-8677 or 326-0388

INTERNATIONAL ACADEMY OF ETHNIC DANCE
595 Massachusetts Avenue
Cambridge, MA 02139
(617) 491-1122

Classes in step dancing.

TIM O'HARE SCHOOL
Detroit, MI
(313) 455-8965

SCHILLING SCHOOL OF IRISH DANCING
Northern New Jersey
(201) 728-1994

Conducts classes in several locations for beginners, novices, advanced dancers and adults.

GOLDEN SCHOOL OF IRISH DANCING
New York City/Long Island, NY
(718) 238-9207

Offers beginning, novice and advanced classes in Brooklyn, The Bronx and Nassau County.

ELLEN PIKE DANCING SCHOOL
c/o Irish Arts Center
553 West 51st Street
New York, NY 10019
(212) 757-3318

BUTLER SCHOOL OF TRADITIONAL IRISH DANCE
Syracuse, NY
(315) 468-2014

Ceili and stepdancing instruction. Adult and children's classes.

MARGARET PIKE STUDIO OF DANCE
1455 Nepperhan Avenue
Yonkers, NY 10703
(914) 961-4226

Irish ceili dancing for adults, step dancing for children. Additional classes in Scarsdale, NY.

TIMONEY IRISH DANCERS
Glenside, PA
(215) 885-2304

Ceili and step dancing for adults and children.

THE PHILADELPHIA CEILI GROUP
c/o The Irish Center
6815 Emlen Street
Philadelphia, PA 19119
(215) 849-8899

TYNAN SCHOOL OF TRADITIONAL IRISH DANCING
Houston, TX area
(713) 893-5380

DENNEHY SCHOOL OF IRISH DANCING
San Antonio, TX
(512) 656-2666 or 492-5292

Classes for adults and children are held on Saturdays.

SAN ANTONIO IRISH DANCERS
San Antonio, TX
(512) 684-5902

Instruction primarily in ceili dancing. For adults.

MAUREEN MALCOM'S ERIN DANCERS
Fairfax, VA
(703) 591-9071

Lessons in ceili dancing for both adults and children.

DIRECTORIES (See also "Irish Studies – Resources")

CENTER FOR STUDY OF COMPARATIVE FOLKLORE
1037 GSM-Library Wing
405 Hilgard Avenue
University of California
Los Angeles, CA 90024
(213) 825-4242

Publishes *The Irish Cultural Directory of Southern California*, compiled by Arthur Gribben and Marsha Maguire. Call or write for descriptive and price information.

GREENWOOD PRESS
88 Post Road West
P.O. Box 5007
Westport, CT 06881
(203) 226-3571

Irish American Voluntary Organizations, edited by Professor Michael Funchion (1983), is the single best source of information on American Irish (and Scots-Irish) organizations of every type. Groups covered – active and defunct, national as well as notable local organizations – include charitable, fraternal, social, nationalist, cultural, religious and educational enterprises. The history, objectives and activities of each are described in detail. Price: $45. Request descriptive brochure.

QUINLIN, CAMPBELL PUBLISHERS
P. O. Box 651
Boston, MA 02134
(617) 787-0178

QPC, a growing publisher and distributor of Irish-related items, recently brought out a *Guide to the New England Irish,* an excellent publication that lists and describes Irish-American activities, organizations and sources of Irish-related products and services throughout the region.

O'NEILL'S FIVE POINTS PRESS
Box 6216
New York, NY 10128

O'Neill's Pocket Guide to Irish New York (1983) is a handy directory covering the wide range of Irish-American activities and resources in the New York City area. Copies are available at many New York Irish book and gift stores as well as from the publisher. $2.95 plus applicable tax.

THE IRISH DIRECTORY
P.O. Box 735
Pearl River, NY 10965

This book includes a state-by-state directory of Irish-American organizations as well as several interesting essays on aspects of Irish and Irish-American culture. Though much of the organizational information is out-of-date, we know of no other source that offers as complete a picture of which Irish-American organizations exist, and where, on the local level. Price: $35.

DOLLS – IRISH-COSTUME

KILTARTON STUDIOS
P.O. Box 403
Oradell, NJ 07649
(201) 261-4759

Sells hand-crafted Irish folk dolls: a girl dressed in woven tweed skirt and shawl, carrying a basket; and a boy wearing an Aran sweater and cap. Also offers a handmade black-faced sheep with genuine wool fleece. Kiltarton says the dolls are suitable for display, or for children's play. Request descriptive literature.

TULLYCROSS
South Street at Hancock
Philadelphia, PA 19147
(215) 925-1995

Sells "Irish colleen" rag-dolls for children as well as handcrafted character dolls intended for display. These include such folk figures as a woman carrying turf, a woman sweeping and a knitter. Request free catalog.

DRAMA GROUPS – IRISH & IRISH-AMERICAN PLAYS

THE TARA PLAYERS
Los Angeles, CA
(818) 796-1273 (Pat Lawless)

Performances are usually staged at the Joey Harris Theater, Santa Monica, or the Century City Playhouse.

THE BODY POLITIC THEATRE
2261 North Lincoln Avenue
Chicago, IL 60614
(312) 871-3000

IRISH HERITAGE PLAYERS
Irish American Heritage Center
4626 North Knox Avenue
Chicago, IL 60630
(312) 282-7035

IRISH THEATRE GUILD
Chicago, IL area
(312) 622-3259

**THE CELTIC THEATRE
COMPANY**
Theatre-in-the-Round
Seton Hall University
South Orange, NJ 07079
(201) 761-9100

THEATRE THIRTY-TWO
c/o The Irish Arts Forum
of Rockland County
P.O. Box 160
Nanuet, NY 10954

**THOMAS DAVIS IRISH
PLAYERS**
c/o Anne Marie Barry, President
6601 Broadway
Bronx, NY 10471
(212) 543-7816

Now in its 54th year of performances.

**THE IRISH ARTS CENTER
THEATRE**
The Irish Arts Center
553 West 51st Street
New York, NY 10019
(212) 757-3318

As resident company of the Irish Arts
Center, this group (formerly The Irish
Rebel Theatre) turns in consistently
outstanding performances of the Irish
dramatic repertoire. The Arts Center
also presents touring drama groups
and entertainers in its small but busy
playhouse.

IRISH FESTIVAL
Villanova Summer Theatre
Vasey Theatre
Villanova University
Villanova, PA 19085
(215) 645-7474

ENTERTAINMENT –
BOOKING AGENTS

The Irish-American newspapers listed
elsewhere in these pages run many
advertisements by singers, instrumentalists and groups specializing in Irish
entertainment. You may also wish to
contact one of the booking agencies
below and discuss the type of
entertainment you're interested in:

IRISH PROMOTIONS, INC.
P.O. Box 1308
Dedham, MA 02026
(617) 484-2275 or 326-5017

Specializes in booking traditional Irish
dancers, singers and instrumentalists
for functions in the New England
states.

ACE ENTERTAINMENT
600 Palisades Avenue
Englewood Cliffs, NJ 07632
(201) 871-4776; (212) 586-7880

Books a variety of Irish talent for
functions nationwide, including bands,
step dancers, instrumentalists, comedians and singers.

BLARNEY PROMOTIONS
c/o Tom O'Donoghue
30 Grant Avenue
Pittsburgh, PA 15223
(412) 781-1666

Handles bookings throughout the U.S.
for leading entertainers from Ireland,
including comedians, singing and
instrumental groups, and individual
performers.

EVENTS, CALENDARS OF –
IRISH-AMERICAN

Several Irish-American newspapers
(See "Newspapers – Irish-American")
regularly publish schedules of forthcoming events, including meetings of
Irish-American organizations, entertainment events and other happenings
of special interest for Irish-Americans
in the states they serve:

THE IRISHMAN
San Francisco, CA

IRISH AMERICAN NEWS
Chicago, IL

THE (BOSTON) IRISH ECHO
Boston, MA

THE IRISH STAR
Boston, MA

THE IRISH ECHO
New York, NY

THE IRISH EDITION
Philadelphia, PA

Depending on where you live, the
following publications and services
may be helpful:

**SOUTHERN CALIFORNIA
IRISH CALENDAR**
c/o Dennis Doyle
1135 Norton Avenue
Glendale, CA 91202
(818) 956-1311

Monthly. Subscriptions: $12/yr.

**THE IRISH INFORMATION
SERVICE**
Baltimore, MD/Washington, DC area
(301) 747-6868

This telephone recording lists
upcoming Irish events in the Greater
Baltimore and Washington area. A
new tape is produced each week.

AN NUAIDEACT ("The News")
c/o Mr. Coilin Owens, Editor
6008 Waynesboro Circle
Springfield, VA 22150
(703) 971-4265

Published four to six times a year, by
the Gaelic League of Washington, this
newsletter covers Irish activities and
organizations in Washington, DC, and
suburban Maryland and Virginia.
Subscription is included with GLW
membership @ $7.50/yr.

IRISH EVENTS NEWSLETTER
c/o EIRE (Emerald Isle Renaissant
Enthusiasts)
5420 Acorn
Houston, TX 77092

This newsletter, covering events in the
Houston area, is available free with
membership in EIRE. Membership
dues are $5/yr. for individuals, $10 for
families.

THE CEILI
c/o Southwest Celtic Music Assn.
P.O. Box 4474
Dallas, TX 75208

Bi-monthly. Devoted to music of
Ireland and the other Celtic nations,
particularly to performances and

festivals in Texas and adjacent states. Includes features, news stories and details of forthcoming events, including listings of Celtic music programs on radio. Subscription comes with SCMA membership @ $25/yr.

THE GUARDIAN
5747 Spring Moon
San Antonio, TX 78247
(512) 656-2666

Bi-monthly. Covers Irish events throughout Texas as well as major events in such neighboring states as Louisiana, Oklahoma, New Mexico, Arizona and Nevada. Subscription: $12/yr.

EXPORTS, IRISH – INFORMATION

Through its two U.S. offices, listed below, the Irish Export Board provides interested American importers, stores and businesses with marketing data and other information about products available for export from Ireland. It also prepares suggested itineraries for U.S. retailers interested in buying trips to Ireland; and arranges for individualized service and assistance to U.S. buying groups during visits to Ireland. In selected cases, the Board cooperates with major U.S. retailers in mounting multi-store promotions of Irish products:

IRISH EXPORT BOARD
North American Headquarters
10 East 53rd Street
New York, NY 10022
(212) 371-3600

IRISH EXPORT BOARD
The Apparel Center
Suite 848
350 North Orleans Street
Chicago, IL 60654
(312) 467-1891

FAMILY-NAME ITEMS

PATRICK MANGAN
37 Westbrook Road
West Hartford, CT
(203) 561-1862

Mangan will hand-paint the coat-of-arms associated with your Irish family name, mounting the painted copper shield on a mahogany base. You may order your wall shield in any of several styles and sizes, and should allow four to six weeks for the order to be made. A $10 deposit is required when you order; it will be refunded if no arms can be found for your name. Request descriptive literature.

B/C CRESTS
100 West Emerson Street
West St. Paul, MN 55118
(612) 457-9224

Offers buttons ($2) and key chains ($4) bearing the coats of arms associated with some 500 Irish family names. Prices include mailing. Send family name and any necessary explanatory information.

ANN CESTREE INNOVATIONS
113 Westover Drive
Cherry Hill, NJ 08034
(609) 428-0556

Offers a variety of items bearing coats of arms of Irish families, including stationery, scrolls, bookplates, jewelry, plaques, ashtrays and mugs. Specimen set of stationery with arms: $2 postpaid.

PLANXTY PRODUCTIONS
376 North Fullerton Avenue
Montclair, NJ 07043
(201) 783-5870 after 6 pm for information and credit-card orders.

Centuries ago, wandering Irish musicians composed special tunes as gifts for their patrons and friends. The recipient's family name was included in the title, and henceforth the tune was associated with that surname. Many a *planxty,* as the melodies were called, has been preserved – and many Irish surnames have their very own. Planxty Productions offers a three-in-one package for each family name it has a planxty for: a transcription of the music on parchment decorated with Celtic-style art and framed in a deep green and gold mat; an audio-cassette recording of the melody by an outstanding traditional musician; and the story behind your family's planxty. The items come in an attractive presentation folder. Each planxty package costs $42.40 postpaid, plus $2.42 tax for NJ residents. Write or phone to find out if a planxty is available for the name of your choice, or consult the list in the advertisement on page 199.

FARNAN JEWELERS
105 North Wayne Avenue
Wayne, PA 19087
(215) 687-1323

14-carat gold family crest rings engraved to order with your family arms.

FASHIONS – IMPORTED (See also "Woolens – Imported")

COUNTY DUBLIN
Ocean at Dolores
P.O. Box 941
Carmel, CA 93921
(408) 624-8324

Irish country clothing for women in traditional, classic styles: coats, capes, jackets, skirts, shawls and throws. Also: Aran handknit sweaters; men's hats; linen handkerchiefs.

THE IRISH SHOP
334 2nd Street
Eureka, CA 95501
(707) 443-8343

Imported clothing for men, women and children: handknit sweaters (Aran, mohair, lambswool and linen); capes; shawls; skirts; caps; hats; ties; plaid kilts; Donegal tweed men's jackets. Also: bedspreads; blankets; throws; and table linen.

THE IRISH SHOP OF
MENDOCINO
45090 Main Street
P.O. Box 1636
Mendocino, CA 95460
(707) 937-3133

See preceding entry.

TIPPERARY FINE IRISH
IMPORTS
5510 College Avenue
Oakland, CA 94618
(415) 428-9222

Emphasizes traditional items, including
Aran sweaters; capes; shawls; scarves;
caps; ties; Donegal tweed hats; and
mohair and wool blankets.

MY IRISH COTTAGE
3302 N.E. 33rd Street
Fort Lauderdale, FL 33308
(305) 564-5542

Designer fashions for men and
women; tweeds; Aran knits.

IRISH IMPORTS
249 Newbury Street
Boston, MA 02116
(617) 267-9024

Sells Donegal tweed jackets and
overcoats; dresses, skirts, coats and
sweaters in mohair and wool, from
Mary Hackett; capes, coats and jackets
by Jimmy Hourihan; blankets, throws
and capes from Avoca Weavers; hand-
knit sweaters in traditional designs;
jumpers and other linen items; Irish-
style work shirts; and mohair capes,
throws and blankets.

IRISH IMPORTS
1735 Massachusetts Avenue
Cambridge, MA 02138
(617) 354-2511

See preceding entry.

THE TALBOT'S IRISH
COLLECTION
Hingham, MA 02043
(800) 225-8200

Offers classic women's and men's
clothing and accessories from Ireland,
including Donegal tweeds, Aran knits
and other woolens; and lace and linen
items. One-year catalog subscription:
$3 for 8 issues.

MARKET IRELAND
1224 Washington Street
Hoboken, NJ 07030
(201) 963-4127

Traditional and designer fashions,
including capes; coats; woolen and
linen shirts; ties; hats; Aran handknits;
scarves, capes, jackets and throws of
handwoven fabric from Tapestry
Ireland.

CARRIG ISLE
118 Ponderfield Road
Bronxville, NY 10708
(914) 337-5115

Imported Irish clothing for women,
including skirts, blouses, scarves,
sweaters, caps and coats.

ST. BRENDAN'S CROSSING
Station Square – #7
Pittsburgh, PA 15219
(402) 471-0700

**AVINGTON OF SLIGO &
KILDARE**
8 East Gay Street
West Chester, PA 19380
(215) 692-2871

This shop specializes in couture and
ready-to-wear collections by Ireland's
leading designers, among them Vonnie
Reynolds, Ruari OSiochain, Evelyn
Cahill and Henry White. Includes
coats, capes, skirts, dresses, blouses,
sweaters and caps. Many items have a
traditional Irish look, though with a
high-fashion cut.

IRISH IMPORTS
Bowen's Wharf
Newport, RI 02840
(401) 847-3331

See entry for Irish Imports, Boston.

**FESTIVALS & *FEISANNA* (See
directory in the *Irish-American
Almanac* section of this book.)**

FILMS – ARCHIVES

THE IRISH NETWORK
Attn.: Jim Gaffney
The Irish Arts Center
553 West 51st Street
New York, NY 10019
(212) 757-0800

Supported by New York's Irish
Institute, the Irish Network has
launched an ambitious but long-
overdue labor: the Media Archive
Project. Its aim: to identify all the

films, videotapes and other audiovisual
media reflecting the Irish and Irish-
American experiences that have ever
been produced. The Network expects
to catalog and cross-index about 2,000
items: documentary, narrative and
experimental. It makes information
about these films and tapes available to
users of all types. If you're a teacher,
historian or scholar – and interested in
this project – the Network welcomes
your ideas on how these media can
best be used in planning curricula and
as teaching aids. If you're a reader,
the Network would like to know about
films or tapes that you've found
particularly valuable or interesting.
And, finally, the Network operates a
circulating library of the programs in
its possession, many of which are
available on both 16mm film and
various video formats. Request a list
of the programs they have available.

FILMS – DOCUMENTARY

**MODERN TALKING PICTURE
SERVICE, INC.**
General Offices
5000 Park Street North
St. Petersburg, FL 33709
(813) 541-7571

Among hundreds of films available
through this distribution service is a
new 16mm title sponsored by
Budweiser. *Irish-Americans: Heart of
a New Land,* traces the Irish contribution to America. Your school, college,
church, club or other organization may
borrow the film without charge for a
limited time, paying return postage and
insurance charges. Contact MTPS for
details, referring to Film #16818.

UNIVERSITY OF MINNESOTA
Audio Visual Library Service
3300 University Avenue, S.E.
Minneapolis, MN 55414
(612) 373-3810

Rents the "Ireland Rediscovered"
series – 12 half-hour 16mm films on
Irish history and literature – produced
by KTCA-TV in cooperation with the
Irish American Cultural Institute.
Request descriptive leaflet.

**CONSULATE GENERAL OF
IRELAND**
515 Madison Avenue
New York, NY 10022
(212) 319-2555

Loans films to educational groups,
Irish-American organizations, etc.
Request information on titles available.

TRIBUNE FILMS
303 Fifth Avenue
New York, NY 10016
(212) 689-3181

Rents about 15 films, all in 16mm with
color and sound and from 10 to 30
minutes long. Included are
travelogues and special-interest films
about such subjects as ancient Celtic
gold ornaments and jewelry; the
Burren, a natural wonder in the West
of Ireland; golfing in Ireland; racing,
hunting, horse shows, trekking and
other horse-related activities in Ireland.
Request descriptive brochure and
reservation application.

FILMS – FEATURE

Hundreds of feature films with Irish or
Irish-American themes have been
produced since the 1910s. Many of
the more familiar, such as *The Quiet
Man*, *Going My Way* and *The Fighting
69th*, are described in the *Irish-
American Almanac* section of this
book. If you'd like to rent a 16mm
print of one of these movies, consult
the classified phone directories for
major cities in your area under "Motion
Picture Film Libraries." If you can't
find the movie you're seeking locally,
request a catalog from one of the
following firms, which have
particularly large rental collections:

**A & C WELLING MOTION
PICTURE COMPANY**
454 Meacham Avenue
Elmont, NY 11003
(516) 354-1066

FILMS INCORPORATED
440 Park Avenue South
New York, NY 10016
(212) 889-7910

Many feature films of Irish interest are
also available on videocassette, of
course. Ask your local dealer to order
titles that are available if he doesn't
have them in stock.

FLAGS & BANNERS

GEORGE LAUTERER CORP.
310 W. Washington Street
Chicago, IL 60606
(312) 332-5584

Request free catalog describing flags in stock. They'll make anything else you want to order.

THE FLAG CENTER
2267 Massachusetts Avenue
Cambridge, MA 02140
(617) 868-2026

Stocks the flag of Ireland in several standard sizes, and will also make flags to order.

THE FLAG GUYS
RD 2 – Bethlehem Road #345
Newburgh, NY 12550
(914) 564-6775

Nylon-fabric Irish tricolor available in four sizes, from 2'x3' up to 5'x8'. Also makes customized banners to your specifications. Request free mail-order catalog.

CELTIC FOLKWORKS
RD #4, Box 210
Willow Grove Road
Newfield, NJ 08344
(609) 691-5968

Specializes in custom-made flags and banners incorporating traditional Celtic and Irish design motifs. Request catalog and other details.

AMERICAN FLAG CENTER
2142 Austin Highway
San Antonio, TX 78218
(512) 655-2898

Ready-made flags of Ireland. Custom-made flags in any size or design.

CHRIS REID COMPANY
P.O. Box 1877
Midlothian, VA 23113
(804) 744-5862

Stocks Irish flag in four sizes – 2'x3' up to 5'x8' – in nylon fabric. Makes other sizes to order. Request free brochure.

FOOD SPECIALTIES (See also "Bakeries")

IRISH IMPORT SHOP
4124 Beverly Boulevard
Los Angeles, CA 90004
(213) 387-0107

Irish-style sausage. Black pudding. White pudding.

O'MALLEY'S CONVENIENT FOOD MART
5277 N. Elston Avenue
Chicago, IL 60630
(312) 286-5277

Carries Irish sausages, black pudding, soda bread, etc.

**WINSTON'S IRISH BAKERY
& SAUSAGE SHOP**
4701 West 63rd Street
Chicago, IL 60620
(312) 767-4353

Irish sausages, soda bread, corned
beef, bacon, black pudding.

**IRISH CROCHET
TREASURES, LTD.**
P.O. Box 1625
562 Milk Street
Fitchburg, MA 01420
(617) 342-1152

Don't let the name fool you. This firm
also sells imported Irish teas, oatmeal,
jams and jellies, steak sauces and tea
biscuits. Request price list.

IRISH IMPORTS, INC.
13251 Michigan Avenue
Dearborn, MI 48126
(313) 584-1404

Makes and sells Irish pork sausage;
pasties filled with beef, chicken and
corned beef/cabbage/ potatoes; home-
made fruit cakes; soda bread. Will
ship orders.

OTTO ROTH & CO., INC.
14 Empire Boulevard
Moonachie, NJ 07074
(201) 440-3600

Imported cheese and biscuit products.

**THE IRISH DELIGHT
COMPANY**
367 West 204th Street
Bronx, NY 10467
(212) 652-6854

Produces Irish-style sausages and
black pudding, sold at this location and
distributed throughout the New York
area. Call for location of nearest
distributor.

ST. JAMES IMPORTING
14 St. James Place
Brooklyn, NY 11205
(718) 706-5969

Two-pound sides of smoked, pre-
sliced Irish salmon shipped by UPS
for $39.95. Phone orders using
AMEX card; mail orders require check
or money order.

TARA FARM
Rural Delivery 2
Campbell Hall, NY 10916

Imported Irish bacon. Lean back
rashers $5.50 per pound – minimum
order 5 pounds. Delivery free to
midtown Manhattan.

**MATTIE HASKINS
SHAMROCK IMPORTS**
205 East 75th Street
New York, NY 10021
(212) 288-3918

Sells bangers; black pudding; Irish
soda bread (raisin and plain); raisin
scones; hot cross buns; and grocery
items.

**IRISH TEA SALES
CORPORATION**
92-16 95th Avenue
Ozone Park, NY 11417
(718) 845-4402

Despite its name, this firm sells a lot
more than Irish tea (and teapots). Its
stock of imported Irish food includes
jams and marmalades, sauces, canned
goods, biscuits, black pudding and
plum pudding. To order by mail,
contact for information and prices.

PATOS LTD.
31-21 68th Street
Woodside, NY 11377
(718) 426-0421

Offers vacuum-packed sides of
smoked Irish salmon.

GAELIC IMPORTS
4882 Pearl Road
Cleveland, OH 44109
(216) 398-1548

Specialist in food items: Irish soda
bread, potato bread, scones; black
pudding, white pudding and Irish
sausage; biscuits, sauces and other
imported grocery items.

**INTERNATIONAL GOURMET
LTD.**
Div. of Howarth Imports
3216 N. Front Street
Philadelphia, PA 19140
(215) 739-1264

**INTERNATIONAL GOURMET
LTD.**
Div. of Howarth Imports
8117 Old York Road
Yorktown Courtyard of Shops
Elkins Park, PA 19117
(215) 576-1274

Specialties include Irish bacon, blood
pudding, Irish sausage, meat pies,
steak & kidney pies, potato scones,
sausage rolls and Irish steak sauce.

BEWLEY'S IRISH IMPORTS
606 Howard Road
West Chester, PA 19380
(215) 696-2682

Established by the immigrant great-
grandson of the founder of Bewley's
Cafes Ltd., a chain of coffee-and-tea
houses known to generations of
Dubliners. BII imports Bewley's tea
and coffee products as well as breads,
cakes and other Irish food products.
In addition to selling through over 400
retail stores across the U.S., the firm
offers mail-order service. Its catalog is
free on request.

FURNITURE – ANTIQUE

**TIPPERARY FINE IRISH
IMPORTS**
5510 College Avenue
Oakland, CA 94618
(415) 428-9222

Imported Irish pine antiques.

ISLAND HOUSE ANTIQUES
Route 7
Wilton, CT 06897
(203) 544-9151

Offers an impressive selection of 18th
and 19th century Irish furniture,
crafted from pine and oak.

WEST COUNTRY ANTIQUES
Route 47
Woodbury, CT 06798
(203) 263-5741

Polished pine and country furniture
crafted in 18th and 19th century
Ireland. Closed Monday and Tuesday.

CENTURY DESIGN IMPORTS
220 North Orlando Avenue
Winter Park, FL 32789
(305) 644-2443

Antique Irish pine furniture, stripped
and waxed. Features armoires, closed
cupboards, wardrobes, open Welsh-
style cupboards and wash benches.

THE IRISH BOUTIQUE
Long Grove Road
Long Grove, IL 60047
(312) 634-3540

Offers a selection of antique pine
furniture typical of what was used by
rural Irish families during the last
century: dressers, cupboards, settle
beds, tables and chairs.

FOXSTONE ANTIQUES LTD.
411 William Street
Fredericksburg, VA 22401
(703) 373-0256

Specializes in "fine country Irish
antiques."

FURNITURE – ANTIQUE – REPRODUCTIONS

Admittedly inspired by English
Georgian models, 18th-century Irish
craftsmen turned out classic pieces of
furniture to grace the homes of the
aristocracy. Generally, however, they
endowed their creations with a distinctively Irish flavor, incorporating such
traditional Irish motifs as shells,
acanthus leaves, masks, animal-like
forms and trifid feet. Two U.S. furniture companies have recently marketed
collections that consist of authentic
replicas of fine furniture pieces found
in some of Ireland's great houses:

**BAKER FURNITURE
COMPANY**
1661 Monroe Avenue, N.W.
Grand Rapids, MI 49505
(616) 361-7321

Many of the Irish pieces in Baker's
Stately Homes of Ireland Collection
reflect the lavish decorative carving
that was common to fine Irish furniture
in Georgian times. Included among
them are chairs, mirrors, cabinets and
tables. The Baker Collection may be
seen at selected stores across the U.S.
For the names of local dealers, or for
further information on the Collection,
contact the company.

KINDEL FURNITURE COMPANY
100 Garden Street, S.E.
Box 2047
Grand Rapids, Michigan 49501
(616) 243-3676

As official furniture licensee of the Irish Georgian Society, Kindel Furniture has brought to market its Irish Georgian Collection. This collection of mahogany reproductions includes 19 chairs, tables, sofas and desks, based on originals at Castletown, the Guinness estate; Leixlip Castle, Kildare; and Glin Castle, Limerick. Contact Kindel for free literature or the names of dealers near you.

GENEALOGICAL RESOURCES – ORGANIZATIONS & RESEARCH COLLECTIONS
(See also "Libraries & Research Facilities")

BRANCH GENEALOGICAL LIBRARY SYSTEM
Church of Jesus Christ of Latter Day Saints (The Mormons)

Genealogy is more than a hobby for members of the Mormon Church, since their faith requires them to have all ancestors who can be identified baptized by proxy as Mormons. As a result, the LDS Church has systematically collected vital records extending centuries into the past from many countries, including Ireland. The Mormons' library in Salt Lake City is the largest depository of genealogical records in the world. Non-Mormons may use most of these materials without charge, and others for a small fee, through any of the 460 local branch libraries the Church maintains in towns and cities throughout the U.S. Without ever setting foot in Ireland, you may discover much about the family lines you're tracing, using, for example, microfilmed birth, marriage and death records the Church has acquired from Catholic, Church of Ireland and other parishes throughout the 32 counties. At the very least, this could save you costly and time-consuming searching once you get to Ireland. For the location of local LDS libraries, consult the phone directories for nearby cities under "Church of Jesus Christ of Latter Day Saints." Or you may request a list of these libraries and information on the services available by writing to: Genealogical Society, Church of Jesus Christ of Latter Day Saints, 50 East North Temple Street, Salt Lake City, UT 84150.

THE NATIONAL ARCHIVES
Pennsylvania Avenue between 7th and 9th Streets, N.W.
Washington, DC 20009
(202) 523-3000

In addition to serving as a repository for U.S. records useful to genealogical researchers – e.g., census records, military pensions, East Coast ship passenger arrivals – the Archives offers a continuing program of courses in genealogical research techniques. You may attend a basic course, or one of the more specialized mini-courses held several times a year on Irish research. Write the National Archives, Attn.: Genealogical Research Courses, and ask to be put on its mailing list for program announcements.

THE NEWBERRY LIBRARY
Local and Family History Division
60 West Walton Street
Chicago, IL 60610
(312) 943-9090

Houses a large collection of
genealogical data relating to New
England and the Midwest.

**NEW ENGLAND HISTORIC
GENEALOGICAL SOCIETY**
101 Newbury Street
Boston, MA 02116
(617) 536-5740

NEHGS, the nation's oldest membership organization for genealogy, has
built up an extensive collection of
genealogical records, particularly on
individuals and families who immigrated to New England. Non-
members may use the library for a fee.

**THE IRISH ANCESTRAL
RESEARCH SOCIETY (TIARA)**
P.O. Box 619
Sudbury, MA 01776

This non-profit, non-denominational
group offers Boston-area residents a
variety of educational programs to aid
them in pursuing Irish genealogical
research: talks by experts in the field;
workshops on the techniques of
genealogical research in general, and
Irish research in particular; monthly
group meetings; and a newsletter
which members use to exhange
information, make inquiries, etc.
Membership dues are $8.50/yr. and
non-members are welcome to attend
meetings. Write for a schedule of
forthcoming events.

**NEW YORK PUBLIC
LIBRARY**
History and Genealogy Department
Fifth Avenue at 42nd Street
New York, NY 10018
(212) 340-0849

NYPL maintains a large collection
useful in researching ancestors who
lived in New York; and major ethnic
collections, including Irish. Anyone
may use the library at no charge.

**GENEALOGICAL RESOURCES
– PUBLICATIONS**

IRISH ROOTS
2004 Kentmere Parkway
Wilmington, DE 19806-2014

Irish Roots, by Donn Devine, is a useful introduction for beginners interested in researching their Irish genealo-
gies. Devine is a professional genealogist as well as genealogy columnist for
the *Irish Edition,* Philadelphia. Send a
$4 check or money order.

**GENEALOGICAL
PUBLISHING COMPANY**
1001 North Calvert Street
Baltimore, MD 21202
(301) 837-8271

GPC offers several works invaluable
for researching Irish roots. Two of
them – Samuel Lewis, *A Topographical Dictionary of Ireland* (two volumes,
$75) and *General Alphabetical Index to
the Townlands and Towns, Parishes
and Baronies of Ireland* ($45) – are
reprints of works published in 1837
and 1861, respectively. They provide

perhaps the best available surveys of both pre- and post-Famine Ireland. Another six-book set, *The Famine Immigrants* ($45 each), gives data on over half a million people who left Ireland for America from 1846 to 1851: name, age, sex, family relationship (where noted), occupation, and when the person sailed, on what ship, from which port. GPC has also republished Margaret Dickson Falley's classic work, *Irish and Scotch-Irish Ancestral Research* (two-volume set: $60), which was first issued in 1962. This is widely considered the best single tool for Irish genealogical research. Volume I "describes genealogical collections and indexes in all major Irish repositories, as well as published indexes, catalogs and source materials in Ireland and the United States." Volume II contains bibliographies of family histories, pedigrees and source data. Finally, *A New Genealogical Atlas of Ireland*, by Brian Mitchell (paper, $18.95) is particularly useful in conjunction with the *Topographical Dictionary* and the *General Alphabetical Index*. With orders, include $1.25 postage for the first book and $.50 per additional volume.

NEW ENGLAND HISTORIC GENEALOGICAL SOCIETY
101 Newbury Street
Boston, MA 02116
(617) 536-5740

Written by experts and published by the Society in 1985, *The Irish in New England* includes chapters describing the Irish-American experience in New England since immigration began; New England sources for Irish-American genealogical research; and the genealogy of the Kennedy family in New England. For a copy, send $3.95 (plus $.50 postage).

NEW YORK IRISH HISTORY ROUNDTABLE
P.O. Box 6216
Yorkville Station, NY 10128

This new group (further described under "Organizations – Irish-American – Local, Selected") is a useful resource for anyone researching Irish-American forebears in the New York metro area. Request a copy of their newsletter, *The New York Irish*, by sending $1 to the address above.

THE GENEALOGICAL HELPER
Everton Publishers
Logan, UT 84321
(801) 752-6022

This bimonthly magazine is filled with articles; reviews; course and meeting notices; and advertisements for genealogical books, materials, courses and services. While only a fraction of the contents deals specifically with Irish and Irish-American genealogy, *Genealogical Helper* contains much information useful to anyone researching his roots, in Ireland or elsewhere. Subscriptions: $17/yr.

THE ALL-IRELAND HERITAGE
2255 Cedar Lane
Vienna, VA 22180
(703) 560-4496

Published quarterly, this genealogical journal is intended to give non-professionals information and research skills that will help them in tracing their Irish roots. A typical issue contains material in several of the following categories: county voter lists; extracts from wills probated in Ireland and the U.S; extracts of births, deaths and marriages from old newspapers; unpublished source material such as church records, census data, etc.; articles on social and economic history;, book-review and problem-solving columns; a researcher's clearing house; and informative extracts from letters sent home by emigrants to America. *A-IH* is edited by Donna Reid Hotaling, a nationally prominent genealogist who has been particularly active in practicing and promoting Irish genealogical research. Subscriptions: $24/volume (four issues); $45/two volumes (eight issues).

GENEALOGISTS – SPECIALISTS IN IRISH FAMILY RESEARCH

DONN DEVINE
2004 Kentmore Parkway
Wilmington, DE 19806
(302) 656-7233

Devine writes a genealogy column for *The Irish Edition*, Philadelphia, in addition to consulting privately with individuals interested in their Irish- or Irish-American roots.

B-ANN MOORHOUSE
222 Hicks Street
Brooklyn, NY 11202
(718) 858-9524

Moorhouse performs all phases of

research involving Irish- and Irish-American genealogy, with particular emphasis on families who entered the United States via the Port of New York.

DONNA REID HOTALING
2255 Cedar Lane
Vienna, VA 22180
(703) 560-4496

Hotaling is not only active in consulting with individuals who wish to trace their Irish roots. She has also organized several international congresses on genealogical and historical research in the 32 counties; she leads regular genealogical tours to Ireland; and she publishes a helpful journal, *The All-Ireland Heritage*. (See "Genealogical Resources – Publications.")

GOVERNMENT OFFICES IN THE U.S. – REPUBLIC OF IRELAND (See also "Exports, Irish – Information," "Industrial Development Opportunities – Ireland – Information" and "Travel – Information")

CONSULATES GENERAL:

CONSULATE GENERAL OF IRELAND
655 Montgomery Street
San Francisco, CA 94111
(415) 392-4214

CONSULATE GENERAL OF IRELAND
400 North Michigan Avenue
Chicago, IL 60611
(312) 337-1868

CONSULATE GENERAL OF
IRELAND
535 Boylston Street
Boston, MA 02116
(617) 267-9330

CONSULATE GENERAL OF
IRELAND
515 Madison Avenue
New York, NY 10022
(212) 319-2555

EMBASSY:

EMBASSY OF IRELAND
2234 Massachusetts Avenue,NW
Washington, DC 20008
(202) 462-3939

UNITED NATIONS MISSION:

PERMANENT MISSION OF
IRELAND TO THE U.N.
1 Dag Hammarskjold Plaza
Second Floor
885 Second Avenue
New York, NY 10017
(212) 421-6934

GOVERNMENT OFFICES IN
THE U.S. – UNITED
KINGDOM (For Business
Relating to Northern Ireland)

CONSULATES
GENERAL/CONSULATES:

U.K. CONSULATE GENERAL
Ahmanson Center – East Bldg
Suite 312
3701 Wilshire Boulevard
Los Angeles, CA 90010
(213) 385-7381

U.K. CONSULATE GENERAL
Equitable Building – 9th Fl.
120 Montgomery Street
San Francisco, CA 94104
(415) 981-3030

U.K. CONSULATE GENERAL
225 Peachtree Street, N.E.
Suite 912
Atlanta, GA 30303
(404) 524-5856/5858

U.K. CONSULATE GENERAL
33 North Dearborn Street
Chicago, IL 60602
(312) 346-1810

U.K. CONSULATE GENERAL
Prudential Tower
Suite 4740
Boston, MA 02199
(617) 437-7160

U.K. CONSULATE GENERAL
845 Third Avenue
New York, NY 10022
(212) 752-8400

U.K. CONSULATE GENERAL
1650 Illuminating Building
55 Public Square
Cleveland, OH 44113
(216) 621-7674

U.K. CONSULATE
c/o Mather & Company
226 Walnut Street
Philadelphia, PA 19106
(215) 925-0118

U.K. CONSULATE
813 Stemmons Tower West
2730 Stemmons Freeway
Dallas, TX 75207
(214) 637-3600

U.K. CONSULATE GENERAL
Dresser Tower – Suite 2250
601 Jefferson
Houston, TX 77002
(713) 659-6270

U.K. CONSULATE GENERAL
820 First Interstate Center
999 Third Avenue
Seattle, WA 98104
(206) 622-9255

EMBASSY:

**EMBASSY OF THE UNITED
KINGDOM**
3100 Massachusetts Ave., N.W.
Washington, DC 20008
(202) 462-1340

UNITED NATIONS MISSION:

**PERMANENT U.K. MISSION
TO THE UNITED NATIONS**
845 Third Avenue
New York, NY 10022
(212) 752-8400

INFORMATION OFFICE:

**BRITISH INFORMATION
SERVICES**
845 Third Avenue
New York, NY 10022
(212) 752-8400

GREETING CARDS & STATIONERY ITEMS

GATEWAY
Box 403
Greenwich, CT 06830
(203) 531-7400

In addition to calendars and a variety
of handcrafted Irish imports, Gateway
carries Irish Christmas cards in
season. Request free catalog.

ARIES GRAPHICS
40 Massabesic Street
Manchester, NH 03053
(603) 668-0811

Cards are available with English or
Gaelic greetings; traditional designs.
Request free literature.

E. CRONIN
RFD #1
Pittsfield, NH 03263
(603) 942-8053

Sells greeting cards and stationery
"adapted from the Celtic tradition" by
artist Mary McSweeney. Also, pen-
and-ink prints (8 1/2"x11") and
notelets with illustrations taken from
Irish life, scenery and culture. Send
$1 for catalog.

CELTIC CRAFT
294 East 204th Street
Bronx, NY 10467
(212) 231-1210

Stocks bilingual Gaelic/English
birthday and Christmas cards.

BRAD BENNETT STUDIO
405 65th Street
Kenosha, WI 53140
(414) 652-9443

Offers greeting cards created from
original watercolors of Irish scenes
painted by Mr. Bennett, whose work
has an international reputation among
art collectors.

**IMMIGRATION & NATURAL-
IZATION – LEGAL COUNSEL
& ASSISTANCE**

**JAMES PATRICK CASEY,
ATTORNEY**
Law Offices of Joel H. Golub
1301 Post Street
San Francisco, CA 94109
(415) 928-0815

**JAMES M. BYRNE,
ATTORNEY**
785 Market Street
San Francisco, CA 94103
(415) 777-4444

**GEORGE A. FINNAN,
ATTORNEY**
463 Pacific Avenue
San Francisco, CA 94133
(415) 398-1823

**DAMIAN B. SMITH,
ATTORNEY**
220 Montgomery
San Francisco, CA 94104
(415) 434-2285

**WILLIAM D. McCANN &
ASSOCIATES**
800 South Broadway
Walnut Creek, CA 94596
(415) 932-7500

**PAUL SHEARMAN ALLEN,
IMMIGRATION LAWYERS**
1625 K Street, N.W.
Washington, DC 20006
(202) 638-2777

**JAMES R. FINNERTY,
ATTORNEY**
205 West Wacker Drive
Chicago, IL 60606
(312) 341-1636

**MARY E. FRANKLIN &
ASSOCIATES, INC.**
Immigration & Naturalization
Consultants
29 S. LaSalle
Chicago, IL 60603
(312) 726-4053

**THOMAS J. SCULLY,
ATTORNEY**
53 West Jackson Boulevard - # 636
Chicago, IL 60604
(312) 663-1090

**ROY WATSON, JR.,
ATTORNEY**
141 Tremont Street
Boston, MA 02111
(617) 423-0968

**BLANE & FRANK,
ATTORNEYS**
4808 Bergenline Avenue
Union City, NJ 07087
(201) 863-9000; in New York City,
call (212) 947-8889

Practice limited to immigration. Free
telephone consultation.

**FREDERICK J. DENNEHY,
ATTORNEY**
900 Route #9
Woodbridge, NJ 07095
(201) 636-8000

**BURKE, BURKE & BURKE,
ATTORNEYS**
147 West 42nd Street
New York, NY 10036
(212) 944-8888

Offers Saturday consultations.

S.D. JEFFRIES, ATTORNEY
Suite 1932
250 West 57th Street
New York, NY 10107
(212) 315-0790

JOHN L. PINNIX, ATTORNEY
Barringer, Allen and Pinnix
P.O. Drawer 1270
Raleigh, NC 27602
(919) 755-0505

JOHN L. PINNIX, ATTORNEY
Barringer, Allen, Pinnix & Burwell
605 NCNB Plaza
Greenville, SC 29601
(803) 232-1045

H. FRED FORD, ATTORNEY
Parkway Towers - Suite 1812
Nashville, TN 37219
(615) 244-3601

IMPORTS – BUSINESSES OFFERING A VARIED SELECTION BY MAIL ONLY

**SAINT BRENDAN'S CELTIC
DESIGN**
1000 Mariposa Street
San Francisco, CA 94107

Request free color catalog.

GATEWAY TO IRELAND
Box 403
Greenwich, CT 06830-0403
(203) 531-7400

Request free catalog, Best of Ireland.
(See advertisement on page 214.)

**THE TALBOT'S IRISH
COLLECTION**
Hingham, MA 02043
(800) 225-8200

Offers classic women's and men's
clothing and accessories from Ireland:
Donegal tweeds, Aran knits and other
woolens; lace and linen items. One-
year catalog subscription : $3.

CELTIC CROSSROADS
96 Stone Hill Road
Pound Ridge, NY 10576
(914) 764-5507

Call or write for free catalog, which
has wide selection of Waterford and
Belleek.

IMPORTS – SHOPS OFFERING A VARIED SELECTION OF IRISH PRODUCTS ON PREMISES

THE IRISH SHOP OF JUNEAU
175 South Franklin Street
Juneau, AK 99801
(907) 586-6055

FLYNN'S GIFTS/ALL THINGS IRISH
1710 West Camelback
Phoenix, AZ 85015
(602) 242-8650

THE IRISH SHOP
334 2nd Street
Eureka, CA 95501
(707) 443-8343

OLD WORLD IRISH SHOP
7561 Center Drive
Unit 64, Front
Huntington Beach, CA 92647
(714) 891-5066

THE IRISH IMPORT SHOP
4124 Beverly Boulevard
Los Angeles, CA 90004
(213) 387-0107

THE IRISH SHOP OF MENDOCINO
45090 Main Street
P.O. Box 1636
Mendocino, CA 95460
(707) 937-3133

SHAMROCK IMPORTS
7949 Laurel Canyon Boulevard
North Hollywood, CA 91605
(818) 764-3935 or 765-9078

TIPPERARY FINE IRISH IMPORTS
5510 College Avenue
Oakland, CA 94618
(415) 428-9222

HOUSE OF IRELAND
238 O'Farrell
San Francisco, CA 94102
(415) 781-1900

IRISH CASTLE GIFT SHOP
2123 Market Street
San Francisco, CA 94114
(415) 621-2200

IRISH IMPORTS
3157 Geary Boulevard
San Francisco, CA 94118
(415) 752-0961

THE KILKENNY SHOP
Ghirardelli Square
900 North Point
San Francisco, CA 94109
(415) 771-8984

TIPPERARY IMPORTS
555 Long Wharf Drive
New Haven, CT 06519
(203) 562-8864

THE THREE-PENNY BIT
3122 M Street, N.W.
Washington, DC 20007
(202) 338-1338

SHAMROCK IMPORT SHOP
429 Branmar Plaza
1812 Marsh Road at Silverside
Wilmington, DE 19810
(302) 475-7117

IRISH IMPORTS GALORE, LTD.
403 Golf View Drive
Boca Raton, FL 33432
(305) 421-6660

MY IRISH COTTAGE
3302 N.E. 33rd Street
Fort Lauderdale, FL 33308
(305) 564-5542

TIERNEY'S IRISH IMPORTS
9825-22 San Jose Boulevard
Jacksonville, FL 32217
(904) 268-0851

KENNEDY'S IRISH COTTAGE
Old Street
P.O. Box 233
Helen, GA 30545
(404) 878-2489

CARA HOUSE LTD.
Ice House Mall
200 Appletree Street
Barrington, IL 60010
(312) 381-3262

DONEGAL IRISH IMPORTS
5358 West Devon Avenue
Chicago, IL 60646
(312) 792-2337

IRELAND HOUSE
132 East Delaware Place
Chicago, IL 60646
(312) 337-2711

IRISH IMPORTS (TEAHAN'S)
2505 North Harlem Avenue
Chicago, IL 60635
(312) 637-3800

SHAMROCK IMPORTS
3150 North Laramie
Chicago, IL 60641
(312) 286-6866

SOUTH SIDE IRISH IMPORTS
3234 West 111th Street
Chicago, IL 60655
(312) 881-8585

MAGGIE'S IRISH IMPORTS
Crystal Lake Plaza
Crystal Lake, IL 60014
(815) 459-1800

HYNES IRISH COTTAGE, LTD.
18218 Harwood Avenue
Homewood, IL 60430
(312) 957-5850

GALLO AND WARD IMPORTS
Louis Joliet Mall
Joliet, IL 60435
(815) 439-1222

A TOUCH OF IRELAND
LaGrange Plaza
140 North LaGrange Road
LaGrange, IL 60525
(312) 579-3473

THE IRISH BOUTIQUE
434 Robert Parker Coffin Road
Long Grove, IL 60047
(312) 634-3540

A TOUCH OF IRELAND
Holiday Inn Arcade
4140 West 95th Street
Oak Lawn, IL 60543
(312) 422-3473

THE IRISH CONNOISSEUR
1232 Waukegan Road
Wilmette, IL 60025
(312) 998-1988

**HARP & SHAMROCK
DESIGNS**
3925 Shelbyville Road
Louisville, KY 40207
(502) 896-2351

THE GALWAY SHAWL
184 Massachusetts Avenue
Arlington, MA 02174
(617) 646-7111

THE IRISH PIPER SHOP
Copley Place
100 Huntington Avenue
Boston, MA 02116
(617) 247-0904

THE IRISH COTTAGE
1236 Burlington Mall
Burlington, MA 01803
(617) 272-1044

EMERALD ISLE
23 Drum Hill Road
Chelmsford, MA 01824
(617) 452-1614

**IRISH JAUNTING CAR
IMPORTS**
89 South Broadway
Lawrence, MA 01843
(617) 683-9007

BOREEN IRISH IMPORTS
9 Boston Street
Lynn, MA 01904
(617) 598-9286

THE LUCKY LEPRECHAUN
54 Court Street
Plymouth, MA 02360
(617) 747-4030

HOUSE OF IRELAND
17 Crescent Street
Waltham, MA 02154
(617) 899-7747

**IRISH COTTAGE IMPORT
GIFT STORE**
196 Apollo Road
Worcester, MA 01605
(617) 852-6532

THE IRISH CENTRE
120 Dock Street
Annapolis, MD 21401
(301) 267-9001

**IRISH COUNTRY STORE,
LTD.**
Harborplace
Baltimore, MD 21202
(301) 659-9304

IRISH IMPORTS
2302 Frederick Road
Catonsville, MD 21228
(301) 788-3700

IRISH IMPORTS, INC.
13251 Michigan Avenue
Dearborn, MI 48126
(313) 584-1404

THE IRISHMAN'S CORNER
Squire's Street Square
Rockford, MI 49341
(616) 866-9924

THE DUBLIN WALK
315 Nicollet Mall
Minneapolis, MN 55401
(612) 338-5203

IRISH TWEED SHOP
Mill Falls Marketplace
Meredith, NH 03253
(603) 279-4312

IRISH TWEED SHOP
Wolfeboro Marketplace
Wolfeboro, NH 03894
(603) 569-2169

**BALLYHUGH IRISH
IMPORTS**
235 South White Horse Pike
Audubon, NJ 08106
(609) 546-0946

ALL IRISH
Carpenter Square
31 Perry Street
P.O. Box 599
Cape May, NJ 08204
(609) 884-4484

ECHOES OF ERIN
1 Klickityklack Depot
Flemington Depot
Flemington, NJ 08822
(201) 782-2427

**CELTIC GALLERIES, INC.
IRISH QUALITY SHOP**
437 Kearny Avenue
Kearny, NJ 07032
(201) 997-3250

THE IRISH CENTRE
1120 Third Avenue
Spring Lake, NJ 07762
(201) 449-6650

IRISH IMPORTS
452 Springfield Avenue
Summit, NJ 07901
(201) 522-1811

THE THATCHED COTTAGE
648 Bloomfield Avenue
Verona, NJ 07044
(201) 239-0858

GUARANTEED IRISH
3605 Kingsbridge Avenue
Bronx, NY 10463
(212) 884-8239

**ALL IRELAND IRISH
IMPORTS**
8515 Third Avenue
Brooklyn, NY 11209
(718) 748-9240

ROCKAWAY IRISH IMPORTS
100-02 Rockaway Beach Boulevard
Brooklyn, NY 11694
(718) 474-8200

GUARANTEED IRISH
Route 145
East Durham, NY 12423
(518) 634-7409

LITTLE BIT OF IRELAND
Mullan's Mountain Spring Hotel
Sunside Road
East Durham, NY 12423
(518) 634-2541

QUEENS IRISH IMPORTS
72-12 Broadway
Jackson Heights, NY 11372
(718) 476-0633

THE CLADDAGH SHOP
252-24 Northern Boulevard
Little Neck, NY 11363
(718) 224-3500

TINKER'S IRISH IMPORTS
The Sheraton Hotel
70 Fulton Street
Middletown, NY 10940
(914) 343-5736

CELTIC CRAFT
294 East 204th Street
New York, NY 10465
(212) 231-1210

JEANNIE CAMPBELL'S IRISH SHOP
5008 Broadway
New York, NY 10034
(212) 567-9029

MATTIE HASKINS SHAMROCK IMPORTS
205 East 75th Street
New York, NY 10021
(212) 288-3918

TARA IRISH SHOP
609 West 207th Street
New York, NY 10034
(212) 569-8644

WILLIAMSON'S IRISH IMPORTS
South Street Seaport
New York, NY 10038
(212) 425-4331

COTTAGE IMPORTS
189 Main Street
Northport, NY 11768
(516) 754-2882

THE IRISH COTTAGE
20 South Main Street
Pearl River, NY 10965
(914) 735-9505

LLOYD'S IRISH IMPORT SHOP
3821 Ridge Road West
Rochester, NY 14626
(716) 225-1050

THE CLADDAGH SHOP
605 Forest Avenue
Staten Island, NY 10310
(718) 442-6400

THE LANCASTER SHOP
774 Castleton Avenue
Staten Island, NY 10310
(718) 273-2583

CASHEL HOUSE
224 Tompkins Street
Syracuse, NY 13204
(315) 472-4438

BROWNE'S IRISH IMPORTS
642 Willis Avenue
Williston Park, NY 11596
(516) 248-6342

IRISH IMPORT SHOP
334 Underhill Avenue
Yorktown Heights, NY 10598
(914) 962-7231

EMERALD IRISH IMPORTS
199 East 228th Street
Euclid, OH 44123
(216) 261-2207

EMERALD IRISH IMPORTS
14722 Detroit Avenue
Lakewood, OH 44107
(216) 221-3378

**KATHLEEN CONNOLLY
IRISH SHOP**
725 S.W. 10th Avenue
Portland, OR 97205
(503) 228-4482

THE IRISH SHOP
824 Lancaster Avenue
Bryn Mawr, PA 19010
(215) 527-1312

THE IRISH SHOP
279 Keswick Avenue
Glenside, PA 19038
(215) 576-5770

THE CELTIC PAVILION
5812 Route 202
Lahaska, PA 18931
(215) 794-3396

**THE GAELIC SHOP OF NEW
HOPE**
25 North Main Street
P.O. Box 6
New Hope, PA 18938
(215) 862-9285

TULLYCROSS
South Street at Hancock
Philadelphia, PA 19147
(215) 925-1995

IRISH DESIGN CENTER
303 South Craig
Pittsburgh, PA 15213
(412) 682-6125

ST. BRENDAN'S CROSSING
Station Square – #7
Pittsburgh, PA 15219
(402) 471-0700

THE TARA SHOP
30 Grant Avenue
Pittsburgh, PA 15223
(412) 781-1666

CROWLEY'S CELTIC MEWS
14619 River Forest Drive
Houston, TX 77079
(713) 493-4329

THE IRISH SHOP
2484 Bolsover
Houston, TX 77005
(713) 521-9270

ALL THINGS IRISH
New Saks Wing
1242 Northstar Mall
San Antonio, TX 78216
(512) 366-2627

THE IRISH WALK
Tavern Square
415 King Street
Alexandria, VA 22314
(703) 548-0118

GALWAY TRADERS
7518 15th Avenue, N.W.
Seattle, WA 98117
(206) 784-9343

THE HARP & SHAMROCK
2704 North Proctor
Tacoma, WA 98407
(206) 752-5012

WEE BIT OF IRELAND
400 Occidental Avenue South
Seattle, WA 98104
(206) 622-9111

INDUSTRIAL OPPORTUNITIES IN IRELAND – CONSULTANTS

PAN ATLANTIC RESOURCES, INC.
50 Exchange Street
Portland, ME 04101
(207) 871-8622

Ireland offers business advantages for manufacturing firms of all types. But no firm would want to invest large sums to open a plant *anywhere* before knowing all the pros and cons. Pan Atlantic, headed by Irish-born David Miley, has prepared feasibility, strategy and market research studies for several leading U.S. firms interested in Irish operations. PAR says opportunities are particularly good for small to medium-size firms. Contact David Miley for information on their services and fees.

INDUSTRIAL OPPORTUNITIES IN IRELAND – INFORMATION

Some 350 American companies now have plants in Ireland, among them such well-known names as IBM, Wang, Apple, Digital Equipment, Pfizer, Microsoft, Memorex and Land O'Lakes. The advantages they cite for their decisions to manufacture in Ireland include low taxes; generous government grants; and a young, technologically oriented labor force. (Ireland produces more college graduates *per capita* in computer science than the U.S.!) If you'd like more information about the general advantages of operating in Ireland, and the specific locations best suited to your company's needs, contact one of the U.S. offices of the Industrial Development Authority of Ireland, as follows:

IDA IRELAND
3000 Sand Hill Road
Building 1 – Suite 100
Menlo Park, CA 94025
(415) 854-1800

IDA IRELAND
1821 Wilshire Boulevard
Suite 317
Santa Monica, CA 90403
(213) 829-0081

IDA IRELAND
P.O. Box 11727
Atlanta, GA 30355
(404) 351-8474

IDA IRELAND
One East Wacker Drive
Suite 2130
Chicago, IL 60601
(312) 644-7474

IDA IRELAND
Three Center Plaza
Boston, MA 02108
(617) 367-8225

IDA IRELAND
Two Grand Central Tower
140 East 45th Street
New York, NY 10017
(212) 972-1000

IDA IRELAND
P.O. Box 22720
Cleveland, OH 44122
(216) 991-6055

IDA IRELAND
1990 Post Oak Boulevard
Suite 317
Houston, TX 77056
(713) 965-0292

**PRICE WATERHOUSE &
COMPANY**
1251 Avenue of the Americas
New York, NY 10019
(212) 489-8900

The Center for International Taxation
at this major international public
accounting firm publishes an informative booklet, *Doing Business in the
Republic of Ireland* (Information
Guide Series), to help promote the
consulting services it offers firms interested in possible ventures in Ireland.
You may request a copy by contacting
the firm as indicated above.

INDUSTRIAL OPPORTUNITIES IN NORTHERN IRELAND – INFORMATION

**INDUSTRIAL DEVELOPMENT
BOARD FOR NORTHERN
IRELAND**
845 Third Avenue
New York, NY 10022
(212) 593-2258

INTERIOR DESIGN – CELTIC-STYLE – FOR HOME, OFFICE OR BUSINESS

CELTIC IMAGE
14A Marine Road
South Boston, MA 02127
(617) 268-6702

Wall decoration using traditional Irish
motifs, such as those from the *Book of
Kells*. Charles Coit of Celtic Image
has decorated lobby walls at Harvard
University, among other commissions.

CELTIC FOLKWORKS
RD#4, Box 210
Willow Grove Road
Newfield, NJ 08344
(609) 691-5968

Bediah Baird, an accomplished graphic
artist specializing in Celtic design,
accepts commissions to decorate
business premises and other spaces.

INTERNATIONAL DELIVERY – EXPRESS LETTER & PARCEL SERVICE TO IRELAND

The following services offer express delivery of letters and packages from the United States to Ireland. Depending on where the delivery originates, and where it is to be made in Ireland, delivery may require as little as one or two days – or as many as four. Check with each service separately for rates, restrictions and other details. And make sure that the service has a facility near you – as well as offering delivery service to the specific place in Ireland you need:

DHL WORLDWIDE COURIER EXPRESS
(800) 225-5345

EXPRESS MAIL INTERNATIONAL SERVICE
United States Postal Service
(Contact your local post office)

FEDERAL EXPRESS
(800) 238-5355

PUROLATOR COURIER
(800) 645-3333

IRISH STUDIES – RESOURCES (See also "Books," "Directories," "Language Study – Gaelic," "Magazines & Journals – Irish-American" and "Organizations – Irish-American")

GREENWOOD PRESS
88 Post Road West
P.O. Box 5007
Westport, CT 06881
(203) 226-3571

GP will publish *Irish Research: A Guide to Collections in North America, Ireland and Great Britain*, by DeeGee Lester, in late 1986. Request price, details.

UNIVERSITY PRESS OF AMERICA
Box 19101
Washington, DC 20036
(301) 459-3366

The Irish-American Experience: A Guide to the Literature, edited by Seamus Metress and published in 1981 by UPA, is perhaps the best survey available of books and articles dealing with the Irish-American community in all its aspects, historical and contemporary. This 226-page work may be ordered in paperback for $12.25; or, with a library binding, for $24. Request free descriptive brochure.

AMERICAN COMMITTEE FOR IRISH STUDIES (ACIS)
c/o Maureen O'R. Murphy, VP
Dean of Students
Hofstra University
1000 Fulton Avenue
Hempstead, NY 11550
(516) 560-6775

ACIS publishes *A Guide to Irish Studies in the United States,* which is revised at intervals, with a new edition due in 1986. This excellent directory surveys, state by state and institution by institution, courses currently taught in various aspects of Irish Studies. It covers both public and private colleges and universities. Most courses come under such disciplines as history, political science, languages, literature, folklore and sociology; some are interdisciplinary. Single copies of the *Guide* are available to non-members of ACIS either free or at a nominal charge, depending on whether a particular edition has been subsidized by a grant-making organization. Contact Dean Murphy for current information.

JEWELRY – TRADITIONAL DESIGNS
(See also "Crafts & Craftspeople – Traditional")

BILL DOWLING
243 North Willow
West Covina, CA 91790
(818) 338-7400

Claddagh rings and pendants; Celtic cross items. Available in 9 and 14 carat gold as well as silver. Request prices and details.

CELTIC JEWELERS
1305 West Northwest Highway
Arlington Heights, IL 60004
(312) 577-5023

Selections include Claddagh rings and earrings; Celtic crosses; etc.

ALL THINGS IRISH
P.O. Box 94
Glenview, IL 60025
(312) 998-4510

Imports Claddagh jewelry and other Irish items in Sterling silver and 9 and 14 carat gold. Many items feature Connemara marble and marcasites. Sells at both wholesale and retail. Request free color catalog.

IRISH CHARM LTD.
P.O. Box 3464
Merchandise Mart Station
Chicago, IL 60654
(312) 670-0150

Imported silver and gold diamond and Claddagh rings.

T.G. MURPHY JEWELRY
619 East Broadway
South Boston, MA 02127
(617) 268-0033

Claddagh rings in 10 and 14 carat gold.

KENNY JEWELERS
308 Main Street
Avon-By-The-Sea, NJ 07717
(201) 775-3336

Offers a wide choice of gold and silver

jewelry in traditional Irish designs, including Claddagh items; St. Brigid's and Celtic crosses; Tara brooches; and harps. Request free color brochure.

MUNSTER
P.O. Box 322
Bronxville, NY 10708

Sells a gold-filled pendant containing an antique Irish pence coin. $18 postpaid.

FINBAR ENTERPRISES
P.O. Box 317
Gardiner, NY 12525
(914) 476-0633

Sells shamrock and Claddagh charms and Claddagh rings in 14 carat gold. Request details.

QUEENS IRISH IMPORTS
72-12 Broadway
Jackson Heights, NY 11372
(718) 476-0633

Claddagh rings, pendants and earrings; Celtic crosses; and St. Brigid's crosses. Available in 14 carat gold or Sterling silver.

TULLYCROSS
South Street at Hancock
Philadelphia, PA 19147
(215) 925-1995

Hand-crafted and -finished jewelry, including Claddagh items; Celtic and St. Brigid's crosses; and pieces modelled after *Book of Kells* designs. Free catalog.

LANGUAGE STUDY – GAELIC – INSTRUCTION OFFERED BY COLLEGES & OTHER ORGANIZATIONS

If you're learning Gaelic for the first time, a live teacher will normally be more effective than a recorded course. Hundreds of colleges and universities throughout the U.S. offer Gaelic instruction. If you live in a large metropolitan area, you might try calling various local institutions of higher learning. (The American Committee for Irish Studies publishes a comprehensive directory of such courses. See "Irish Studies – Resources")

Instruction is also available through many local Irish-American organizations and private teachers. Consult announcements in Irish-American newspapers serving your area or contact local organizations.

LANGUAGE STUDY – GAELIC – MATERIALS FOR SELF-INSTRUCTION

EDUCATIONAL SERVICES
1725 K Street, NW - 408
Washington, DC 20006
(202) 298-8424

Sells a newly published course in Irish Gaelic prepared and recorded by Coilin Owens, a teacher at George Mason University. Two cas-settes provide 1 1/2 hours of lessons and guided practice in commonly used words and phrases. Topics covered include traditional music, dances, pub culture, seasonal greetings, festivals, religion, theatre, sports and pastimes. The course comes in a vinyl album with a phrase dictionary. Price: $14.95.

AN DROICHEAD/THE BRIDGE
c/o Ull Mor
3 York Street
New York, NY 10013

This recently inaugurated magazine is perhaps the only English-Gaelic publication easily available to Americans studying Gaelic – or interested in refreshing their knowledge of it. *An Droichead,* which is published quarterly, covers a wide range of cultural material, from poetry, drama and short stories to painting, photography, film, sculpture, crafts, music, natural history, new books and book people. Each article appears in Gaelic with parallel English text and extensive photos and illustrations. Order a one-year subscription to the magazine alone for $12. Or, for $40 ($42.31 in N.Y.State), receive not only the magazine itself, but a cassette with each issue containing the entire contents read in Gaelic by native speakers of the language. (See advertisement on page 228.)

CONVERSA-PHONE INSTITUTE, INC.
1 Commack Loop
Ronkonkoma, NY 11779
(516) 467-0600

Offers a one-record introductory course in Irish Gaelic, including 20 lessons with an instruction manual. Request details.

LINGUAPHONE
World Language Courses, Inc.
313 Nolana Avenue
McAllen, TX 78504
(800) 531-7505; in Texas,
(512) 687-6761

Linguaphone's Irish Gaelic course consists of 30 lessons prepared and recorded by native speakers. They cover both beginning and intermediate levels, and are recorded on audio-cassette. Three illustrated textbooks and a carrying case are also provided.

The course costs approximately $150. Request free brochure.

LIBRARIES & RESEARCH FACILITIES
(See also "Irish Studies – Resources")

Following are some of the more important Irish research collections in the U.S. If you're doing serious research as a student, scholar or journalist, you will normally receive permission to use a collection by writing the chief librarian:

SAMFORD UNIVERSITY
Harwell G. Davis Library
800 Lakeshore Drive
Birmingham, AL 35209

19th and 20th-century materials on Ireland.

UNITED IRISH CULTURAL CENTER OF SAN FRANCISCO
2700 45th Avenue
San Francisco, CA 94116
(415) 661-2700

90,000 volumes covering Irish history; drama; poetry and other literature; folklore; genealogy; and the 32 counties. Irish and Irish-American newspapers and periodicals are also available.

UNIVERSITY OF CHICAGO
The University Library
Department of Special Collections
1100 East 57th Street
Chicago, IL 60637
(312) 753-4308

Social and cultural history of Ireland, 17th-19th centuries.

COLBY COLLEGE
Library – Special Collections
Waterville, ME 04901
(207) 873-1131

Literary manuscripts and other papers of 19th and 20th century Irish authors, including Shaw.

BOSTON COLLEGE
Bapst Library – Irish Collection
Chestnut Hill, MA 02167
(617) 969-0100

7,500 books and several dozen journals and serials. Collection covers Irish political and social history; art; archaeology; education; government; and literature – Gaelic and Anglo-Irish.

COLLEGE OF ST. THOMAS
The Celtic Collection
c/o The Library
St. Paul, MN 55105

Collection includes nearly 5,000 items covering history, literature, folklore and philology.

SETON HALL UNIVERSITY
The McManus Collection
McLaughlin Library
405 South Orange Avenue
South Orange, NJ 07079
(201) 762-9000

4,000 volumes on Irish literature, history and politics – particularly the Home Rule question. Also: autographs, clippings and correspondence.

AMERICAN IRISH HISTORICAL SOCIETY
991 Fifth Avenue
New York, NY 10028
(212) 228-2263

Holdings include manuscript collections and archives dealing with Irish individuals, families and organizations, mainly from the 19th and 20th centuries.

ELIZABETH SETON COLLEGE
The Library
1061 North Broadway
Yonkers, NY 10701
(914) 969-4000

Irish music manuscripts.

LIFE INSURANCE – FRATERNAL

HIBERNIAN LIFE INSURANCE
790 South Cleveland Avenue
Suite 221
St. Paul, MN 55116
(612) 690-3888

Originally founded by the Minnesota Ladies' Auxiliary, Ancient Order of Hibernians (AOH), Hibernian Life now administers all life insurance programs offered by AOH units throughout the U.S. The company offers three types of whole-life policies, which are available to any or all family members: (1) whole-life policies requiring premium payments until age 85; (2) policies requiring a single, lump-sum premium payment; and (3) 20-pay whole-life policies, whose total premiums are paid over a 20-year period. HLI is licensed to sell policies by mail to residents of all 50 states, and also sells to Chicago-area residents through a local agency. Contact HLI for details on eligibility requirements and insurance application forms. (See advertisement on this page; Hibernian Life also funds two scholarship programs of special interest to Irish-Americans. See "Scholarships.")

LINENS -- IMPORTED

CARR & PAYNTER
P.O. Box 592
Harrison, NY 10528
(914) 967-8358

U.S. distributor for Fingal Irish Linen products. Imports pure linen tea towels in about 50 colorfast designs, including traditional blessings, recipes, maps, calendars and pictures. The towels also make attractive wall hangings. Also distributes Irish linen damask tablecloths in various sizes and designs. These items are commonly carried by import shops (See "Imports"). Although it doesn't sell directly to the public, Carr & Paynter will be pleased to refer you to a dealer near you that handles its products.

ULSTER WEAVING COMPANY, LTD.
148 Madison Avenue
New York, NY 10016
(212) 684-5534

Importer and wholesale distributor of household linens and piece goods made in Ireland by its parent company. These include large selections of table linen, with many items incorporating Celtic designs; printed tea towels, including maps of Ireland, stories of Irish traditions, Irish verse and blessings; guest towels; and men's and women's handkerchiefs, including many hand-embroidered and lace-edged items. Ulster Weaving will give you the names of stores in your area that stock its products.

MAGAZINES & JOURNALS – IRISH-AMERICAN

ADRIFT
c/o Irish American Cultural Project
239 East 5th Street – #4D
New York, NY 10003

A semi-annual journal devoted to original works by new Irish and Irish-American poets and writers. Also includes reviews of new works. $7/yr. for two issues; $3.50 per single issue.

AN GAEL
c/o The Irish Arts Center
553 West 51st Street
New York, NY 10019
(212) 757-3318

An illustrated quarterly devoted to traditional Irish culture and its perpetuation and revival in America. Subscriptions: $10/yr.; $11 in Canada; $12 elsewhere.

DUCAS
c/o The Irish American Cultural Institute
2115 Summit Avenue
Box 5026
St. Paul, MN 55105
(612) 647-5678

A newsletter devoted to brief items on Irish and Irish-American history, culture and miscellany as well as IACI news. Issued eight times a year, in months when *Eire-Ireland* (see below) is not published. A subscription is included with membership in the Irish American Cultural Institute @ $25/yr. (tax-deductible).

EIRE-IRELAND
c/o Irish American Cultural Institute
2115 Summit Avenue
Box 5026
St. Paul, MN 55105
(612) 647-5678

A scholarly journal of Irish studies
covering history, music, literature,
traditional Irish culture, folklore, etc.
A four-issue subscription – plus eight
issues of *Ducas* (see above) – is
included with membership in IACI @
$25/yr. (tax-deductible).

FOLK HARP JOURNAL
P.O. Box 161
Mt. Laguna, CA 92048

A quarterly journal covering all aspects
of this traditional Irish and Celtic
instrument: its history and evolution;
its construction; playing techniques;
music written for it; and contemporary
use throughout the world. Subscriptions: $12/yr. (U.S.); $14 elsewhere.
Request free descriptive flyer.

IRISH AMERICA
P.O. Box 5141
Grand Central Station
New York, NY 10163
(212) 725-2993/2994

This attractive new monthly, started in
1985, is the first magazine in the
United States devoted to regular news
coverage and features of Irish-
American interest. Subscriptions: $20/
yr.; $36/two yrs. A growing number
of newsstands and Irish import shops
also carry this publication. (See
advertisement on page opposite inside
front cover.)

**IRISH LITERARY
SUPPLEMENT**
Attn.: Robert G. Lowery, Editor
114 Paula Boulevard
Selden, NY 11784
(516) 698-8243

Published twice yearly, ILS contains
literary criticism and reviews of recent
works of Irish or Irish-American
history, poetry, drama, fiction,
literature and literary criticism. Covers
about 75 books per issue from Irish,
American and British publishers. Also
publishes news of the Irish literary
world and of happenings of interest to
readers of Irish literature.
Subscriptions: $5/ yr. for two issues.

IRISH STUDIES
Cambridge University Press
32 East 57th Street
New York, NY 10022
(212) 688-8885

An annual interdisciplinary journal
presenting research on Ireland by
leading scholars in such fields as
history, economics, literature, politics
and sociology. Each volume is
devoted to a central unifying theme,
such as "Ireland: Land, Politics and
People;" "Ireland and the European
Community;" and "The Irish in
America." Current prices are $30 per
volume for individuals; $55 for
institutions. Back volumes are
available.

JAMES JOYCE QUARTERLY
The University of Tulsa
Tulsa, OK 74104

Offers critical essays on the works of
Joyce and other major Irish writers as

well as notes, book reviews and checklists. Individual subscriptions (U.S.) – $12/yr., $23.50/two yrs.; for institutions – $13/yr., $25.50/ two yrs.

JOURNAL OF IRISH LITERATURE
Proscenium Press
P.O. Box 361
Newark, DE 19711

An irregular title, normally issued once or twice a year. Publishes poetry, drama, fiction, literary criticism, book reviews and bibliographies of Irish interest. Subscriptions: $12/yr. for individuals; $18 for institutions. Back issues are available. Request free price list.

MAILING LISTS – IRISH-AMERICAN

AMERICAN COMMITTEE FOR IRISH STUDIES (ACIS)
Mary Helen Thuente, Secretary
c/o Department of English
Indiana University
Fort Wayne, IN 46805
(219) 481-6841

The ACIS membership list contains over 1,200 names, mostly teachers and scholars in the humanities and social sciences. Members share a common interest and specialty: Ireland and/or Irish America.

DIRECT COMMUNICATIONS
Attn.: Chris Mayka
75 Main Street
Fair Haven, VT 05743
(802) 265-8144

This firm brokers a variety of lists, including U.S. subscriber lists for *Ireland of the Welcomes; Irish America,* and *The Irish Echo;* and mail-order customer lists for such businesses as Gateway to Ireland, Genuine Irish and Rego Irish Records & Tapes. Most lists require a minimum order of 5,000 names; and rental is subject to approval by the owner or its represent-ative. Request details on available lists, formats, prices, etc.

MAPS – ANTIQUE

GEORGE RITZLIN BOOKS & MAPS
P.O. Box 6066
Evanston, IL 60204
(312) 328-1966

Rare maps, atlases and books. Mr. Ritzlin's wife is a McMichael by birth, so he tries to keep old Irish items in stock but finds that they sell quickly.

THE ARGOSY BOOK STORE
116 East 59th Street
New York, NY 10022
(212) PL3-4455

Stocks a good selection of maps of Ireland (and parts of Ireland) published between the 16th and the 19th centuries. Will send items on appro-val: you send payment for what you keep, if anything – and return the rest undamaged, without obligation.

MAPS & TRAVEL GUIDES – CONTEMPORARY

PHILEAS FOGG'S BOOKS AND MAPS FOR THE TRAVELER
540 University Avenue
Palo Alto, CA 94301
(415) 327-1754

Maps and travel guides to Ireland.

MASON MAP SERVICE
553 West Las Tunas Drive
San Gabriel, CA 91776
(213) 281-8757

RAND McNALLY MAP STORE
595 Market Street at 2nd
San Francisco, CA 94105
(415) 777-3131

RAND McNALLY MAP STORE
23 East Madison
Chicago, IL 60602
(312) 267-6868

AMERICAN MAP CORPORATION
46-35 54th Road
Maspeth, NY 11378
(718) 784-0055

Request free 35-page catalog.

FACSIMILE BOOK SHOP
16 West 55th Street
New York, NY 10019
(212) 581-2672

Carries several road maps of Ireland as well as specialized maps.

RAND McNALLY MAP STORE
10 East 53rd Street
New York, NY 10022
(212) 751-6300

FORSYTH TRAVEL LIBRARY
P.O. Box 2975
9154 West 57th Street
Shawnee Mission, KS 66201

Request free descriptive price list, which includes several maps and travel guides to Ireland.

WIDE WORLD BOOKS & MAPS
401 N.E. 45th Street
Seattle, WA 98105
(206) 634-3453

Travel books, guides, and maps of Ireland including the Ordnance Survey maps, which show topographical features and are ideal for hikers. Also, atlases of Ireland and roadmaps published by Bartholomew's, Michelin and Geographia. Contact for further details.

MOVERS – OVERSEAS – SPECIALISTS IN SHIPMENTS BETWEEN U.S. & IRELAND, INCLUDING HOUSEHOLD & OFFICE RELOCATIONS

GROVE STORAGE COMPANY
7001 South Chicago Avenue
Chicago, IL 60637
(312) 624-7200; (800) 348-2187

JOHN RYAN TRUCKING, INC.
4838 North Paulina Street
Chicago, IL 60640
(312) 334-6749

AIR-SEA-PAC
2300 East Higgins Road
Elk Grove, IL 60007
(312) 640-8033

MOVERS INTERNATIONAL
1337 Industrial Drive
Itasca, IL 60143
(312) 773-3772

OVERSEAS MOVING SPECIALISTS, INC.
112 North 12th Street
Brooklyn, NY 11211
(718) 963-4200; (800) 631-4911
outside New York State

OMEGA SHIPPING COMPANY
176-24 148th Street
Jamaica, NY 11434
(718) 656-7630; (800) 232-0037
outside New York State

INTERNATIONAL PACKING & REMOVALS LTD.
37-31 10th Street
Long Island City, NY 11101
(718) 721-3000

LIFFEY MOVERS
336 East 73rd Street
New York, NY 10021
(212) 794-2795

LYNCH INTERNATIONAL, INC.
34-37 65th Street
P.O. Box 1112
Woodside, NY 11377
(718) 672-8900; Call toll-free
(800) 672-7266 from other A/Cs

Serves the Boston and Philadelphia areas as well as Greater New York.

MUSEUMS

THE HOUSE OF IRELAND
Balboa Park
San Diego, CA 92101
(619) 466-7654

This authentic replica of a rural Irish cottage dates from the 1930s. Open Sundays from 1:30 to 4:30, the cottage is the focus of musical, song, artistic, dance and other activities designed to preserve and promote an appreciation of Ireland's traditional culture. Tea and soda bread are served to visitors in the Kennedy Kitchen.

UNITED IRISH CULTURAL CENTER OF SAN FRANCISCO

2700 45th Avenue
San Francisco, CA 94116
(415) 661-2700

The Center's impressive All-Irish Library, which houses about 90,000 books, periodicals and other items, also maintains a mini-museum that displays Irish artifacts and paintings.

MUSEUM OF FINE ARTS

465 Huntington Avenue
Boston, MA 02115
(617) 267-9300

MFA exhibits items representing various aspects and periods of Irish culture. On display are ancient Celtic ornaments; Irish lace; Irish silver; portraits by John Singleton Copley, who became an expatriate in London but had been born in Boston of Irish descent; paintings by Yeats; Irish Chippendale furniture; and a Waterford crystal chandelier.

DETROIT INSTITUTE OF ARTS

5200 Woodward Avenue
Detroit, MI 48202
(313) 833-7900

Among the Institute's many excellent exhibits is North America's largest collection of ancient Irish gold jewelry from the pre-Celtic Bronze Age period (2000 B.C. to 200 B.C.).

NEW YORK STATE IRISH AMERICAN HISTORY MUSEUM

The Neil Hellman Library
College of Saint Rose
979 Madison Avenue
Albany, NY 12203
(518) 454-5180

Founded with a State grant, this new museum is housed temporarily at the College of Saint Rose. A panel of Irish-American state legislators will pick a permanent site. For now, the museum will concentrate on acquiring books and periodicals on Irish affairs and history, which will be available to students, scholars and the public. It will also host Irish-American events. Exhibits depicting aspects of the Irish and Irish-American experiences will be assembled and installed.

THE IRISH CLASSROOM

The Cathedral of Learning
University of Pittsburgh
Pittsburgh, PA 15213

One of 18 "international classrooms" grouped around the Commons Room of the Cathedral of Learning, the Irish Classroom – the only stone room –features elements from both northern and southern Ireland. It has the shape, size and materials of a sixth-century Irish oratory, or small chapel. The vestibule entrance is copied from Killeshin Chapel, County Laois.

MUSICAL INSTRUMENTS –
TRADITIONAL –
INSTRUCTION

There are clearly many more individuals who teach traditional Irish instruments than those listed here. Many of these will be identified and included in our next edition. Meanwhile, you may also be able to locate suitable instructors through local Irish centers and societies, including chapters of Comhaltas Ceoltoiri Eireann, the Traditional Irish Musicians Association. (See "Organizations – Irish-American – National"):

WORLD OF STRINGS
1738 East 7th Street
Long Beach, CA 90813
(213) 599-3913

Will arrange Irish fiddling lessons.

LAURIE RILEY
Mendocino, CA
(707) 964-5569

Celtic harp instruction. Beginning and experienced players welcome.

PHIL WHITE
San Diego, CA
(619) 222-4606

Lessons on the uillean pipes.

CAIT REED
San Francisco, CA
(415) 661-7358

Irish fiddling lessons for children of all ages; solo and groups for adults.

SUE RICHARDS
Washington, DC and suburbs
(301) 424-9239

Lessons in Irish harp for children and adults.

NOEL RICE SCHOOL OF IRISH MUSIC
Irish American Heritage Center
2540 Happy Hollow Road
Glenview, IL 60025
(312) 564-1338

Beginning and advanced classes in flute, fiddle, accordion, Irish harp, tin whistle, bodhran drums, concertina, bagpipe and Uillean pipes.

JOHN WILLIAMS
3632 West 61st Street
Chicago, IL 60629
(312) 585-5264

Accordion. Concertina. Tin whistle. Flute.

MICHAEL FLATLEY
12000 South 93rd Street
Palos Park, IL 60464
(312) 448-4448

Flute instruction.

MARY MEYER
10475 Doris Court
Rosemont, IL 60018
(312) 699-6471

Tin whistle.

BILLY CAPLES
Boston, MA area
(617) 646-5211

Accordion.

SEAMUS CONNOLLY
Boston, MA area
(617) 926-8170

Irish fiddling.

EAMON FLYNN
Boston, MA area
(617) 327-8723

Irish fiddling.

ROBERT GRADY
Boston, MA area
(617) 298-0429

Bodhran.

JOE JOYCE
Boston, MA area
(617) 325-8386

Accordion.

WILLIE MAHON
Boston, MA area
(617) 491-8556

Flute.

DAVID O'DOHERTY
Boston, MA area
(617) 876-1471

Flute.

MAIREAD O'DOHERTY
Boston, MA area
(617) 653-7480

Irish harp.

MICHAEL QUINLIN
Boston, MA area
(617) 254-2179

Flute.

GOLDEN FLYN
637 56th Street
Brooklyn, NY 11220
(718) 839-2595

Accordion. Tin whistle. Flute.

THE TOMMY DOYLE SCHOOL
Long Island, NY
(516) 826-9017 or
783-1424 (after 5 p.m.)

Private and group classes in Irish
button accordion, tin whistle, banjo
and other traditional instruments.

BILL OCHS
New York, NY
(212) 247-3231

Tin whistle and Uillean pipes for
adults. Small groups. No musical
background required.

ROSALYN BRILEY
Philadelphia, PA
(215) 697-7348

Harp instruction.

MARK CARROLL
Philadelphia, PA and vicinity
(215) 482-1957

Teaches harp, hammered dulcimer, tin
whistle and anglo concertina.

MUSIC BARN, INC.
625 West Street Road
Warminster, PA 18974
(215) 674-5505

Lessons in traditional Irish and Celtic
harp-playing.

**MUSICAL INSTRUMENTS –
TRADITIONAL – SOURCES**

CASWELL HARPS
14690 Carrier Lane
Guerneville, CA 95446
(707) 869-0997

A highly rated maker of ancient and
neo-Celtic harps. Also sells hardware,
strings and accessories. Request free
catalog.

LARK IN THE MORNING
Box 1176
Mendocino, CA 95460
(707) 964-5569

Irish harps by Caswell and Witcher.
Uillean and other bagpipes.
Bodhrans. Concertinas. Irish-style
flutes. Hammered dulcimers. Send
$2.50 for catalog.

**DRAGONWHISPERS BY
BETTY R. TRUITT**
P.O. Box 211
Sunrise Highway
Mt. Laguna, CA 92048
(619) 473-9010

Handcrafted folk harps, including
Irish, neo-Irish and Celtic styles in
sizes from 3 to 5 feet high. Harps may
be custom-carved, painted and
decorated to your specifications. Also
sells harp stands; strings; electronic
tuners. You may visit the workshop
by appointment. Request free product
literature.

ROBINSON'S HARP SHOP
P.O. Box 161
Mt. Laguna, CA 92048
(619) 473-8556

This shop, operated by Roland
Robinson, makes harps and harp components in a variety of styles and sizes.
Robinson's also publishes plans for
building harps, and sells instruction
books, harp strings and recorded harp
music. Roland Robinson was instrumental (no pun intended!) in establishing the Society of Folk Harpers and
Craftsmen and the *Folk Harp Journal*.
Request free brochure covering harps,
books, records and cassettes.

**IRISH ACCORDIONS &
RECORDS**
1357 Geary Boulevard
San Francisco, CA 94118
(415) 752-0961

Harps handmade by Brian McGirr, a
highly regarded craftsman in County
Tyrone; accordions; bodhrans; and tin
whistles. Also: instruction books and
instrumental music collections.

FOLK MOTE MUSIC
31 West Canon Perdido
Santa Barbara, CA 93101
(805) 962-0830

Specialists in traditional Irish instruments, including bodhrans, harps, bouzoukis, tin whistles and hammered dulcimers. Also: books of traditional Irish music; records and tapes. Harp lessons available. Request free catalog.

TRIPLETT HARPS
325 East Cabrillo Boulevard - #1
Santa Barbara, CA 93101
(805) 966-5489

Manufactures and repairs folk harps and hammered dulcimers. Also offers kits; assembled instruments that require finishing; books; records; and tapes. Request free catalog.

HOBGOBLIN MUSIC
P.O. Box 5311
South San Francisco, CA 94080
(415) 991-4040

Stocks traditional musical instruments and supplies, both Irish and other. These include fiddles; Uillean pipes; bodhrans; Caswell harps and harp kits; accordions; concertinas; melodeons; and bones. Also carries a limited selection of records; song and tune books; and used instruments. Request free catalog.

KEVIN J. O'DWYER, HANDCRAFTED MUSICAL INSTRUMENTS
P.O. Box 9303
Savannah, GA 31412
(912) 238-5206

Stocks a variety of fine traditional instruments, handmade by leading craftsmen in Ireland, Britain and the U.S. Included in O'Dwyer's stock are Uillean (and other) pipes; bodhrans; bones; bouzoukis and citterns; button accordions; concertinas; flageolets; flutes; harps; mandolins; and tin whistles. Request descriptive price list.

HOUSE OF MUSICAL TRADITIONS
7040 Carroll Avenue
Takoma Park, MD 20912
(301) 270-9090

Traditional Celtic instruments, books, recordings. Catalog: $2.

CASTIGLIONE ACCORDION COMPANY
P.O. Box 05369
12644 East Seven Mile Road
Detroit, MI 48205
(313) 527-1595

Shamrock accordions and other brands. Irish musette tuning. Write or call collect for catalog.

FEADAN, LTD.
P.O. Box 5244
Manchester, NH 03108
(603) 434-2426

Irish tin whistles.

ANNE HABERMEHL, AG
3925 North Main
Marion, NY 14505
(315) 926-5318

Fine traditional Irish metal-strung
harps by Witcher. Request free
literature.

DEIRO'S MUSIC HEADQUARTERS
123 Greenwich Avenue
New York, NY 10014
(212) 675-5460

Irish folk harps. Bodhrans.
Pennywhistles. Concertinas.
Bagpipes. Uillean pipes. Music
books. Reeds.

IMBUSCH HARPS
c/o Kevin Imbusch
86 West 12th Street – #1E
New York, NY 10011
(212) 691-7486

For decades, some of the world's
finest folk harps were made by George
Imbusch, who died in his native
Limerick in 1985. His son, Nial,
learned the craft from his father, and
now carries on the family tradition.
The "Imbusch harp" is 4 feet 6 inches
high, has a range of four octaves and
is completely handcrafted from the
finest woods. To acquire one – or
obtain further information – contact
Kevin Imbusch, another of George's
sons, as indicated above.

GEORGE BRITTON FOLK STUDIO
616 Germantown Pike
Lafayette Hill, PA 19444
(215) 828-7537 or 247-7802

Sales, rental and repair of traditional
Irish instruments, including bodhrans,
fiddles, Uillean pipes, Irish tenor
banjos, bones, concertinas and button
accordions. Lessons also given.
Contact for details.

BUCKS COUNTY FOLK MUSIC SHOP
40 Sand Road
New Britain, PA 18901
(215) 345-0616

Sells bodhrans; rosewood Irish
whistles; Irish bouzoukis; Irish harps;
pennywhistles; mandolins; concertinas;
rosewood and maple fifes; Irish books
and records.

THE MUSIC BARN
625 West Street Road
Warminster, PA 18974
(215) 674-5505

Irish and Celtic folk harps.

NEEDLE ARTS – TRADITIONAL IRISH TECHNIQUES & DESIGNS
(See also "Crafts & Craftspeople – Traditional")

IRISH CROCHET TREASURES
P.O. Box 1625
562 Milk Street
Fitchburg, MA 01420
(617) 342-1152

Imports woolen cushion covers embroidered with designs from the famous *Book of Kells*. Contact for sizes, prices and other information.

NEWSPAPERS & MAGAZINES – IMPORTED – NEWS DEALERS

HAROLD'S HOMETOWN NEWSSTAND
484 Geary
San Francisco, CA 94102
(415) 474-2937

IRISH IMPORTS
3157 Geary Boulevard
San Francisco, CA 94118
(415) 752-0961

DONEGAL IMPORTS
5358 West Devon Avenue
Chicago, IL 60646
(312) 792-2377

O'MALLEY'S CONVENIENT FOOD MART
5277 North Elston Avenue
Chicago, IL 60630
(312) 286-6866

SHANNON IMPORTS
5726 West 95th Street
Chicago, IL 60453
(312) 424-7055

OUT OF TOWN NEWS
Zero Harvard Square
Cambridge, MA 02138
(617) 354-7777

National and county newspapers – and selected magazines – flown in regularly from Ireland.

JEANNIE CAMPBELL'S IRISH STORE
508 Broadway
New York, NY 10034
(212) 567-9029

National and county newspapers from Ireland.

HOTALINGS NEWS AGENCY, INC.
Foreign News Depot
142 West 42nd Street
New York, NY 10036
(212) 840-1868

National and county newspapers flown in regularly from Ireland.

NEWSPAPERS & MAGAZINES – IMPORTED – U.S. SUBSCRIPTION AGENTS

IRELAND OF THE WELCOMES
Subscription Forwarding
P.O. Box 2744
1255 Portland Place
Boulder, CO 80323

This bi-monthly publication, published by the Irish Tourist Board, is a travel magazine – and more. Through color and black-and-white photos and informative articles, it provides an all-around *entree* to Irish culture today – and the heritage of Ireland's past. *Ireland of the Welcomes* covers virtually any subject of interest dealing with Ireland and those of Irish heritage. Recent issues, for example, have contained stories on such diverse subjects as the renaissance of Irish quilting; contemporary buildings and town planning in Ireland; Irish emigration to Australia during the age of sail; the rocks and geological formations of Ireland; the master stonecarvers of Durrow, County Laois, who carry on the tradition started with the great high crosses; the many attractions of Fota Island, County Cork; the story of the Gaelic Athletic Association; and Graninne Ui Mhaille (Grace O'Malley), the legendary 16th century chieftainess who built a kingdom on the west coast of Ireland based on trade and piracy. You may order a one-year subscription – at a special rate – by sending a check or money order for $9.95 to the address above. Individual issues may also be purchased at many Irish book and import shops.

QUINLIN, CAMPBELL PUBLISHERS
P.O. Box 651
Boston, MA 02134
(617) 787-0178

Sells subscriptions to *FORTNIGHT: Magazine of Ulster Opinion* (26 issues @ $45/yr.).

IRELAND DIGEST
P.O. Box 2455
Clifton, NJ 07015

A biweekly, four-color tabloid of news and features covering politics, business, the arts, sports and a wide range of other Irish events and subjects. *Ireland Digest*, written by leading Irish journalists and writers, is edited and published in Ireland for an international readership by Martin O'Shea, an American-born journalist. Subscriptions: $25/yr. in North America via "accelerated bulk postage"; $40/yr. anywhere in the world via air mail. Also available at some Irish import and book stores.

IRELAND'S NEWSPAPERS
Attn.: Stanley Plitt
230 East 44th Street
New York, NY 10017

Offers "fast mail delivery" of newspapers from the 26 counties in the Republic, and of the major daily and Sunday Dublin newspapers. Write for price list and other information.

IRISH STUDIES
114 Paula Boulevard
Selden, NY 11784
(516) 698-8243

Serves as subscription agent for *Poetry Ireland* ($12/yr. for four issues).

NEWSPAPERS – IRISH-AMERICAN (See also "Events, Calendars of – Irish-American" and "Magazines & Journals – Irish-American")

THE IRISHMAN
P.O. Box 11278
San Francisco, CA 94101
(415) 392-0766

Monthly. Subscriptions: $14/yr. Concentrates on covering the California Irish-American community and its activities.

THE IRISH HERALD
2123 Market Street
San Francisco, CA 94114
(415) 621-2200

Monthly. Subscriptions: $10/yr.

IRISH AMERICAN NEWS
P.O. Box A66218
Chicago, IL 60666
(312) 882-4410

Monthly. Covers not only Chicago, but most of mid-America, through a network of correspondents in cities from Ohio to Texas. Subscriptions: $12/yr. in U.S.; $20/yr. in Canada. (See advertisement on page 244.)

THE IRISH ECHO (Boston Edition)
1874 Centre Street
Boston, MA 02132
(617) 327-0110

Weekly. Subscription: $14/yr.

THE IRISH STAR
395 West Broadway
P.O. Box 6
Boston, MA 02127
(617) 268-4747

Weekly. Subscriptions: $10/yr.

BOSTON IRISH NEWS
14 Franconia Street
Dorchester, MA 02122
(617) 825-1400

Monthly. Subscriptions: $10/yr.

THE IRISH ADVOCATE
15 Park Row
New York, NY 10038
(212) 233-4672

Weekly. Subscriptions: $10/yr.

THE IRISH ECHO
309 Fifth Avenue
New York, NY 10016
(212) 686-1266

Weekly. In-depth coverage of New York City and suburbs, as well as weekly reports from correspondents as far afield as Chicago. Subscriptions: $18/yr. (See advertisement on page 245.)

THE NATIONAL HIBERNIAN DIGEST
c/o James Brennan,
Advertising Director
207 North Zane Highway
Martin's Ferry, OH 43935

Bi-monthly. Subscriptions are normally available only to members of the Ancient Order of Hibernians, and are included with membership. (See "Organizations – National") Advertising space is available in the *Digest*, however, and sample copies and rate information are available by writing the address above.

THE IRISH EDITION
P.O. Box 44102
Philadelphia, PA 19144
(215) 849-4404/4405

Monthly. Covers Philadelphia and the mid-Atlantic states. Subscriptions: $10/yr.

NOVELTIES – IRISH

KILTARTON STUDIOS
P.O. Box 403
Oradell, NJ 07649
(201) 261-4759

Imports and sells Irish sheepskins, which are suitable for use as throw rugs and furniture coverings. Request details.

ANCESTRAL LAND COMPANY OF IRELAND, LTD.
P.O. Box 53
Island Park, NY 11558
(516) 432-3177

You can "own a piece of Ireland" for just $20. For this sum (plus local sales tax for New York State residents), Ancestral Land Company will transfer to you or someone you designate a 21-year leasehold on a numbered square foot of land located in County Sligo. The firm reports it has sold 10,000 square feet since 1984 -- most of them bought as Christmas or birthday gifts, or by companies who use them to promote their business. For each square-foot parcel, ALCI issues an attractive four-color, parchment-like certificate inscribed with the "owner's" name. Request a free brochure by contacting the address above. If you're interested in a quantity order for promotional or other purposes, phone (207) 871-8622.

ORGANIZATIONS – IRISH-AMERICAN – IRISH CENTERS

UNITED IRISH CULTURAL CENTER OF SAN FRANCISCO
2700 45th Avenue
San Francisco, CA 94116
(415) 661-2700

This modern center offers a ballroom accommodating 1,000; modern kitchen and bar facilities; a cocktail lounge with stage for floor-show entertainment, dancing area, seating for 300 and dining area; rooms for meetings and receptions by clubs and private parties; a large library of Irish materials; and recreational facilities.

IRISH AMERICAN HERITAGE CENTER
4626 North Knox Avenue
Chicago, IL 60630
(312) 282-7035

This recently opened center, housed in a former junior-college building and renovated at a cost of $3 million, serves the Chicago Irish-American community with a variety of facilities. Rooms are available for organizational meetings, and an auditorium seats 900 for large meetings and performances. There is a full-service kitchen on premises, and plans call for adding a library, a museum, a chapel and an "Irish-American Hall of Fame" in the fairly near future. The Heritage Center is located in the near northwest section of Chicago, convenient to major highways and public transit.

**IRISH CULTURAL SOCIETY
OF NEW ORLEANS**
3600 Chestnut Street - 3rd Floor
New Orleans, LA 70115
(504) 488-3338

Founded several years ago, this group
now has limited permanent facilities in
a private home. These include a
meeting and a library room. Activities
held here or elsewhere, as needed,
include ceilis; Irish dancing instruction;
a genealogy club; Irish history lectures;
Gaelic classes; evening discussions of
Irish literature and poetry; and
traditional music performances.

**GAELIC LEAGUE & IRISH
AMERICAN CLUB OF
DETROIT**
2068 Michigan Avenue
Detroit, MI 48216
(313) 964-8700

Opened in 1920, this center features
banquet facilities for 300; a library; and
meeting rooms of various sizes.

**THE IRISH CENTER/
COMMODORE BARRY CLUB**
6815 Emlen Street
Philadelphia, PA 19119
(215) 843-8051

Located in Philadelphia's Mt. Airy
section, the Irish Center/ Commodore
Barry Club is the main focus for Irish-
American activities in the city. The
organization is housed in a large older
building whose facilities include one of
the city's largest ballrooms; many
smaller rooms for meetings and other
functions; a bar/lounge with dancing
area; a kitchen for catering; and a
library. Many independent Irish-

American groups make their homes
here, and the regular activities schedule
includes classes in stepdancing,
Gaelic, Irish harp and other instruments; evening ceilis; performances of
Irish drama; and meetings of the local
Gaelic Athletic Association and other
societies.

**IRISH CENTRE OF
PITTSBURGH**
6886 Forward Avenue
Pittsburgh, PA 15217
(412) 521-9712

Set on a 4 1/2 acre site, the Pittsburgh
Centre contains an extensive library; a
large hall with stage for dancing, concerts, exhibitions and lectures; as well
as offices and a kitchen for catering.
There's even an outdoor swimming
pool. The activities schedule, equally
impressive, includes an Irish choral
group; stepdancing and Irish music
classes; speakers; and special events,
including an annual feis. The Centre's
focus is educational, cultural and
social, with a large family membership.

**ORGANIZATIONS – IRISH-
AMERICAN – LOCAL –
SELECTED (See also
"Organizations – Irish-American
– Irish Centers")**

NOTE: There are thousands of local
Irish-American organizations – and
chapters of national organizations –
throughout the U.S. Those listed
below are merely *a handful* of the more
prominent. To find out about the
activities of organizations in your area

– and how to contact them – consult appropriate Irish-American newspapers (See "Newspapers – Irish-American") and calendars of events (See "Events, Calendars of – Irish-American"). For most of the Midwestern and Rocky Mountain states, and those in between, the best single source is the monthly calendar published in *The Irish American News,* Chicago.

THE CHARITABLE IRISH SOCIETY
Box 850
Lynnfield, MA 01940-2314

This group merits mention if only because it is the oldest Irish organization in the U.S., founded in 1737. While the exodus to the suburbs has helped bring membership down to 500 or so, the CIS still carries on one of its original aims: helping assist the poor in Ireland, the U.S. and elsewhere. The Society holds quarterly meetings as well as a gala dinner each March at Boston's Copley Hotel. Over the years, it has hosted speeches by such noted Irish-Americans as John F. Kennedy (a member) and Babe Ruth. Sen. Edward Kennedy, John Boyle O'Reilly and former Mayor of Boston Patrick Collins have also been members.

EIRE SOCIETY OF BOSTON
23 Pointallerton Avenue
Hull, MA 02045
(617) 925-0665

Since it began in 1937, the Eire Society has been working to promote the "knowledge of Irish culture through the encouragement of study in the arts, sciences, literature, language and history of Ireland." One means it uses is an excellent *Bulletin,* which contains fascinating articles on Irish and Irish-American culture and history. The Society also sponsors monthly lectures from October through April. It awards a Gold Medal each year to a prominent individual. Recipients have included Fianna Fail leader Charles Haughey; journalist Bob Considine; film director John Ford; U.S. House of Representatives Speakers John W. McCormack and Thomas J. "Tip" O'Neill; and Archbishop of Boston Richard Cardinal Cushing. Each year, the Society co-sponsors an "Irish Night at the (Boston) Pops" with the Charitable Irish Society. Eire Society dues are $20/yr., including the bulletin.

THE IRISH ARTS CENTER/AN CLAIDHEAMH SOLUIS
553 West 51st Street
New York, NY 10019
(212) 757-3318

This organization conducts most of its activities in New York, but it's more than a local New York institution. This is due in large part to its excellent quarterly magazine, *An Gael: Irish Traditional Culture Alive in America Today* (See "Magazines & Journals – Irish-American.") Though modest and aging, the Center's three-story quarters bustle with a continuous round of activities. There are classes in Irish music, dance, history and language; and first-rate theatrical performances by the Irish Arts Centre Theatre, its resident company, and other groups. Elsewhere in the city, the Center sponsors regular ceilis as well as an annual festival of traditional Irish music and dance. National membership ($20/yr.) includes a subscription to *An Gael;* free courses; and 20% discounts on plays, ceilis and other cultural events. Sponsor ($50) and Patron ($100) memberships bring you these and additional benefits. Request a free sample issue of the Center's bimonthly newsletter, *Litr Nuacht.*

NEW YORK IRISH HISTORY ROUNDTABLE

P.O. Box 6216
Yorkville Station, NY 10128

Founded in 1984, this organization works to promote study of Irish-American history in New York City and surrounding areas. It also helps provide its members – scholars and laypeople alike – with information on source materials available in local libraries, archives and other institutions. Meetings are held twice a year, and membership dues are $10. To join, write local libraries, archives and other institutions. Meetings are held twice a year, and membership dues are $10. To join, write to the address above, enclosing payment. Or send $1 for a sample copy of *The New York Irish,* the group's newsletter.

ORGANIZATIONS – IRISH-AMERICAN – NATIONAL

AMERICAN IRISH HISTORICAL SOCIETY

991 Fifth Avenue
New York, NY 10028
(212) 288-2263

A non-sectarian, non-political organization that works to promote a better appreciation of the Irish role in American history and society. AIHS maintains a library of 25,000 volumes, chiefly covering Irish and Irish-American history and genealogy. Publishes an annual journal, *The Recorder.* Membership dues are $50/yr. Write for membership information and application form.

AMERICAN COMMITTEE FOR IRISH STUDIES (ACIS)

c/o Maureen O'R. Murphy, VP
Dean of Students
Hofstra University
1000 Fulton Avenue
Hempstead, NY 11550
(516) 560-6775

This nationwide organization, with a membership of 1,200-plus scholars and others, works to foster scholarship on Ireland and Irish America in such varied disciplines as history, literature, political science, folklore, economics, archaeology, art, sociology and linguistics. Members present papers at a spring national conference and at regional conferences in the fall. ACIS publishes a quarterly newsletter; an annual membership directory; and *A Guide to Irish Studies in the United States,* a directory to courses offered at institutions across the country. Members also receive the *Irish Literary Supplement*. Dues for calendar-year membership are $11.50 for students and retirees; $14 for U.S. residents; $18 for non-residents.

ANCIENT ORDER OF HIBERNIANS IN AMERICA (AOH)
National Office
5034 Wisconsin Avenue, N.W.
Washington, DC 20016
(202) 244-0005

Celebrating its 150th anniversary in 1986, AOH is the nation's largest Irish-American organization, with a reported 91,000 members affiliated with divisions and chapters throughout the U.S. AOH traces its roots to an Irish society founded in the 16th century. Membership is currently restricted to Roman Catholic men of Irish heritage. There is a parallel ladies' auxiliary, the Ladies Ancient Order of Hibernians (LAOH). And there has been at least one attempt – so far unsuccessful – to accept Irish-American men of non-Catholic heritage. Nationally and locally, AOH works to promote awareness and action on Irish-related public issues; provides social and fraternal activities for members; sponsors scholarships and other awards; and offers members reasonably priced fraternal life insurance. (See "Life Insurance – Fraternal.") Members receive a bimonthly newspaper, *National Hibernian Digest*.

COMHALTAS CEOLTOIRI EIREANN
Traditional Irish Musicians Assn.
c/o Bill McEvoy, North American Coordinator
928 Hawkins Avenue
Lake Grove, NY 11755
(516) 588-3709

This international society, headquartered in Ireland, has 30 local chapters – and over 4,000 members – in North America. Its goal is to preserve traditional Irish music in all its forms – instrumental, song and dance – and to promote a better appreciation of Gaelic. Local chapters usually hold monthly functions open to both members and non-members. Annual dues are $12, and include a subscription to the quarterly magazine, *Treoir* ("The Message"). To find out where your nearest chapter is located, call or write Mr. McEvoy.

EMERALD SOCIETIES
(Independent societies in various cities)

Unique among Irish-American groups, the Emerald Societies are organized along occupational lines. They are generally open to those of Irish birth or heritage who share a common, often governmental, employer – for example, a police department, fire department, board of education, sanitation department or other agency. Emerald Societies offer members an opportunity to meet other Irish-Americans in the same trade or profession and work to foster appreciation of Irish culture and traditions as well as pursuing charitable and nationalist objectives. Emerald Society pipe bands are a fixture in many St. Patrick's Day parades; there are 10 such bands in New York alone. The first Emerald Society was established in New York City in the early 1950s, and similar groups have followed in Boston, Chicago and other cities. The tri-state New York/New Jersey/Connecticut area alone now claims over 40 Emerald Societies coordinated by a Grand Council.

THE GAELIC LEAGUE
(Independent chapters are located in several U.S. cities.)

The American units of this prestigious international society, each chartered independently by the Irish parent organization, seek to promote the goals put forth in 1893 by their Irish founders, Douglas Hyde (a leading Gaelic scholar and the future first President of Ireland) and historian Eoin MacNeill, later chief of staff of the Irish Volunteers. These were to keep the Gaelic language alive where it was still spoken and to promote wider study and appreciation of the language as well as the musical, dancing and other cultural activities associated with it. The League was instrumental in persuading the Irish government to require Gaelic instruction in schools, but neither it nor the government has been able to make Gaelic the everyday language of Ireland's people. It is among Irish-Americans that Gaelic is becoming an increasingly popular subject of study, and Gaelic League chapters in several U.S. cities do a worthy job of promoting language instruction and wider cultural activities. The organization is non-sectarian in membership and outlook. You may find out whether there is a chapter near you by contacting the Irish American Cultural Institute (see next entry).

IRISH AMERICAN CULTURAL INSTITUTE
2115 Summit Aveune
Box 5026
St. Paul , MN 55105
(612) 647-5678

This international foundation is devoted to promoting the cultural heritage of Ireland and Irish America, and has no religious, political, social or fraternal objectives in the normal sense. It carries out its aims through a variety of activities and programs, which have included (1) the production of 53 half-hour television programs and 13 half-hour films on various aspects of Irish culture; (2) publication of *EIRE-IRELAND*, a highly regarded quarterly journal of Irish studies; (3) annual awards of $10,000 to Irish writers and artists; (4) bringing dramatic and musical productions and art exhibitions to the U.S. from Ireland; (5) sponsorship of "Irish Perceptions," which brings leading Irish writers, artists and scholars to lecture and perform in several U.S. cities six times a year; (6) sponsorship of local chapters in over a dozen U.S. communities; (7) the Irish Way program, which offers summer experiences in Ireland for U.S. high school students; and (8) Irish Books and Media, an affiliate that sells books from Ireland by mail. IACI depends for its funds on memberships (Basic, $25/yr.; Bronze, $50/ yr.; Silver, $100/yr.; and Gold, $150/yr.) as well as on gifts from individuals, companies and foundations. Donations are tax-deductible. Request literature.

THE IRISH GEORGIAN SOCIETY
455 East 51st Street
New York, NY 10022
(212) 759-7155

As the American arm of the IGS, this organization works to help preserve, maintain and restore the architectural and artistic treasures created in Ireland from the late 17th through the early 19th century. There are 22 local chapters throughout the U.S. Membership benefits include (1) lectures on aspects of Irish Georgian culture and arts; (2) occasional information bulletins; (3) chapter tours to Ireland, which include visits to great houses and art collections not open to the general public. Regular membership dues are $15/yr.; contributing membership, $100/yr.; life membership, $1,000.

KNIGHTS OF EQUITY AND FRIENDLY SONS OF ST. PATRICK
National Headquarters
2010 15th Street
Altoona, PA 16601
(814) 943-2210

Founded in 1895, this fraternal and cultural organization has local chapters with 4,500 members in Michigan, New York, Ohio and Pennsylvania. Men of Irish descent who are practicing Catholics are eligible to join. (Women may join the Daughters of Erin, an auxiliary organization.) The Knights' activities include promoting appreciation of Irish history and culture through lectures and other means; assisting orphanages, homes for the aged and young men interested in becoming priests; sponsoring courses in Gaelic language and culture;

buying athletic trophies for Catholic schools; and providing over two dozen scholarships each year for members' children. The organization also issues a monthly newsletter and presents an annual Celtic Culture Award to a group or individual. For further information or to find the location of your nearest chapter, contact Joseph L. Moran, Supreme Secretary, as indicated above.

PEAT (TURF) BRIQUETTES – IMPORTED

ARDAGH IMPORTS
3 Warwick Court
Streamwood, IL 60103
(312) 884-0464

Sells compacted briquettes of Irish peat to give your fireplace that sweet, nostalgic aroma that only this traditional fuel can provide. Twenty bricks for $10. Delivery in Chicago area at no charge, depending on location.

CLARK & WILKINS INDUSTRIES, INC.
1871 Park Avenue
New York, NY 10035
(212) 534-5110

Imports and sells genuine Irish peat, the fuel used for centuries to heat Irish homes and to cook. The peat comes in compressed briquettes: a 28-pound box costs $30., including delivery by UPS. May only be available in the Eastern states.

P&M SALES, INC.
1019 East Tioga Street
Philadelphia, PA 19134
(215) 423-2988

Sells Irish peat "Turfettes," which cost
$2 each and weigh two to three
pounds. Shipping charges are
additional.

PHOTOGRAPHS – IRELAND

**THE IRISH HERITAGE
PHOTOGRAPHY PROJECT**
c/o National Office
Ancient Order of Hibernians
5034 Wisconsin Avenue, N.W.
Washington, DC 20016
(202) 244-0005

Offers photographs of landscapes from
throughout Ireland, in either linen or
oil painting seal finish and in sizes
from 8x10 to 16x20 inches. Each
photo costs from $35 to $120,
depending on the finish and frame
ordered. Request a free brochure
covering the county or counties you're
interested in. (Allow several weeks:
requests are forwarded to Ireland and
the information is mailed from there.)

PIPE BANDS – IRISH-AMERICAN

**CHICAGO RIVER BRIDGE
PIPERS**
Chicago, IL
(312) 825-4014 or 698-0126

**SHANNON ROVERS IRISH
PIPE BAND**
Chicago, IL
(312) 775-8946

TRI-COUNTY PIPE BAND
Bergen County, NJ
(201) 836-6403

COUNTY TYRONE PIPERS
Long Island, NY
(718) 746-7700 or
(516) 671-6332

**EMERALD SOCIETY PIPE
BAND**
New York City Police Department
New York, NY
(718) 474-2448 (eves/weekends)

EMERALD PIPE BAND
Philadelphia, PA
(215) 487-0166 or 637-5765

POSTCARDS – ANTIQUE

**OLD WINDSOR
DISTRIBUTORS**
RD 2 – Bethlehem Road
New Windsor, NY 12550
(914) 564-6775

Stocks a large selection of old Irish
postcards. You may order cards on
approval, paying for those you keep
and returning the rest undamaged.
Suitable for framing, gifts or collecting. Request details.

POSTMARKS – U.S. – "IRISH" PLACE-NAMES

Whether you're doing a mailing to customers of your Irish-related business or to members of your Irish-American organization; or just sending St. Patrick's Day or other greetings to special friends or relatives, you can add a memorable touch by having your mail postmarked in any of several U.S. communities with special Irish names. Enclose your stamped envel-ope(s) in a larger envelope addressed to: **U.S. Post Office, Attn.: Postmaster, (Town or city of your choice, with zip code, from the list below).** Enclose a brief note asking that the stamps on the enclosed envelopes be cancelled with the local postmark and mailed. If you're doing a large mailing, you should write or phone the post office first for instructions:

Erin, NY 14838

Erin, TN 37061

Hibernia, NJ 07842

Ireland, IN 47545

Ireland, TX 76536

Shamrock, NC 28205

Shamrock, OK 74068

Shamrock, TX 79079

Shamrock Station, PA 19552

If there's an Irish town or county with special meaning for you, check the list under *Irish Names upon Our Land* (see *Irish-American Almanac* section of this book) to see whether there's a place of the same name in the U.S. If there is, you can ask your local post office for the correct zip code, and follow the procedure explained above.

POTTERY & CERAMICS – IMPORTED

MARKET IRELAND
1224 Washington Street
Hoboken, NJ 07030
(201) 963-4127

Carries handmade dinnerware and other pottery from the Stoneware Jackson Pottery, County Kilkenny. Contact for details.

SIMON PEARCE
385 Bleecker Street
New York, NY 10014
(212) 924-1142

Sells traditional dinnerware and pottery items handmade at the Philip Pearce and Stephen Pearce potteries in Shanagarry, County Cork. Made from Blackwater River clay and fired (in the case of Stephen Pearce Pottery) in turf-burning kilns, the line includes plates, bowls, mugs, pitchers, servers and other dinnerware and kitchen items. The shop also stocks traditional hand-blown lead glassware from the Simon Pearce Glass Mill, Quechee, VT. (See "Crafts & Craftspeople – Traditional") Send $2 for catalog.

PRINTS – ANTIQUE

ARGOSY BOOK STORE
116 East 59th Street
New York, NY 10022
(212) PL3-4455

Offers a variety of old Irish prints –
typically hand-colored engravings –
portraying such subject matter as noted
Irish people; town and city plans; and
scenic views. No catalog is available,
but Argosy will send items to you on
approval: you keep what you like,
forwarding payment, and return the
rest undamaged without further
obligation.

PUBS – IRISH-AMERICAN

If you're fond of the camaraderie and
good drink that characterize the typical
Irish-American pub, you probably
already have your own favorite(s). In
any event, there are thousands of pubs
across the country – simply too many
to begin to list them here. If you'd like
to shop around, however, the best bets
are the ads run by pubs in various Irish-
American newspapers. In addition,
each issue of *Irish America* magazine
contains a guide to selected pubs in
New York City and Boston. Finally,
if you live in or near Boston, there's a
new book entitled, *Irish Pubs of
Boston – A Guide to the Pubs, Music,
Dance, Food & Drink... Including
Favorite Irish Songs*, by Richard K.
Wesson. You may order a copy by
sending $7.95 to the publisher:
Boardworks Publishing, 35 Eldridge
Road – #110, Jamaica Plain, MA
02130. (617) 522-5493.

RADIO PROGRAMS – IRISH-AMERICAN

There are probably hundreds of radio
programs broadcast locally throughout
the United States for Irish-American
audiences. Their formats generally
emphasize music, news and commen-
tary about Ireland, news and announcements of local Irish-American activities, or some combination. We
haven't attempted to list these programs or stations here. There are
simply too many – and a fair percentage come and go rather quickly, or at
least change their time slots. To find
out which programs can be heard
where you live, we suggest you check
the radio schedules published in the
Irish-American newspapers serving
your area. (See "Newspapers – Irish-
American.")

REAL ESTATE – IRISH – FOR RENT

House and cottage owners throughout
Ireland welcome vacationers who'd
like to rent their homes instead of stay-
ing in the usual hotel. Irish-American
newspapers – especially *The Irish
Echo,* New York, and *The Irishman,*
San Francisco – regularly run advertisements for such rentals. And U.S.
consular offices can also refer you to
appropriate real estate agents in either
the Republic or Northern Ireland. (See
"Government Offices in the U.S. –
Republic of Ireland" and "Government
Offices in the U.S. – United
Kingdom") The Irish Tourist Board
also has two helpful, free booklets you
may wish to request: *Rent an Irish*

Cottage and *SelfCatering Accommodation.* (See "Travel – Information" for addresses of U.S. offices.)

Shannon Development Company serves as agent for a number of rental-cottage developments in the south and west of Ireland. Your travel agent may obtain information or make reservations for you by calling, toll-free, one of the wholesale tour operators listed in this directory under "Travel to Ireland – Wholesale Tour Brokers & Operators."

REAL ESTATE – IRISH – FOR SALE

You needn't be an Irish citizen to own property in Ireland. For current listings, check for classified and display advertisements in various Irish-American newspapers, especially *The Echo* and *The Irishman.* (See "Newspapers – Irish-American.")

You may also contact the nearest Irish or British consulate – depending on the county of interest – and request the names and addresses of local real-estate agents. (See "Government Offices in the U.S. – Republic of Ireland" or "Government Offices in the U.S. – United Kingdom.")

RECORDS & TAPES – IRISH MUSIC

THE EVEREST RECORD GROUP
2020 Avenue of the Stars
Los Angeles, CA 90067
(213) 557-0303

Request free catalog describing Irish records and cassettes.

DOWN HOME MUSIC
1-341 San Pablo Avenue
El Cerrito, CA 94530
(415) 525-1494

DHM's free catalog, *Folk Music of the British Isles and Europe,* features one of the largest selections available of Irish traditional and folk music. Also included: books of Irish tunes and song lyrics; and instrumental instruction books. Sells through its own retail store as well as by mail and phone.

IRISH ACCORDIONS & RECORDS
3157 Geary Boulevard
San Francisco, CA 94118
(415) 752-0961

LPs and cassettes of traditional Irish musical groups; show bands; ceili music; and leading Irish singers, past and present.

GREEN LINNET RECORDS
70 Turner Hill Road
New Canaan, CT 06840
(203) 966-0864

Green Linnet's free catalog of traditional and folk music recordings serves up
a generous helping of Irish fare. Each
recording is described in detail. Mail
orders only.

IRISH RECORDS INTERNATIONAL
Box 196
Accord, MA 02018
(617) 878-7936

Stocks a good selection of albums by
the leading Irish recording artists, including the Clancy Brothers, the Irish
Rovers, the Dubliners and James
Galway. Serves mail-order and wholesale customers. Request free catalog.

QUINLIN, CAMPBELL PUBLISHERS
P.O. Box 651
Boston, MA 02134
(617) 787-0178

Carries recordings of traditional Irish
music, including privately produced
titles. Free brochure.

BRIGGS AND BRIGGS, INC.
1270 Massachusetts Avenue
Cambridge, MA 02138
(617) 547-2007

Stocks a good selection of Irish records, including many hard-to-find
imported traditional items.

SANDY'S RECORD SHOP
896A Massachusetts Avenue
Cambridge, MA 02138
(617) 491-2812

Offers a wide selection of Irish
traditional and folk music. Fills mail
orders.

SHANACHIE RECORDS
Dalebrook Park
Ho-Ho-Kus, NJ 07423
(201) 445-5562

One of the largest sources in U.S. for
recordings of traditional Irish music.
Free catalog.

CELTIC CRAFT
294 East 204th Street
Bronx, NY 10467
(212) 231-1210

Stocks about 400 Irish record and tape
titles as well as recordings from other
Celtic nations.

PRIME RECORDS
P.O. Box 7156
Garden City, NY 11530
(516) 292-1521

Records and tapes featuring popular
Irish bands in the New York
metropolitan area. Request free
catalog and price list.

REGO IRISH RECORDS & TAPES, INC.
64 New Hyde Park Road
Garden City, NY 11530
(800) 854-ERIN; (516) 328-7800 in
New York State

Sells LPs and tapes featuring popular
singers and musicians as well as
traditional groups.

FIESTA RECORD COMPANY
251 Broadway
Lynbrook, NY 11563
(516) 599-5522

Request free price list of international
recordings, including over 25 Irish
selections. Most come on both
cassette and LP.

RELEASE RECORDS
225 Washington Street
Mount Vernon, NY 10550
(914) 667-8900

Imports or produces and distributes
"the largest collection of Irish traditional and ballad material." Most titles
come on LP or cassette. Request free
catalog. Mail orders only.

FOLKWAYS RECORDS
TRF Music, Inc.
40 East 49th Street
New York, NY 10017
(212) 753-3234

Carries about 40-50 titles of traditional
Irish songs and instrumental music
played on authentic traditional
instruments. Request free catalog.

ALCAZAR PRODUCTIONS, INC.
Box 429
Waterbury, VT 05676
(802) 244-5178

Distributes records on about 350
different labels, including a wide
variety of Irish selections. Request free
catalog, which lists Irish items under
"British Isles."

RELIGIOUS GOODS & BOOKS

ST. PAUL CATHOLIC BOOK & FILM CENTER
172 North Michigan Avenue
Chicago, IL 60601
(312) 346-4228

THOMAS P. EGAN & SONS
518 Gallivan Boulevard
Dorchester, MA 02122
(617) 436-4360; (800) 442-2099 in
Massachusetts; (800) 235-0003
in other states.

Religious articles and church supplies,
including statues, rosary beads,
religious pictures and memorials.

M.J. CURLEY COMPANY
1360 Hancock Street
Quincy, MA 02169
(617) 770-1205

Religious articles; books; records and cassettes; candles; memorials.

RESORTS – IRISH-AMERICAN

New York's Catskill Mountains are better known for their "Borscht Belt," a mecca for vacationing Jewish-Americans. But two communities to the northeast – East Durham and Cairo -- are the Irish-American equivalent. Whether for a weekend or longer, these resorts offer Irish-style food, gift-shopping, entertainment, and hotels for every budget. For information on attractions and accommodations, contact:

EAST DURHAM VACATIONLAND
Box 67
East Durham, NY 12423
(518) 622-3243

Though no other resorts rival these Catskill communities, several other Northeastern resorts have hotels and establishments catering primarily to Irish-Americans. Among these are the New Jersey seaside towns of Atlantic City, Ocean City and Cape May; and several Cape Cod communities. For details on these, check ads in Irish-American newspapers serving New York, Philadelphia and Boston. (See "Newspapers – Irish-American.")

SCHOLARSHIPS

COMHALTAS CEOLTOIRI EIREANN/THE TRADITIONAL IRISH MUSICIANS ASS'N

This international group works to preserve traditional Irish music through performances, teaching and other means. Local chapters generally offer scholarships to permit talented young performers to pursue formal music studies. (See "Organizations – Irish-American – National" for contact information.)

HIBERNIAN LIFE INSURANCE
790 South Cleveland Avenue
Suite 221
St. Paul, MN 55116
(612) 690-3888

HLI funds several scholarships each year, under two programs: (1) non-public high school scholarships; and (2) scholarships for The Irish Way, which support summer study and travel in Ireland under a program operated by the Irish American Cultural Institute, St. Paul, MN. (See "Travel to Ireland – Student Travel & Travel/Study Programs.") For details on scholarship eligibility requirements and application forms, contact HLI.

JOHN McCORMACK SOCIETY OF AMERICA
c/o John P. Keveny
853 Felter Avenue
Maywood, NJ 07607

Awards a competitive scholarship for song and concert singing.

SHILLELAGHS & BLACKTHORN STICKS

GAELIC TRADING COMPANY, LTD.
345 North Broadway
Yonkers, NY 10701
(914) 965-9870 or 965-4456

SOUVENIR ITEMS – FOR FUNDRAISING, FESTIVALS, PROMOTIONS, ETC.

ERIN INTERNATIONAL COMPANY
15 Denmark Avenue
Milton, MA 02186
(617) 696-1470

Sells a variety of "Irish" items, including Claddagh, shamrock and U.S.A./ Ireland flag pins; keychains; jewelry; music boxes; caps; tee shirts; and stick-ons. Send for free catalog.

CENTURY IRISH ITEMS
2 Cliff Estates
North Scituate, MA 02055
(617) 545-2788

Offers family-crest buttons for over 500 names; keychains and other items. Request free brochure.

SPORTS – COMPETITIONS

THE SHAMROCK GAMES
Attn.: Mr. Dan Doyle, Director
Irish American Sports Foundation
740 North Main Street – Suite M
West Hartford, CT 06117
(203) 233-3692

First held in Ireland in 1985, the Shamrock Games will take place in Worcester, MA, until Summer 1990, at least. The Games feature competition in some 20 sports events over a four-day period in July and/or August, and are meant to raise funds for the work of the Irish American Sports Foundation (see "Sports – Organizations"). The events are crew, basketball, cycling, golf, gymnastics, karate, lacrosse, 10K road race (and a Walk for Ireland), rugby, soccer, touch football, softball, tennis, track and field, volleyball, wrestling and Gaelic sports. These are amateur competitions and are open to citizens of the U.S., Canada, Ireland and Israel, regardless of previous athletic experience or achievement. Event winners earn free trips to Ireland to take part in sports exhibitions and competitions with Irish athletes. For more information, contact the Games staff at the address above.

SPORTS – GAELIC – IN THE U.S.

Since its founding at Thurles, County Tipperary, in 1884, the Gaelic Athletic Association has worked to foster traditional Irish sports as part of a broader effort to preserve traditional Irish culture. Hurling and Gaelic football have been the mainstays of GAA competition from the beginning; handball, a centuries-old Gaelic sport, and camogie, a women's version of hurling, have joined the GAA repertoire more recently. In the U.S., officially sanctioned Gaelic sports competition comes under the auspices of two separate and mutually exclusive GAA bodies: the GAA of New York governs local teams and competition in New York, Connecticut and New Jersey; all other states come under the jurisdiction of the GAA/North American Board.

Each spring, before the start of its regular season, the New York GAA hosts exhibition matches at Gaelic Park, The Bronx, against all-star hurling and football teams from Ireland. U.S. GAA teams make occasional playing visits to Ireland. Now that the Central Division of the GAA/North American Board has moved into its splendid new stadium in the Chicago suburbs, we can expect more exchanges of this type involving teams outside New York.

All New York GAA games are played at:

GAELIC PARK
4000 Corlear Avenue
Bronx, NY 10463
(212) 548-9568

Schedules for New York GAA events are published in the *Irish Echo* at least two weeks in advance. Games under the GAA/North American Board are held at facilities throughout the country, including a new permanent Gaelic sports park in Chicago:

GAELIC PARK
6119 West 147th Street
Orland Park, IL 60462
(312) 687-9323

The latest annual schedule of games under the GAA/North American Board is available from:

GAELIC ATHLETIC ASSOCIATION
North American Board
9145 South Central Park
Evergreen Park, IL 60642
(312) 636-8560

SPORTS – LIVE BROADCASTS FROM IRELAND

NORBERT HENNESSY
5824 Broadway
Bronx, NY 10463
(212) 601-3833

Hennessy, who runs the "Irish Sports Results" telephone line and distributes videocassettes of Irish sports matches through Irish Video, can also arrange for your group to hear live radio broadcasts of football, hurling and other Irish sports matches via transatlantic connection.

SPORTS – ORGANIZATIONS
(See also "Sports – Gaelic – in the U.S.")

NORTH AMERICAN CURRACH ASSOCIATION
Attn.: James Gallagher, Secretary
351 Boston Post Road
East Lyme, CT 06333
(203) 739-8216

This group works to revive and foster the traditional craft of building cur-rachs, small boats used for centuries along the western coast of Ireland. It also sponsors races among crews from currach clubs in various cities, which include New London, CT; Annapolis, MD; Boston; New York; and Pitts-burgh. The races are usually held as part of festivals designed to keep alive the broader Irish cultural traditions associated with currach building.

IRISH AMERICAN SPORTS FOUNDATION
Attn.: Mr. Dan Doyle
740 North Main Street – Suite M
West Hartford, CT 06117
(203) 233-3692

This foundation works to help young people throughout Ireland's 32 count-ies by funding several sports-related programs. These include (1) building gymnasiums and other athletic facilities in Ireland; (2) providing scholarships to bring athletically talented Irish young people to the U.S. to study; (3) sending American coaches to Ireland to conduct sports clinics; and (4) bringing Irish young people to the U.S. to attend sports camps. IASF welcomes all contributions, which are tax-deductible. You may ask to receive its quarterly publication, *IASF News-letter*, without charge or obligation.

ST. BRENDAN CUP COMMITTEE IN AMERICA
Suite 505
2000 P Street, N.W.
Washington, DC 20036
(202) 833-9624

Established in 1981 to commemorate St. Brendan's legendary voyage to America in the sixth century –and to pro-mote sportsmanship and friend-ship between the Irish and American peoples. The Committee sponsors St. Brendan Irish festivals in selected cities, featuring sail races with various boat classes represented – and currach races as well. Ashore, the races are complemented by social and cultural events celebrating Ireland's maritime heritage. The Committee maintains a network of local clubs and is working to inaugurate a regular transatlantic sail race from Ireland to the U.S. – the St. Brendan Cup – beginning in 1986 or 1987.

SPORTS – RESULTS FROM IRELAND

IRISH SPORTS RESULTS LINE
(212) 601-3800

A three-minute recording that reports the latest team sports scores from Ireland. A new tape goes on-line each Sunday at about 2 p.m. This free service – you pay only for the phone call – maintains over 20 lines to handle your incoming calls.

STAMPS, POSTAGE – IRISH – COLLECTORS

EIRE PHILATELIC ASSOCIATION
Attn.: Robert C. Jones, Sec'y
Eight Beach Street
Brockton, MA 02402
(617) 587-6382

Affiliated with an Irish parent organization, the Eire Philatelic Association is open to adults interested in Irish stamps and other philatelic items, especially as collectors. EPA currently has ten chapters across the U.S. with about 800 members. It holds informal meetings coordinated with major U.S. stamp expositions; conducts mail auctions of Irish stamps and related materials; publishes an informative quarterly, *The Revealer;* and holds an annual meeting, sometimes irregularly. Dues are $7/yr. Write for membership details and application.

TELEVISION PROGRAMS – IRISH-AMERICAN

NEWS EUROPE
San Francisco, CA
(415) 821-1728

Frank Ahern, who produces this show, formerly produced a program called *Irish Magazine* in the same time spot. He hopes to revive this all-Irish program within the next year or two. Meanwhile, *News Europe* offers in-depth coverage of news from various European countries, using a network of correspondents on location. Stories from Ireland are aired when these are judged particularly interesting or important. *News Europe* can be seen on cable Channel 25 from 8:30 to 9:00 pm each Monday, and on Wednesday nights at 8:30 on Marin Channel 31.

IRELAND ON THE MOVE
Box 583
Hyde Park, MA 02136
(617) 364-3041

A one-hour program that covers news of Irish-American activities in the Greater Boston area, including sports, politics, festivals and personalities. Each progam also offers a feature segment and an interview with an author, businessperson, sports figure, entertainer or other personality of Irish-American interest. A new program is aired every week. Can be seen in the Boston area on cable Channel A3 (BNN – Public Access) Thursdays from 8:00 to 9:00 pm, with the same show repeated at the same hour on Friday of the following week. In some other parts of Massachusetts, *Ireland on the Move* may be seen on cable Channel 28.

IRISH CIRCLE NEWS MAGAZINE
P.O. Box 1339
New York, NY 10156
(212) 689-4853

Typical program includes coverage of Irish and Irish-American news; sports; a cultural feature; a guest editorial; and a brief Gaelic lesson. Telecast on Manhattan Cable TV, Channel J, each Sunday from 9:00 to 9:30 pm.

THE IRISH NETWORK
Attn.: Jim Gaffney
The Irish Arts Center
553 West 53rd Street
New York, NY 10019
(212) 757-0800

The Irish Network, a private partnership, will launch a weekly hour-and-a-half show dealing with matters Irish and Irish-American in the second half of 1986. It will be telecast over local cable networks as well as non-network TV stations. The Network welcomes program ideas and suggestions, as well as inquiries from individuals interested in serving as local correspondents for this show.

TRAVEL TO IRELAND – BOOKINGS – RETAIL TRAVEL AGENTS

Nearly any travel agency can handle the arrangements you need for a trip to Ireland. Those we list below are agencies owned and/or operated by Irish-Americans, many of them Irish-born. They are likely to have more specialized Ireland-related experience than the average agency, and be better able to help you plan a satisfying visit:

IRELAND TRAVEL HEADQUARTERS
3355 Mount Diablo Boulevard
Lafayette, CA 94549
(415) 283-7521

O'CALLAGHAN TRAVEL
1527 Wilshire Boulevard
Los Angeles, CA 90017
(213) 413-2525

LOPEZ TRAVEL
Attn.: Mrs. Pat Foley
303 A Street
San Diego, CA 92101
(619) 232-2128

HIBERNIA INTERNATIONAL TRAVEL SERVICE/IRISH AIR AGENCY
2123 Market Street
San Francisco, CA 94114
(415) 863-1126

IRELAND TRAVEL CONSULTANTS/ KIVLEHAN TRAVEL
3150 California
San Francisco, CA 94115
(415) 567-2882

IRELAND TRAVEL HEADQUARTERS
680 Beach
San Francisco, CA 94109
(415) 885-5563

IRISH TRAVEL SERVICE
3157 Geary Boulevard
San Francisco, CA 94118
(415) 752-0961

TARA TRAVEL, INC.
681 Market Street
San Francisco, CA 94105
(415) 777-4555

ROUND TOWER TRAVEL
6754 Diversey Street
Chicago, IL 60635
(312) 889-7533 or
(800) 621-7442

GAFFNEY TRAVEL SERVICE
4604 West 103rd Street
Oak Lawn, IL 60453
(312) 636-1683

ROUND TOWER TRAVEL
11700 Old Columbia Pike
Silver Spring, MD 20904
(301) 421-9042 or (800) 225-9988

HOLIDAIR TRAVEL
210 Boylston Street
Chestnut Hill, MA 02167
(617) 969-4650

JULIA'S TRAVEL SERVICE
126 Alden Street
Dedham, MA 02026
(617) 326-0388

ROUND TOWER TRAVEL
18 Central Street
Norwood, MA 02062
(617) 762-9090

ABBEY TRAVEL SERVICE
657 Adams Street
Quincy, MA 02169
(617) 479-7990

**IRELAND-AMERICAN
FLIGHTS & TOURS/ IRELAND
TRAVEL CENTER**
15 Crescent
Waltham, MA 02154
(617) 899-7733

IRISH TRAVEL SPECIALISTS
1896 Centre
West Roxbury, MA 02132
(617) 327-1300

TARA TRAVEL
389 Highway 35
Middletown, NJ 07701
(201) 530-2020

GRIMES TRAVEL AGENCY
95 Madison Avenue
Morristown, NJ 07960
(201) 539-6674

**CELTIC INTERNATIONAL
TOURS**
161 Central Avenue
Albany, NY 12206
(518) 463-5511

**DONOGHUE HEALY
O'SULLIVAN TRAVEL**
22 East Kingsbridge Road
Bronx, NY 10468
(212) 733-4600

MURPHY & BROWN TRAVEL
25 East Bedford Park Boulevard
Bronx, NY 10468
(212) 584-2224

**SHAMROCK WORLDWIDE
TRAVEL SERVICE**
6045 Riverdale Avenue
Bronx, NY 10471
(212) 549-8898

TARA TRAVEL
265 West 231st Street
Bronx, NY 10463
(212) 548-6500

GLENWOOD TRAVEL
1485 Flatbush Avenue
Brooklyn, NY 11210
(718) 434-4344

BRENDAN WARD TRAVEL
86-16 Queens Boulevard
Elmhurst, NY 11373
(718) 651-6161; (800) 251-6161

BRIAN MAY TRAVEL
3712 82nd Street
Jackson Heights, NY 11372
(718) 458-0030

SHANNON TRAVEL SERVICE
75-24 37th Avenue
Jackson Heights, NY 11372
(718) 639-0667 or 639-7530

**DILLON'S MANHATTAN
TRAVEL SERVICE**
One East 42nd Street
New York, NY 10017
(212) 490-3510

GRIMES TRAVEL AGENCY
1860 Broadway
New York, NY 10023
(212) 307-7797

LISMORE TRAVEL
106 East 36th Street
New York, NY 10016
(212) 685-0100

**O'CONNOR'S FAIRWAYS
TRAVEL, INC.**
800 Second Avenue
New York, NY 10017
(212) 661-0550

ROUND TOWER TRAVEL
Suite 1507
745 Fifth Avenue
New York, NY 10151
(212) 371-1064; (800) 522-7560
from New York State; (800)
221-4611 from other states

HEALY O'SULLIVAN TRAVEL
22 South Main Street
Pearl River, NY 10965
(914) 735-9500

ROCKAWAY TRAVEL
100-02 Rockaway Beach Boulevard
Rockaway, NY 11694
(718) 747-8200

GRIMES TRAVEL AGENCY
54 Mamaroneck Avenue
White Plains, NY 10601
(914) 761-4550

**PAT LYNCH'S WOODSIDE
TRAVEL**
60-25 Roosevelt Avenue
Woodside, NY 11377
(718) 478-9016

ROUND TOWER TRAVEL
3016 Township Line Road
Drexel Hill, PA 19026
(215) 853-3050; (800) 225-9988

DURKIN WORLD TRAVELS
156 West Chelten Avenue
Philadelphia, PA 19144
(215) 843-4800

TRAVEL TO IRELAND – INFORMATION

The Irish Tourist Board operates several U.S. offices. Its New York office, however, is best equipped to serve individuals. For general information and literature; brochures on attractions, accommodations, car rentals and escorted tours; or answers to more specific questions, contact:

IRISH TOURIST BOARD
757 Third Avenue
New York, NY 10017
(212) 418-0800

For similar assistance involving Northern Ireland, contact:

NORTHERN IRELAND TOURIST BOARD
40 West 57th Street
New York, NY 10019
(212) 581-4700

TRAVEL TO IRELAND – PILGRIMAGE TOURS

Tours to Ireland's traditional pilgrimage sites can, of course, be booked through many, if not most, travel agents – usually without problems. In the past, however, some pilgrims have been victimized by tour operators who offered overpriced packages or failed to deliver on certain promises. To help remedy this, the Vatican in 1985 established a special office in New York. The U.S. Catholic Office for Pilgrimages helps put U.S. Catholics in touch with operators who have a "good track record" for offering tours that are reasonably priced and conducive to spiritual growth. For information, contact:

U.S. CATHOLIC OFFICE FOR PILGRIMAGES
1011 First Avenue
New York, NY 10022
(212) 371-1000

TRAVEL TO IRELAND – SPECIAL- INTEREST PROGRAMS

HAMILTON TRAVEL AND INCENTIVE CORPORATION
3 East 54th Street
New York, NY 10022
(212) 751-9360

Ireland has long been famous for its horses, so seeing parts of the island on horseback seems a particularly apt way to go. Hamilton Travel offers several riding holidays in Ireland, including horseback tours of Connemara, Killarney and Sligo; an eight-day trek through Kerry's Dingle Peninsula; and cross-country riding at Horetown House in County Wexford or around the Castle Leslie Equestrian Centre in Glaslough. Request brochures and further details.

NRCSA
823 North 2nd Street
Milwaukee, WI 53203

Whatever your hobby – or the special interest you've been wanting to develop – chances are there's a suitable program waiting for you in Ireland. For example, you can learn traditional wool spinning or lacemaking techniques...study Irish genealogy – and how to research yours...go pony trekking...birdwatch in some of Ireland's most picturesque spots...immerse yourself in Irish theatre...or learn to sail. In fact, Ireland offers hundreds of unusual programs, and most are detailed in the *NRCSA Program Directory for Britain and Ireland,* available for $9.98 (postpaid) from the address above. NRCSA staff will also answer your questions and make arrangements for any program you may wish to participate in.

TRAVEL TO IRELAND – STUDENT TRAVEL & TRAVEL/STUDY PROGRAMS

PROGRAM IN IRISH SOCIETY AND POLITICS
c/o Center for Irish Studies
Catholic University of America
620 Michigan Avenue, N.E.
Washington, DC 20017
(202) 635-5488

U.S. college students accepted for this one-semester program have an opportunity to work in Dublin as research assistants to members of the Irish parliament. Request details and application form.

THE IRISH WAY PROGRAM
c/o The Irish American Cultural
Institute
2115 Summit Avenue
Box 5026
St. Paul, MN 55105
(612) 647-5678

This summer program is designed to give American high-school students a six-week Irish experience that includes educational, cultural, recreational and social aspects. Based at Gormanston College, a superbly equipped campus north of Dublin, participants spend six weeks in planned activities including (1) classes and field trips dealing with Irish history, current events, literature, language, music, song and dance; (2) horseback riding, golf, tennis, swimming and other sports; (3) evening activities such as movies, ceilis, discos, group talent shows and the like. Each teenager also spends about 10 days as the guest of an Irish family. Program costs are about $1,500 per student, plus airfare and money for personal expenses such as gifts, snacks, etc. A limited number of scholarships are funded by various Irish-American organizations. For further information, application forms and (if desired) a scholarship application, contact the program administrator at the address above. Applications should be submitted as soon as possible after January 1st of the year in which the student wishes to participate.

COUNCIL ON INTERNATIONAL EDUCATIONAL EXCHANGE (CIEE)
205 East 42nd Street
New York, NY 10017
(212) 661-1414

CIEE offers two summer travel/ study programs for college students, co-sponsored with the Union of Students in Ireland – Travel (USIT). **Encounter Ireland,** a three-week, $895 program, includes presentations and discussions on Irish history and culture as well as a home-stay with an Irish family; an independent travel pass; and scheduled round-trip air transportation between New York and Dublin. The **Trinity College Program** provides five weeks at historic Trinity College, Dublin, in a wide-ranging course of study on various aspects of modern Irish life and culture. Field trips; a home stay with an Irish family; independent travel and other extracurricular activities supplement classroom sessions. The program runs from early July through early August, with applications due by June 1st. Academic credit can be arranged – up to six credits, depending on class attendance and performance on examinations. The total cost is $1,800, including round-trip airfare from New York. Contact CIEE for information and application forms for either program.

IRISH TOURIST BOARD
757 Third Avenue
New York, NY 10017
(212) 418-0800

ITB publishes an informative booklet, *Discover Young Ireland: Learning and Leisure Opportunities,* which describes a wide range of programs throughout Ireland for young people. Among them are experiences involving travel, study, voluntary service, summer camp, hostelling and home stays. The booklet also covers programs in bird-watching, golf, hang-gliding, inland cruising and many other special interests. Copies are free, subject to availability. Other helpful ITB publications include Information Sheet #39 – *Youth Hostels.*

U.S. IRISH STUDENT TRAVEL SERVICE
356 West 34th Street
New York, NY 10001
(212) 239-4247

This is the U.S. office of the Union of Students in Ireland – Travel (USIT), and operates to help further a cultural exchange agreement designed to help college students in both countries enjoy unique educational and cultural experiences on both sides of the Atlantic. USISTS offers American students discount travel arrangements, both to Ireland and within Ireland itself.

TRAVEL TO IRELAND – WHOLESALE TOUR BROKERS & OPERATORS – COMMERCIAL

BRENDAN TOURS
15137 Califa Street
Van Nuys, CA 91411
(818) 785-9696; (800) 252-0351 in California; (800) 421-8446 outside California

CELTIC INTERNATIONAL TOURS
161 Central Avenue
Albany, NY 12206
(518) 463-5511; (800) 433-4353 in New York State; (800) 833-4373 outside New York State

O'SHEA TOURS LTD.
195 South Broadway
Hicksville, NY 11801
(516) 681-2223; (800) 632-2302 in
New York State; (800) 645-7462
outside New York State

LISMORE TOURS
106 East 31st Street
New York, NY 10016
(212) 685-0100; (800) LISMORE
outside New York City

LYNOTT TOURS
350 Fifth Avenue
New York, NY 10001
(212) 760-0101; (800) 537-7575
in New York State; (800) 221-
2474 outside New York State

EMERALD TOURS
113 South Washington Street
Alexandria, VA 22314
(703) 684-2129 from metro DC;
(800) 368-3267 nationwide

**TRAVEL TO IRELAND –
WHOLESALE TOUR
BROKERS & OPERATORS –
OFFICIAL**

**C.I.E. TOURS
INTERNATIONAL**
122 East 42nd Street
New York, NY 10168
(212) 972-5600; (800) 522-5258 in
N.Y.State; (800) CIE-TOUR from
other states nationwide

This is Ireland's official transportation
authority, which specializes in *booking*
wholesale travel arrangements involving Ireland, the United Kingdom and/
or the Continent. (The Irish Tourist
Board, by contrast, is responsible for
promoting travel to Ireland by providing information and other services.)
C.I.E. operates the most modern fleet
of tour buses in Europe, and says it
stresses quality in booking arrangements, whether in cottage rentals; self-
drive tours; guided tours; or whatever.
In addition to the 64-page brochure it
mails to thousands of U.S. travel
agents each year, C.I.E. publishes a
128-page *Irish Touring Guide*, which
is given without charge to individual
travel customers when they arrive in
Ireland.

**TYPESETTING – GAELIC
(See also "Calligraphy &
Graphic Design – Celtic-Style")**

ARIES GRAPHICS
40 Massabesic Street
Manchester, NH 03053
(603) 668-0811

Provides typesetting in Gaelic for
publications, promotional purposes,
etc. Contact for samples and rate
information.

**VIDEO – RECORDINGS (See
also "Films – Archives")**

TRAVEL ADVENTURES
Suite 345
#3 Golf Center
Hoffman Estates, IL 60195
(312) 882-3343

Sells an 80-minute video travelogue, *Ireland,* which takes you on an armchair tour of the Emerald Isle. Covers such sights and places as Dublin, Blarney Castle, Kilkenny, the Rock of Cashel, Cork, the River Shannon, Knock, Aran, Limerick and the Cliffs of Moher. Send $39 per copy (plus $3 postage) and specify VHS or Beta format. Call for further details or mail your order with check or money order.

IRISH VIDEO
5824 Broadway (at 238th Street)
Bronx, NY 10463
(212) 601-3833 or 549-9698

Distributes recordings of recent Irish sports matches in hurling, rugby, football and soccer. Tapes are normally available one or two days after an event, and are supplied on American-standard (NTSC) cassettes in either VHS or Beta format. Request details.

REGO IRISH RECORDS, TAPES & VIDEO, INC.
64 New Hyde Park Road
Garden City, NY 11530
(516) 328-7800

Write or call for free catalog.

TRIBUNE FILMS
303 Fifth Avenue
New York, NY 10016
(212) 689-3180/3181

Sells several video programs about Ireland, including *Destination Donegal, Lovely Leitrim, Reflections – Ireland, The Magic of Ireland* and *Ireland – Bird's Eye View.* Prices

range from $14 to $20, plus $2 postage and handling for each tape. Available only in VHS. Request descriptive price list.

BANBA, INC. – VIDEO DEPOT
22690 Shore Center
Euclid, OH 44123
(216) 261-0867 or 531-5068

Irish sports events, drama, music and movies are among the subjects featured on the videocassettes Banba distributes. Available on U.S.-standard VHS or Beta format. Request free catalog.

VIDEO – STANDARDS CONVERSION SERVICE

IMPORTANT NOTE: It *seems* simple. Aunt Brigid sends you a videocassette of, let's say, your Irish cousin's First Communion. Her VCR is VHS-format, like yours, so you pop the cassette into your machine and settle back for... static! The problem is, European and American videocassette recorders may *look* the same, and the same cassettes fit both. But unless the tape was recorded using the *electronic* format your system uses, it won't play back. Irish videocassette recorders use the so-called PAL standard, while their American counterparts are designed to record and play back in NTSC. (We're not referring to video format – for example, VHS, Beta or 3/4" U-Matic. The standards problem affects all three equally.) So, if you're sending a tape to Ireland – *or receiving one from someone there* – make sure it's converted to the correct standard before expecting it to play. Following is a sampling of services available to convert your tape(s):

VIDEO RECORDS PRODUCTIONS
3 Bayview Drive
San Carlos, CA 94070
(415) 593-4617

PAL VIDEO
19061 Tina Place
Tarzana, CA 91356
(818) 344-1603

GLOBAL VIDEO COMMUNICATIONS CORPORATION
774 West Church Street
Orlando, FL 32805
(305) 423-8299

A.N.S. INTERNATIONAL VIDEO, LTD.
396 Fifth Avenue
New York, NY 10018
(212) 736-1007

DEVLIN PRODUCTIONS, INC.
150 West 55th Street
New York, NY 10019
(212) 582-5572

GLOBAL VIDEO COMMUNICATIONS CORPORATION
333 West 52nd Street
New York, NY 10019
(212) 581-7543

IRISH VIDEO
5824 Broadway
Bronx, NY 10463
(212) 549-9698 or 601-3833

WOOLEN PRODUCTS (See also "Fashions – Imported")

NOREEN BRENNAN
P.O. Box 8001
La Crescenta, CA 91214-0001
(818) 957-6570

A native of County Clare, Ms. Brennan knits various types of Irish sweaters by hand. Aran fisherman sweaters are her specialty. She fills custom orders for both individuals and businesses.

BECKWITH ENTERPRISES
Irish Imports Division
101 First Street – Suite 164
Los Altos, CA 94022

Handknit 100% virgin wool fisherman sweaters. Available in unisex sizes and three styles: crew-neck pullovers; traditional and crew-neck cardigans. Request descriptive leaflet/order form.

MOLLY MALONE
934 High Ridge Road
Stamford, CT 06905
(203) 322-2160

Sweaters, cardigans, hats, tweed caps, blankets, gloves, scarves and mittens. Request free catalog.

IRISH CROCHET TREASURES
P.O. Box 1625
562 Milk Street
Fitchburg, MA 01420
(617) 342-1152

Sells sweaters handknit in County
Sligo: Aran fishermen's sweaters in
cardigan and pullover styles; Icelandic-
design pullovers; and mohair pullovers
for women. Custom orders welcomed. Request free price list.

MARKET IRELAND
1224 Washington Street
Hoboken, NJ 07030
(201) 963-4127

Irish-made wool shirts, socks, shawls
and blankets as well as hand-knit
fisherman's sweaters for adults and
children. Color catalog of mail-order
offerings: $2 postpaid.

K.M. O'CONNOR COMPANY
221 West 82nd Street
New York, NY 10024

Hand-knit pure wool items from
Donegal, in "blackberry" stitch: men's
and women's cardigans, pullovers, ski
caps and tams.

SKIPPER ARANWEAR
Mail Order/Patos Ltd.
31-21 68th Street
Woodside, NY 11377
(718) 426-0421

Request free color catalog.

MRS. McKENNA'S
6 Anderson Avenue
Ardmore, PA 19003
(215) 642-8110

Imported hand-knit fishermen's
sweaters. Scarves. Mittens. Hats.
Request free brochure.

IRISH SWEATERS
103 Berman Street
Newtown Square, PA 19073
(215) 642-8110; 664-4529

Handknit fishermen's sweaters from
Donegal: heavy men's and women's
pullovers; ladies' cardigans; and
ladies' vests. Inquire about sizes,
prices, other details.

IRISH DESIGN CENTER
303 South Craig Street
Pittsburgh, PA 15213
(412) 244-1867; 682-6125

Handwoven pure wool shawls, 54
inches square, made by Avoca
Handweavers, Ireland's oldest
handweaving mill, dating from 1723.

ABOUT THE EDITORS

About the Managing Editor:

BRIAN EVANS COOPER, who conceived and directed *The Irish-American Almanac & Green Pages*, is founder and president of Pembroke Press. Reared in Stewart Manor, NY, Mr. Cooper earned degrees at Princeton University (A.B., *Magna cum laude* in history) and the University of Michigan (M.A. in history). He subsequently spent 14 years in public relations, advertising and marketing posts with various organizations, including the Port Authority of New York & New Jersey (Airport Promotion Staff); Treadway Inns Corporation; Harcourt Brace Jovanovich, the publishing conglomerate; and St. Regis Paper Company. Before launching Pembroke Press, Mr. Cooper worked as a senior account executive at Hill and Knowlton, the leading international public relations firm, where he counseled major multinational clients on corporate and financial communications. He is a member of the American Committee for Irish Studies (ACIS) and the American Irish Historical Society (AIHS). Mr. Cooper's Irish forebears include members of the Daugherty (also spelled Doherty, O'Dochartaigh, etc.) Ferguson and Bryan families..

About the Contributing Editors:

MARTHA MOORE BATTLES is a full-time researcher with Hill and Knowlton, the world's largest public relations firm. She previously worked at the Horatio Alger Association, where she edited the book, *Only in America: Opportunity Still Knocks*; and at Sullivan & Cromwell, a leading New York law firm. Mrs. Battles attended Trinity College, Dublin, while her father, John D. J. Moore, was U.S. Ambassador to Ireland from 1969 to 1975. She completed an undergraduate degree in English at Smith College, Northampton, MA.

ANN KATHLEEN BRADLEY is the author of *A History of the Irish in America*, published in 1986 by Chartwell Books (London). After earning a B.A. at Bryn Mawr College she did graduate work at the University of Massachusetts and Harvard University. Ms. Bradley currently works as an editor in New York City. She is a member of the American Committee for Irish Studies (ACIS).

JOHN VINCENT CODY, PH.D., was born and reared in Chicago, earning his undergraduate degree at Loyola University in that city. He received a doctorate in Classics from Princeton in 1971, and has taught Classics and literature at Loyola, Lehigh and Northwestern universities. Relocating to San Francisco in 1977, Dr. Cody served as managing editor of *Literature of Liberty*, a libertarian journal formerly published by the Cato Institute. He is currently a freelance editor and software developer, consulting with corporations, publishers and universities in California.

KAREN S. DAUGHERTY, a native of Greenwich, Connecticut, took a B.A. in English at St. Lawrence University, Canton, NY, and also holds a master's from Columbia University School of Journalism. She works as a television newswriter and producer in New York. While employed by NBC News, Ms. Daugherty helped cover the Pope's visit to Japan in 1981.

JOAN MOODY, who has lived nearly all her life in San Antonio, is active in organizing and promoting Irish-American events in Texas, which she notes is "the fourth-largest state in Irish America." She publishes *The Guardian*, a newsletter covering local and regional Irish events, and also writes regularly on Texas Irish activities for both the *Irish American News*, Chicago, and the *Irish Advocate,* New York. A former teacher, Ms. Moody holds a B.A. in English from Incarnate Word College, San Antonio, and has also studied marketing and management. She is currently a communications consultant.

TIMOTHY ROGUS, a lifelong Chicagoan, is employed as an associate foreign language editor at National Textbook Company in nearby Lincolnwood. He holds a bachelor's in French language and literature from Loyola University, Chicago, and a master's from Northwestern University, Evanston, IL.

HELP US MAKE A GOOD BOOK BETTER

With your help, the next edition of *The Irish-American Almanac & Green Pages* can be even bigger and better. If you have information to add, corrections to suggest, new listings for *The Green Pages* — in fact, comments or suggestions of any kind — please use the space below, referring to specific pages in the book where possible. Make photocopies of this form if needed, or attach additional sheets.:

The Irish-American Almanac:

The Green Pages:

General comments/suggestions:

Please include source(s) for information above, as appropriate, and fill in your name, address and phone number below so we may contact you for further details or clarification:

Your name _____ Date _____

Street/P.O. Box _____

City _____ State/Zip _____

Phone: Area code (___) _____ Days? ☐ Evenings? ☐

How did you learn about this book?

Please mail completed form to: Irish-American Almanac & Green Pages, Pembroke Press, Suite 201, 127 East 59th Street, New York, NY 10022.

Order Form for Additional Copies of
THE IRISH-AMERICAN ALMANAC
& GREEN PAGES

☐ Please send me _____ copies of *The Irish-American Almanac & Green Pages* @ $11.45 (U.S.) each, including shipping charge of $1.50 per copy. (New York State residents *must* add applicable sales tax.) I enclose payment in check or money order for $_____ (U.S.).

☐ Please send information on quantity-discount orders.

Send to:

Name _____

Organization _____

Street/P.O. Box _____

City _____ State/Zip _____

(We can normally have your order delivered to you within 2 weeks of receiving it. Since we may on rare occasions be temporarily out of stock, you should allow 4-6 weeks for delivery. Money-back guarantee: If you are not completely satisfied with this book, you may return up to two copies to us within 30 days and receive a full refund.)

Complete form and send with payment to:

Pembroke Press, Publishers
Suite 201
127 East 59th Street
New York, NY 10022

Reader's Notes

Reader's Notes

Reader's Notes

Reader's Notes

Reader's Notes

ADVERTISERS IN THIS EDITION OF
THE IRISH-AMERICAN ALMANAC
& GREEN PAGES

Page

If your company or organization is interested in advertising in a future edition of *The Irish-American Almanac & Green Pages,* request a rate card and media kit by writing: Irish American Almanac & Green Pages, Attn.: Advertising Department, Pembroke Press, Publishers, Suite 201, 127 East 59th Street, New York, NY 10022.